WASHINGTON

WASHINGTON

by JAMES RESTON

Macmillan Publishing Company   Collier Macmillan Publishers
New York   London

Macmillan Publishing Company
866 Third Avenue, New York, N.Y. 10022
Collier Macmillan Canada, Inc.

The articles in this book all appeared in slightly altered form in *The New York Times.*

Library of Congress Cataloging-in-Publication Data
Reston, James, 1909–
  Washington.

  Includes index.
  1. United States—Politics and government—1945–
I. Title. II. Title: Washington.
E839.5.R44   1986   973.92   86-12431
ISBN 0-02-602310-5

Macmillan books are available at special discounts for bulk purchases for sales promotions, premiums, fund-raising, or educational use. For details, contact:

Special Sales Director
Macmillan Publishing Company
866 Third Avenue
New York, N.Y. 10022

10 9 8 7 6 5 4 3 2 1

Printed in the United States of America

BOOK DESIGN BY BARBARA MARKS

For my eldest son,
Richard Fulton Reston

CONTENTS

INTRODUCTION

In 1967, the late Alfred A. Knopf, who usually had better judgment, published a collection of my columns from the pages of *The New York Times*. The collection was called *Sketches in the Sand*, out of respect for Walter Lippmann's definition of a columnist: "a puzzled man making notes, drawing sketches in the sand which the sea will wash away."

Since then, the sea has washed away many puzzled men and many forests of newsprint. But the job of observing the flowers and the beer cans floating in the stream of history is as endless as the tides. So I toss another handful of pebbles into the flood, just for fun.

My excuse for inflicting those first sketches on a sympathetic publisher was that I was then impressed by something the British novelist J. B. Priestley wrote during the dark days of the German blitz in London in the last world war.

I was a youngster then, when the British people were digging Anderson shelters in their back yards and their children were running up the back stairs to toss the Luftwaffe's fire sticks off the roof. In those days, criticism of the British Government, then staggering and blundering, seemed almost intolerable.

Yet Priestley, while engaged in a series of patriotic broadcasts for the BBC, insisted on the importance of private criticism of public policy.

"We should love our country," he wrote, "as women behave toward the men they love. A loving wife will do anything for her husband, except to stop criticizing and trying to improve him.

"That," he added, "is the right attitude for a citizen. We should cast the same affectionate but sharp glance on our country. We should love it, but also insist on telling its faults."

This is not a popular theme in America as I write in the last years of the 1980s. Maybe it hasn't been since Franklin D. Roosevelt was elected four times by running against Herbert Hoover and the faults of the Great Depression.

But we are living in a different world in the last quarter of the century. Science has changed everything faster than we can change ourselves or our institutions. With its new machines, it has transformed the production and distribution of goods between nations; with its pills, it has revolutionized the relations between the sexes; and with its nuclear missiles, it has carried our struggles beyond the earth and into outer space.

I am concerned here, however, only with the revolution of communications and its influence on politics, primarily in the United States.

When I stumbled into journalism in Dayton, Ohio, almost fifty years ago, the daily newspaper was the first and main source of news. Only old geezers of my generation are likely to remember when, after some thunderclap in the news, little boys ran through the streets in the night shouting "Extra! . . . Extra!"—a startling and haunting cry, now forgotten.

The radio, being faster, took over that first announcement of the news. And soon after, the television, with its magic cameras, brought the scenes of the battlefield and the football field into our living rooms and forced the daily newspapers to think—which was not their favorite pastime—and to think particularly about the past and the future.

At first, the newspapers resented those new electronic characters who came in with a bit of a swagger. Even *The New York Times* refused for a while to print their daily programs. But while radio and TV took the old away from their front porches and their papers—in the process killing some of the best of those papers, including my favorite names in journalism: *The World* in New York, and the best name of all, *The Evening Star* in Washington—and brought them inside to watch snowy pictures on their screens, I think the pioneers of radio and television did the newspapers a great favor in the long run.

For they forced the papers to think not only about the fire in the night but to consider what started the fire in the first place, to analyze the causes of human conflict and not just the effects.

In the process, the daily newspapers changed for the better. They no longer tolerated the old dictator-publishers who presented the news and opinion on the news in accordance with their personal prejudices. They now hired a new and better-educated generation of reporters, more qualified to speak the languages and interpret the increasingly complicated economics and politics of the world.

And they changed in other ways, as well. They provided more access in the "opposite-editorial" pages to include the opinions of scholars, businessmen, and politicians who were increasingly informed on the problems of other nations and cultures.

This, however, produced as never before a conflict between the principal executives of government in Washington and the press. Officials increasingly relied on television to put their arguments and policies before vast national audiences, but an increasingly critical press was analyzing and challenging not only many official policies but many of the facts on which those policies were based.

There can be little doubt, at least in the end of the 1980s, that the balance of power between the modern politicians using modern television on the one hand and a more critical newspaper and periodical press on the other is running against the press. The politicians have discovered that if they can master the arts of television, personality may be more important than policy or even than fact and therefore more important in the struggle to win the next election.

If I am right about this, or even partly right, Priestley's insistence on private criticism of public officials is even more essential today than it was in the 1930s. Not because public officials of today are demonstrably less interested in the truth—in general, they are probably more interested in it—but because the truth about complicated contemporary issues is harder to find and because the instruments for persuasion and deception available to those public officials are now so much more powerful.

So here are a few more sketches, not only in the sand but in the mud and dirt of politics. They're just a few examples of the old argument that as power increases it must be watched more carefully. And so we continue to watch, not only the power of the government and of television and the combination of the two but the power of the press as well.

I am grateful to *The New York Times* for permission to publish this second volume of my columns and also to Sam Howe Verhovek, Eric Schmitt, Amy Wallace, and James Newton, my associates, who had the hard task of rescuing these survivors from the past.

—JAMES RESTON
WASHINGTON, D.C.
MARCH 3, 1986

PART I

REFLECTIONS

1 THE NATION NEEDS A PRESIDENT WHO WILL LEAD IT, NOT FOLLOW IT

WASHINGTON, June 20, 1960—If it is true that America needs and lacks a sense of purpose, the history of the nation suggests a remedy.

For if George Washington had waited for the doubters to develop a sense of purpose in the eighteenth century, he'd still be crossing the Delaware. In fact, most of the great political crises of the American past have been resolved, not by the zeal and purpose of the people, but usually by the willpower or obstinacy of their leaders.

No doubt the massive thirst of a long-tormented majority brought back 3.2 beer, but the plain fact is that in most other emergencies, a resolute minority has usually prevailed over an easygoing or wobbly majority whose primary purpose was to be left alone.

John Adams estimated that one-third of the population was against the American Revolution, one-third for it, and one-third indifferent. And this is the way it has usually been.

Some farsighted character like Thomas Jefferson or Teddy Roosevelt was always buying Louisiana or the Panama Canal when nobody was looking, and writers have always been grumbling, mainly to each other, about the feebleness of the national will.

The main difference between today's lamentations and those of the past is that the language is milder and the pay better.

Thomas Paine, roaring about America's mulish indifference in 1775, makes today's orators sound complacent. And even Ralph Waldo Emerson, who was really a pretty cheery fellow, could wail in 1847:

"Alas for America, the air is loaded with poppy, with imbecility, with dispersion and sloth. . . . Eager, solicitous, hungry, rabid, busybodied America: catch thy breath and correct thyself."

Thus, criticism of the American people for lack of purpose is not new. What is new is that leaders now seem to think they must follow the nation instead of leading it. What is new is that a hostile coalition of nations now has the military power to destroy the Republic. The margin of error granted to us in past wars and crises has vanished. What could be won before with partial effort, late starts, feeble alliances, and mediocre administration can no longer be won in a contest with the Communists.

It is not that they are so efficient but that they are so purposeful. They are all working on the main target and we are not. Life, tyranny, and the pursuit of capitalists is the Russian way of life. They have obliterated the difference between war and peace. They are always at war, all of them, women as well as men—teachers, philosophers, scientists, engineers, lady discus throwers, airmen, and three or four million foot soldiers.

None of this need trouble us very much except for *their* national purpose, which is simply to replace our system of individual freedom with their system of state control wherever they can, including regions vital to our security such as Germany, Japan, and even Cuba.

I must say they have been very frank about it. They have given us timely if not fair warning. They are directing all the energies of all their people to that goal. They are not arguing about the conflict between private interests and the national interest. They have simply eliminated private interest. They have put everybody to work on "burying" capitalism, and since our national purpose, among other things, is to avoid being buried, this creates an awkward and even nasty situation.

How, then, shall we approach the problem? I was brought up

on the Church of Scotland's shorter catechism, the first question of which is: "What is the chief end of man?"

Accordingly, I am all for self-direction and self-criticism. Nevertheless, I have my doubts about the imminence of any self-induced renaissance or epoch of austerity.

When I consider attacking the problem through the people, I think of Harry Ashmore's old story about the man who acquired a reputation for training mules with honeyed words and kindness. Hearing about this remarkable achievement, the Society for the Prevention of Cruelty to Animals dispatched a lady emissary to present the mule-trainer with a medal.

Upon arrival, she asked for a demonstration. The trainer obligingly trotted out a young mule, reached for a long two-by-four, and clouted the beast over the head. As the mule struggled back to his feet, the good lady exclaimed in horror, "Good heavens, man, I thought you trained these animals with kindness."

"I do, ma'am," he replied, "but first I got to git the critters' attention."

I don't know how just anybody gets the attention of 180 million people these days. They are engaged in the pursuit of happiness, which, incidentally, the Declaration of Independence spells with a capital H, and to be frank about it, I suspect that public debates on the national purpose give them a pain.

It will not, I think, be wise to underestimate America's current resistance to exhortations from the preachers, professors, columnists, and editorial writers of the nation. For unless I miss my guess, the Americano, *circa* 1960, is in no mood to rush off on his own initiative to "emancipate the human race," or to set any new records as the greatest benefactor of all time, or engage in any of the other crusades mapped out for him in Cambridge, Mass.

He may do many of these things because he is honest enough to know that he doesn't know all the facts of this dangerous and complicated era, but he is not likely to set out to do them because of his own "reflection and reason" or the arguments of talkers or writers he seldom sees.

Accordingly, we must, I think, start with the national leadership, partly because this is the engine that has pulled us out of the mud before and partly because this is an election year, when we will be picking a President, probably for most of the nineteen sixties.

The President of the United States is the one man who can get the attention of the American people. If he says the nation is in trouble, they will listen to him. If he addresses himself to their doubts and questions, they will hear him out. If he presents programs and legislation to do what he thinks is necessary for the safety of the Republic and explains and keeps explaining why these are essential, he may very well prevail.

All the magazine articles on the national purpose, all the reports by all the foundations on all our manifold weaknesses, all the speeches by Adlai Stevenson, Jack Kennedy, Lyndon Johnson, and Stuart Symington on the wickedness of the Republicans, all the exhortations to return to the faith of our fathers—all are nothing compared to serious programs, eloquently expressed and strongly pushed by a determined President of the United States.

"His is the only national voice in affairs," wrote Woodrow Wilson. "Let him once win the admiration and confidence of the country and no other single force can withstand him, no combination of forces will easily overpower him. His position takes the imagination of the country. . . . His is the vital place of action in the system. . . ."

Of course, he has to act. He cannot ask for half-measures and run away. But once he expresses the national need, once he decides to try to remove rather than to perpetuate the illusions of the past, then his specific remedies will affect the spirit and direction of the nation.

I remember when the Marshall Plan for Europe was devised in Washington. It was perfectly obvious that the sickness of the European economy was creating a crisis of great magnitude, and the bare bones of a four-year plan, costing perhaps as much as twenty billion dollars, were worked out and approved by President Truman.

I printed a long story about it one Sunday in *The New York*

Times, and by ten o'clock that morning, the late Senator Arthur H. Vandenberg of Michigan, then Chairman of the Foreign Relations Committee, called me at home and said: "You must be out of your senses. No administration would dare to come to the Senate with a proposal like that."

Yet once the lead was taken and the need documented, Senator Vandenberg ended up as a key supporter of what almost everybody agrees was the most farsighted piece of legislation since the war.

I do not underestimate the task. I agree with much that has been said about the slackness of our society, but I find the present mood understandable, perhaps inevitable, under the circumstances, and not without hope.

At the end of the last war, the American people made a genuine effort to clear the wreckage and understand the new situation. They went through the biggest geography and history lesson in their history, always with the false optimism that they were dealing with a temporary situation that would eventually go away.

Instead of going away, the problems became larger and more complex: After Europe, it was the Middle East; after the Middle East, the Far East; after the Far East, Africa; after Africa, outer space; and after outer space, a lot of inner tensions over U-2, me-too, inflation, deflation, rising cost of living, balance of payments, nuclear testing, sputniks, luniks, and a lot of other things that everybody seemed to be differing about.

There was no panic about any of this. The people merely turned from what they did not understand to what they did understand. They turned inward from the world to the community and the family. In the fifteen years of the atomic age, they increased the population of the nation by more than forty million, which is not the action of a frightened people and which is interesting when you think that the entire population of the country at the start of the Civil War one hundred years ago was only thirty-one million.

A distinction has to be made, I think, between the façade of America and the other, more genuine America. There is, of course, this big obvious clattering America of Hollywood and

Madison Avenue and Washington, but there is also the outer, quieter America, which has either kept its religious faith or at least held on to the morality derived from religious tradition.

I do not wish to glorify the multitude. Much can be said about the dubious effects on the American character of very early marriage, easy credit, cheap booze, cheaper TV, low education standards, and job security even for sloppy work.

Nevertheless, there is more concern for the outside world, more interest in its problems, more generosity, and more resourcefulness in this society than in any free society I know anything about.

If it is true, as I believe, that this generation of Americans is doing less than it could, it is also true that it has done everything it was asked to do. It may be more concerned about its private interests than about the public interest, but if a man is offered a choice between a Cadillac and a swift kick in the pants, we should not be surprised if he doesn't bend over.

What has it been asked to do that it has not done?

It was asked to restore the broken economy of Europe, and it helped bring that continent, within a decade, to the highest level of prosperity in history.

It was asked to accept high taxation and military conscription to police the world, and it has done so from the North Cape of Norway to Japan and Korea.

It was asked to keep a standing army of a quarter of a million men in Western Europe, and it has done so for fifteen years, with scarcely a murmur of protest from a single American politician.

It was asked to abandon its tradition of isolation, and it took on more responsibilities involving more risks—in Korea and elsewhere—than the British ever did at the height of their imperial power.

These are not the acts of a slack and decadent people. There is nothing in the record of free peoples to compare with it. This is not a static society. The problem is merely that the pace of history has outrun the pace of change. Ideas and policies have lagged behind events, so that by the time policies were formulated, debated, and put in force, the situations they were intended to remedy had changed.

Thus, in a torrent of change, in a revolution of science, a social revolution at home, and an unprecedented political revolution in Asia, Africa, and Latin America, it is scarcely surprising that there is a crisis of understanding in the nation. This is all the more true because there has been a serious weakening of the ties between the men of ideas and the men of politics in this country during the last decade.

"Our slow world," wrote Woodrow Wilson in 1890, "spends its time catching up with the ideas of its best minds. It would seem that in almost every generation men are born who embody the projected consciousness of their time and people.

Their thought runs forward apace into the regions whither the race is advancing, but where it will not for many a weary day arrive. . . . The new thoughts of one age are the commonplaces of the next.

The men who act stand nearer to the mass than the men who write; and it is in their hands that new thought gets its translation into the crude language of deeds. . . .

It cannot be said that the men of ideas in the country have not performed in these last few years their traditional tasks. They have observed the convulsions of our time and let their minds run ahead to the logical consequences for the nation.

I cannot remember a time when there has been more purposeful thought on contemporary problems in the universities and foundations than now. Their reports and conclusions would fill a good-sized library, but the alliance between them and the White House has been feeble, and somehow it must be restored.

What, then, can be done?

We can, at least, look at the world as it is instead of the world as we would like it to be. In the forty-three years since the Soviet revolution—of which twenty-five have been devoted to establishing their regime and fighting the last world war—they have brought their industrial production to about 45 percent of ours.

Since the war, their rate of growth has been between 9 and 10 percent, while ours has been in the neighborhood of 3 percent.

They are having trouble with their agricultural production, but if they and we both continue at the present rates of growth, the experts figure they will have approximately as much effective industrial production as the United States in 1975.

On the face of it, this may not worry the American people, but it is perfectly obvious that the trend is running against us in this field, and that, as former Secretary of State Dean Acheson says, the likelihood is that Moscow will do three things with this new production: (1) increase their military capabilities; (2) increase their resources for economic penetration in the underdeveloped nations; and (3) by a combination of these two, demonstrate to the uncommitted countries of the world that the Soviet Union is the country of spectacular growth and that the Communist system is the way to lift new countries in a short time into the new scientific age.

It is this latter point, rather than the threat of nuclear war against the United States, that concerns most students of the problem.

The Russians have already increased their exports to underdeveloped countries to about three million dollars. They have five thousand people administering these programs. And they are directing them primarily in six countries of considerable political importance to the U.S.S.R.

It is much harder to understand the threat of this kind of economic penetration than it is to understand the threat of indirect Communist aggression, as, for example, in Korea. But the threat is there just the same.

Since the last war, 1.2 billion people have changed their form of government in the world, and 800 million of these have achieved independence for the first time. These new nations are determined to be industrialized, ready or not. Hunger and pestilence are not new in the world, but the two billion hungry people are less willing to tolerate hunger and pestilence now that they know something can be done about it.

How these new governments develop, in freedom or by the quicker way of state control, may very well determine not only the climate of freedom in the world but the balance of power as well.

Thus, the primary problem of foreign affairs may very well be not the East-West problem we hear so much about, but what Sir Oliver Frank calls the North-South problem: whether the nations of the South, in Africa, Asia, and Latin America, develop along the lines of the free industrialized nations of the North or the state-controlled methods of the two large Communist Northern states of the Soviet Union and China.

We have tended to make several assumptions about this: that most nations wanted to develop like the United States; that knowledge cannot develop except in a climate of freedom; and that the Western powers could deal with the underdeveloped nations without interfering much with present concepts of sovereignty or commercial practice.

All these assumptions are now under challenge. The Soviet Union has shown that spectacular scientific progress can be made in a closed society. Cuba, to take only one example close at hand, has not only indicated contempt for the American system of free enterprise but is now organizing its whole society under state control.

The problem is not that the Soviet Union produces better engineers than the United States—though it certainly produces more—but that it can direct its engineers into these new countries or anywhere else that helps promote the purpose of the state.

As Dean McGeorge Bundy of Harvard has pointed out:

It may be that we are at the edge of a time in which authoritarian societies, controlling and using this new investment, the human mind, will be able to produce revolutions in power and in growth as remarkable to us as our own revolution, the industrial and technological revolution of the last 150 years, is remarkable today to the people who inhabit the world of rising expectations.

To me, this hazardous possibility that centralized control of technology and of science behind it may lead to a new order of growth, of power, and of change in the hands of people with a high degree of political purpose and centralized and ruthless control . . . seems to be the real danger in the growth of Soviet and Chinese power.

My conclusions about all this mysterious sociology and economics are unoriginal, vague, and even modest. All I know about the "rate of growth" is what happened to three boys of my own in the last twenty-three years, and even that is a little confusing. It would be pleasant to think, however, that all this concern in the nation among serious men about the higher rate of growth in the U.S.S.R. was seriously discussed and not dismissed as another left-wing trick to increase the size of government or elect some Democrat.

First, therefore, an honest debate on the issue might not be a bad idea. Maybe we cannot do everything everywhere. Maybe after 125 years of isolation and a generation of internationalism, somebody should call out once more to America: "Catch thy breath and correct thyself."

But anyway, a revival of honest plain talk in the country wouldn't do any harm.

Second, in the face of the clear facts, anything less than the highest possible standard of education for the children of America is obviously a disgrace. We cannot punch kids out like cookies and drop them into slots, and wouldn't if we could; but we ought to be able to spend more money on their education than we do on all that sexy advertising.

Third, offhand, I would guess we were kidding ourselves in thinking we could do this job with the kind of people now working on it overseas or that we could do it without far more cooperation and coordination among the allies.

If the main war now is the battle in the underdeveloped areas, why not offer talented young men of draft age the option of using their brains in a civilian service in Indochina rather than sentencing them to Army KP in Hoboken?

It is not fair or accurate to say that the voluntary system cannot compete with the directed system in recruiting men for service in the underdeveloped areas, for no really imaginative effort has been made to attract the volunteers.

Thus, wherever you look it is hard to escape the conclusion that our response is unequal to the threat. We are in what Professor Walt Whitman Rostow of the Massachusetts Institute of

Technology calls one of those "neurotic fixations of history." These are periods when nations are confronted by radically new situations but hang on to old policies that are increasingly divorced from reality.

This is what George III of England did when confronted by what he called the "rebellion" of the American colonies, what Edward VIII did when he hung on to Wally Simpson, what Stanley Baldwin did when he refused to rearm Britain in the face of Hitler's challenge, and what the United States did when it clung to isolation after the rise of Nazi Germany.

Isolation is now gone, but the hangover of the old habits of the days of isolation remain; in our assumptions that we can meet the Soviet challenge with the same school system, the same political patronage system, the same diplomatic system, the same attitudes toward politics and the public service, and the same old chestnut about private interests inevitably serving the public interest.

It is not so much that we have lost our way forward, but that we have lost our way home. This is the country of freedom, youth, experimentation, and innovation; of pioneers and missionaries and adventurers.

If you ask whether we can meet the Soviet challenge by concentrating on our private interests instead of on the public interest, by losing a great many of our best young brains in poor schools before they ever get to the college level, by not using our intelligent women when the Russians are using theirs, by not making a genuine effort to get our best brains into the most effective jobs to serve the nation, why I'm bound to say that the answer is no.

I believe, however, that there is still a lot of spunk and spirit in this country that can be brought by free methods into the service of the nation, provided Presidential power is used to clarify where the nation stands.

The first national purpose is to know who we are and what we stand for; it would be an impertinence to try to improve on the second paragraph of the Declaration of Independence as a guide to the problem.

"We hold these truths to be self-evident," it says in the first sentence. It thereupon lists, as if they were the indisputable facts of last Sunday's American League batting averages, a whole catalog of wonderful things that are not only not "self-evident" in 1960 but are actually in violent dispute among men all over the world, including quite a few in our own country.

"All men are created equal," it says, and, of course, this is just the trouble, for you can get an argument on that one anywhere in the province of Georgia, U.S.S.R., or the state of Georgia, U.S.A.

In the minds of the Founding Fathers, the moral idea came before the political, and the latter was merely an expression of the former. This, too, was apparently the idea Matthew Arnold had in mind when he came to this country before the turn of the century and discussed our national purpose in New York.

He made two points:

We must hold fast to the austere but true doctrine," he said, "as to what really governs politics, overrides with an inexorable fatality the combinations of so-called politicians, and saves or destroys states.

Having in mind things true, things elevated, things just, things pure, things amiable, things of good report: having these in mind, studying and loving these, is what saves states.

However, the old gentleman, when writing these exuberant sentences, had no illusion about their being put into force by the majority. These moral concepts would prevail, he said, only as they were upheld by "the remnant" of leaders and thinkers who loved wisdom; for the majority, he insisted, was full of "prosperities, idolatries, oppression, luxury, pleasures, and careless women. . . . That shall come to nought and pass away."

"The remnant" in America of those who love wisdom and have the ability to compete with any nation in the world is very large. It has greatly increased as the population of the nation has increased, but it needs to be brought to bear on the great purposes of the nation more than it is today, and this is obviously one task of Presidential leadership.

Meanwhile, there is no cause to despair over the evidence of disorder and menace, for in all the golden ages of history, disorder and hazard have existed alongside vitality and creativeness.

"Surely our age shares many characteristics with the earlier golden times," Caryl P. Haskins, president of the Carnegie Institution of Washington, has written. "Theirs is the wide feeling of insecurity, the deep-lying anxiety, the sense of confusion, not unlike the earlier times in general character. . . .

"But there is likewise the same intense concern with new ideas and new concepts, the same eagerness for widened vistas of understanding. . . ."

What Mr. Haskins did not say was that these golden ages were also periods of great leaders who knew how to bring ideas and politics together, and this seems to me to be the heart of our present problem.

2 THE PARADOX OF AMERICA

WASHINGTON, March 5, 1968—Go across the full length of this great country and what do you find? Material progress beyond the dreams of kings. Vast soaring commercial palaces of glass even in the middle cities. The bulldozer and the pneumatic drill, energy, noise, change, the fantastic beauty of the Los Angeles Art Center, and the slums of Watts. The lowest national unemployment rate in many years and the highest black teenage rate of unemployment and crime on record.

The paradoxes are endless: We have probably never had so much moral concern or moral indifference at the same time in our history. But business in America has never been more savagely competitive or more conscious of its social responsibilities. It is filling the central cities with some of the finest architecture of the age and the suburbs with some of the most vulgar monstrosities in the long sad story of commercial construction.

We have never had more prosperity and poverty at the same time as we have now, never more problems or opportunities existing side by side. It is impossible to go across this country without being impressed by the fundamental decency and fair-mindedness of the American people. They want to do what's right when they are really confronted with the hard facts. They are deeply divided about the war in Vietnam and the war in the cities, both of which are far away from their daily personal and professional lives, but they hear about it on the TV and in the newspapers, and they are talking about it in the privacy of the family much more than is generally realized.

The Three Questions

Three things seem to get in the way of a rational conclusion about what should be done about the war in Vietnam and the war in the cities. The first is that the Vietnam War is thousands of miles away and the black revolution is on the other side of town. They know both exist, but they don't *feel* it. The new circular highways around the cities fly over and bypass the slums. The mysteries about Vietnam are beyond comprehension. The people are worried about Harlem in New York and Hough in Cleveland and Watts in Los Angeles, but most of them know little more about life in these places than about life in Saigon.

Second, when the people turn to their institutions for help, they feel abandoned. The churches are divided about the war and even about the black revolution. The universities are in turmoil. The military draft is obviously unequal. The press is a confusion of advice between hawks and doves on the war, and the pro- and anti-black arguments in the cities.

Finally, the Johnson Administration asks for confidence and trust for policies which are not succeeding either at home or abroad, so there is no trust or confidence, and the people are left to their own doubts and suspicions.

"A demoralized people," Walter Lippmann wrote in 1932 at the height of the economic depression, "is one in which the individual has become isolated.

. . . He trusts nobody and nothing, not even himself. He believes nothing, except the worst of everybody and everything. He sees only confusion in himself and conspiracies in other men. That is panic. That is disintegration. That is what comes when in some sudden emergency of their lives men find themselves unsupported by clear convictions that transcend their immediate and personal desires.

There is a lot of this in the nation today. And yet, despite all the doubts and confusions and prejudices, there is also a lot of honest debate in America about great issues. The country, one feels, is looking for a new lead, for somebody who will come forward with a new philosophy, and it is not finding the answer in Johnson or any of his political opponents.

The Fatal Divisions

Washington is now the symbol of the helplessness of the present day. The Congress is up in arms against the President's policies, but is impotent to deal with the present trend toward more men and arms for Vietnam. The Republicans are dividing once more between the Rockefeller and Goldwater factions. Even the President's own aides are beginning to have the most serious doubts about a policy which rests on an ineffective and corrupt Government in Saigon.

Yet the political opposition offers no alternative that commands the confidence of a majority of the people. The main crisis is not Vietnam itself, or in the cities, but in the feeling that the political system for dealing with these things has broken down.

3 THE STRANGLED CRY

WASHINGTON, April 6, 1968—The nation is appalled by the murder of Martin Luther King, but it is not appalled by the conditions of his people. It grieves for the man, but not for his cause. This is the curse and tragedy of America.

At least the extremists have kept their promises. The white racists said they would kill King, and the black racists said they would burn us to the ground. And we will not hear again that strangled cry or the rolling Biblical cadences of that magnificent voice; and the smoke is drifting this weekend through the cherry blossoms by the Jefferson Memorial, and the rest of us have not kept our promises to the black people.

The Real Crime

This is the real crime of which the assassination of Dr. King is but a hideous symbol. It will not be redeemed by the capture of the murderer. It can only be redeemed by the transformation of the lives of blacks, and even now America has not faced up to the cost of this historic debt.

When President Johnson's riot commission surveyed the results of the twenty major outbreaks of racial violence recently, it reached the conclusion that despite all the turmoil and the efforts of many concerned citizens and officials, the main reaction in the ghettos of Los Angeles, Detroit, Cleveland, New York, and the other trouble spots was that "nothing much changed— one way or the other."

The Balanced Costs

When Gunnar Myrdal, the Swedish social philosopher who has followed the black problem in America for forty years, came back here recently, he felt that a great deal had changed for the better, but concluded that we had greatly underestimated the scope of the black problem. It would take a revolution in the white attitudes, and twenty years, and "trillions of dollars" to deal with it, he felt, and the cost of not dealing with it would in the long run be much more.

The revolution in the white attitudes is probably the main thing. Neither the Congress nor the Court will solve it. President Johnson may appeal to the conscience of the nation and get another civil rights bill passed, and that may help some, but it is not the answer.

For the problem is not that the Congress is unrepresentative of the American people on the question of jobs and open housing for blacks, but that it is representative. It may even be ahead of the people. Even if the war in Vietnam ended this month, the chances of getting Congress in its present mood to transfer the war appropriations to the ghettos would be extremely remote, and the reasons are fairly clear.

Despite the progress of the last decade in black education, jobs, and housing, the evidence is that a majority of the people are opposed to open housing and many other black demands for an equal and integrated society; and while black violence may produce concessions, it is rapidly reaching the point where it will produce fear and counter-violence that could reverse the trend toward a more compassionate society.

One of the many tragedies of Dr. King's death is that it has silenced the most eloquent black voice for nonviolent protest and tipped the balance toward the black nationalists who call for war and guns. Here the need is for the transformation of the attitudes of the young black militants and their hoodlum gangs. For there is a violent strain in the American people, and if the black arsonists carry the torch from the ghettos to the white communities, it will take more than troops to quell the bloody reaction.

At this critical point, therefore, the leaders of every community—all of them, black and white, labor and management, educational and religious—will have to mobilize to deal with their local situation, whatever it is. The revolution will not be contained by Federal and state officials and appropriations alone, or even by local mayors, and fortunately, we now have the beginnings of a structure for doing just this through the Urban Coalition led by John Gardner, the former Secretary of Health, Education, and Welfare.

Further Polarization

For this is not a problem of government alone, but of American attitudes and assumptions. There was an outcry from some quarters when the President's riot commission suggested that we were moving toward two separate nations, one white and the other black. But the fact is that for most white and black people in the North, this is already a fact, and violence on both sides will merely hasten the process.

The evidence is plain before our eyes. For violence, while it can destroy indifference, which is the curse of the moderate middle class, cannot choose. It destroys good as well as evil. Brute coercion and savage intolerance of blacks must be destroyed, but they cannot be burned away by raging demons intoxicated with illusion.

4   REPEAL THE BILL OF RIGHTS?

WASHINGTON, April 18, 1970—You can put it down as a fairly reliable rule that periods of war or fierce domestic controversy tend to threaten or restrict the constitutional liberties of the American people. And with the war in Vietnam and a crime wave at home, we are clearly going through another such time.

The reasons are plain. The uses of physical violence against the people, property, and institutions of the United States in defiance of the law have created a climate of fear in the country, and under the dominion of fear, a great many people now seem willing to choose order at the expense of some of their liberties, or at least at the expense of somebody else's liberties.

The Counterrevolution

It is hard to estimate just how far this counterrevolution has gone, but recently, CBS News took a nationwide poll which at least gives us a clue. It concluded that the majority of American adults now seem willing to restrict some of the basic freedoms constitutionally guaranteed by the Bill of Rights.

Specifically, about three-fourths of the 1,136 people interviewed in the telephone poll said extremist groups should not be permitted to organize demonstrations against the Government, even if there appeared to be no clear danger of violence.

Over half of those questioned would not give everyone the right to criticize the Government, if the criticism were thought to be damaging to the national interest, and 55 percent added that newspapers, radio, and television should not be permitted to *report* some stories considered by the *Government* to be harmful to the national interest.

On this ground, no group characterized by the Government as "extremist" could even organize a peaceful assembly against the war. The Government could draft them into war they oppose, but they wouldn't even be able to exercise their First Amendment right to demonstrate against such action.

It would not be hard to demonstrate that any serious criticism of the present Government's war effort in Vietnam gives comfort to the enemy and, therefore would be considered by the Government as damaging to the national interest; so should there be no criticism of a war the people have to fight and finance?

The suggested prohibition on reporting things the *Government* thinks damaging to the national interest is even sillier. Most governments think reporting battlefield losses and certainly battlefield atrocities like Mylai are damaging, but even Vice President Agnew hasn't suggested that these reports should be suppressed.

Nor do individual liberties in criminal matters win the support of a majority of those polled by CBS. Nearly three out of every five adults (58 percent) said that if a person is found innocent of a serious crime, but new evidence is uncovered after trial, he should be *tried again*, despite the protection against double jeopardy. And three out of five questioned added that if a person is *suspected* of a serious crime, the police should be allowed to *hold* him in jail until they can get enough evidence to charge him with the crime.

What Goes On?

Well, save my old habeas corpus, what goes on here? Are we to fight a war for the liberties of the Vietnamese people and lose our own in the process? Let the Government take us into an obscene war by stealth at the cost of over forty thousand American dead and not be free to criticize its stupidities or even report its blunders?

The Nixon Administration has already mounted an attack on the press and on the Senate for exercising their constitutional freedoms. Chief Justice Burger has just written a long dissent in the Supreme Court insisting on a far stricter definition of "double jeopardy" than any of the other conservatives on the Court. And Attorney General Mitchell is advocating the right of "preventive detention" of suspected criminals.

Those 462 Words

This, of course, is not wholly new. After the French Revolution, we had the Alien and Sedition Acts of 1789. During the Civil

War, military trials were often substituted for civil trials, and habeas corpus was often suspended. The fear of anarchists led to a wave of repressive measures after the First World War, and the fear of Communist subversion turned us over to the tender mercies of Joe McCarthy after the Second World War. But usually the people fought for their liberties, and now they seem to be acquiescing in their erosion.

In face of all the present civil disorder, it may be understandable, but it is tolerable only if you don't think about it. Maybe we ought to read the Bill of Rights again. After all, it's only 462 words, and we really ought to keep them, at least until the two hundredth anniversary of the Declaration in 1976.

5 THE PAINLESS REVOLUTION

WASHINGTON, Jan. 28, 1971—Change and revolution are generally supposed to be two of the most painful processes in human experience, but most of the talk in Washington now is about painless change and painless revolution.

According to the official rhetoric of the new year, everything is going to get better and nobody is going to get hurt. Under the Vietnamization program, the United States is going to bring the boys back home and South Vietnam is going to be secure. And that's not all.

Under the Nixon Doctrine, the U.S. is going to reduce its overseas commitments, but even the Pentagon is going to be happy, because the defense budget for 1971–72 is going to go up.

The cities and states are going to get more money, the people are going to get more power, more freedom, more jobs, more health care, and a generation of peace, but no more taxes, and eventually no more military conscription.

The theoretical explanation of this remarkably pleasant prospect, of course, is that all this is going to be possible because there is going to be far more wealth to go around. The G.N.P. is now running at the rate of over a trillion dollars a year, so the Government will be able to increase the defense budget, pay more for a volunteer army, and have enough left over to bail out the bankrupt cities and states and provide for the economic and social reconstruction of the people.

Well, America is still the land of wonders, and all this is not quite so contradictory as it sounds; but still, there is something wrong with this alluring picture, and what is wrong is that it leaves out people, and at best, it minimizes the problems of the rest of the world.

The evidence of recent years, and centuries for that matter, is that the human race does not accommodate itself to these dreams, at least not without quite a lot of pain. The people are multiplying faster than the jobs, even in the United States. The distribution of the people and of the money needed to sustain them is uneven and cruel, and if history tells us anything, it is that we are not immune to the miseries and conflicts of the rest of the world.

Although agricultural production is now going up dramatically, Robert McNamara, president of the World Bank, testifies that at least a third to a half of the world's people suffer from hunger or malnutrition.

Infant mortality is four times as high in the poor countries as in the rich, and there are over one hundred million more illiterates in the world today than there were twenty years ago.

In these same poor or developing countries, approximately 20 percent of the entire male population is unemployed. In short, the gap between the rich and the poor countries is not getting narrower, but wider, and while the nations of the world are spending over two hundred billion dollars a year on military arms, the rich industrial countries are not even meeting their goal of providing seven billion a year for the poor countries—and this at a time when even the illiterates are beginning to understand that poverty is not inevitable, but intolerable.

In the face of all this, it is clear that there is still a fundamental difference between thoughtful men about what is the most serious threat to the security of the Republic and the order of the world. The Administration has come forward with some imaginative ideas on welfare reform, government reform, and budget reform, but it is still hard to believe that it has accepted the full scale of the national or world economic and social crisis.

It is talking about "the new American Revolution" to come from revenue-sharing and Government reorganization, and better management of the resources and environment of the nation, but men like McNamara and Lester Pearson of Canada are talking about the world revolution—indeed, about a kind of class war between the rich and poor nations—that is going on right now.

"A planet," said Pearson in his report to the United Nations, "cannot, any more than a country, survive half-slave and half-free, half engulfed in misery, half careening along toward the supposed joys of almost unlimited consumption."

"In that direction," adds McNamara, "lies disaster, yet that is our direction today unless we are prepared to change course, and do so in time. . . . There are really no material obstacles to a sane, manageable, and progressive response to the world's development needs. The obstacles lie in the minds of men. We have simply not thought long enough and hard enough about the fundamental problems. . . ."

As it happens, McNamara agrees with many of the innovations suggested by President Nixon, but he sees a larger and more dangerous revolution that cannot be removed by military arms—and he clearly believes that dealing with it is essential, costly, and even painful.

6 A DEBT OF HONOR

WASHINGTON, Feb. 7, 1973—After the return of the prisoners from Vietnam, after all the consoling ceremonies at the White House, and the family reunions and tears on television, the reality for the prisoners coming home at last will begin in private. When they come home from Vietnam, what will they find?

The rest of us will never really understand. Most of us in this big continental country never had a son or relation killed or maimed in Vietnam. America lost over 46,000 dead, but for most of us, this was a statistic in the papers and not a tragedy in the family or down the street.

For the liberated prisoners and their families, however, it is an intensely personal crisis. On the television, it looks like a reunion of lovers and families, but in reality, it is a reunion of strangers.

The prisoners come back different men, usually helpless or rebellious. They have had to surrender to endure. Many of them have literally been "killing time," which means killing their fears, blotting out the present, romanticizing the past, and dreaming of a family and an America that are changed beyond their imagining.

In the history of the Republic, the Vietnam War will probably look like a capricious incident, but the United States was already involved in it casually but carefully under President Eisenhower in 1953, twenty years ago, and much more deeply involved under President Kennedy in 1963. In family terms, this is a very long time.

The Census Bureau in Washington tells us that over half the people in the United States are now under twenty-eight years of age. This means that most of our people cannot even remember much before we were involved in Vietnam. And in the lives of the prisoners now coming home, most of whom are under twenty-five, Vietnam dominates everything.

They not only come home different men but come home to the same but different and older wives, different children, a different country, with different memories and different values. After the reunion and the celebration, trying to sort all this out at home and in the community is bound to be an agony.

The least that can be done for these returning prisoners is to see that they are given good jobs and relieved of the economic anxiety of taking care of the security of their wives and the education of their children. But even this is not enough.

No doubt the communities they return to will see that they are employed, but after a few years, it is easy to forget. So while the President and the Congress are now celebrating the courage and endurance of the prisoners, maybe they should agree on a prisoners bill that would ensure the economic security of these families during the coming years, when they will still be struggling with the consequences of Vietnam, long after most people have forgotten.

After all, the prisoners amount to only a few hundred, and their sacrifice is not as great as the tens of thousands who were killed in the struggle, but they are a symbol of the tragedy of the Vietnam War and the conscience of America, and if the Government is as sympathetic and grateful as it now says, maybe it should not only welcome them home but give them a chance for a secure economic future after the celebrations are over.

If the returning American prisoners are to be dealt with practically, and not merely politically or romantically, legislation must be introduced now, with the support of the President and the leaders of the Congress, to relieve these families of their economic anxieties.

The Government cannot wipe out their memories. The war has gone on too long and many of them have been in prison for too many years to regain a normal family life or readjust to the values and styles of America that changed so much while they were in prison.

Some of the prisoners will have been strengthened by sacrifice and adversity, and will come back to families ennobled by sorrow and fidelity; but others will be overwhelmed by remorse, and even the austere and faithful families may have trouble with their wayward children.

For a returning prisoner to deal with all this, even in the best of circumstances, to make decisions when for years he had no power of decision, to get to know himself at another time of life, and his wife, and his growing and transformed children—this is a challenge beyond the reach of most men.

Right now, however, when the President and the Congress are conscious of the returning prisoner's problems, there is at least a chance to ease his economic burdens in a time of inflation and unemployment, and give him time to think and sort things out.

Speeches of gratitude from the President, which are undoubtedly sincere, and homecoming celebrations and parades on Main Street, are not really enough. These prisoners and their families need to be relieved for a time of economic worries to deal with their personal and family anxieties, and a Government that speaks of "peace with honor" owes them a debt of honor, which so far has not been paid.

---

7 CONFUSION OF LOYALTIES

WASHINGTON, Sept. 28, 1975—In recent days, we have had strikes of teachers in New York and many other places, of policemen in San Francisco, and of professional football players in Boston. Also, spectacular kidnappings, murders, demonstrations against busing and abortion, and two threats on the life of the President of the United States.

It is hard and maybe even silly to try to generalize about all these events, which run from madness to justifiable grievances and to honest expressions of conscience, but coming together within the short space of a few weeks, they seem almost absurd. Is there any way to explain all this disorder and reduce all this inexplicable diversity to some kind of identity?

One thing is fairly obvious. A great many people in this country are now modifying their loyalty to the authority and purposes of the Federal, state, and local governments, and transferring it to personal commitments or to unions, business associations, or social cults of various kinds.

After all the analysis of the Watergate and Vietnam tragedies, there seemed to be a general consensus that the men around Johnson and Nixon had somehow got trapped in a confusion of loyalties. But despite all the mystifying clarifications of these two events, the confusion of loyalties seems to go on.

The loyalty of the striking policemen in San Francisco and even of the striking teachers in some cities was not to the law but to their own associations and personal interests. The workers who refused to load the grain for the Soviet Union substituted their own foreign policy for President Ford's and Secretary Kissinger's.

The Boston Patriots put "union solidarity" ahead of their obligations to their "loyal fans," who pay high prices to park and watch their heroes, and the Washington Redskins, averaging over fifty thousand dollars a season, joined the strike.

Defiance of the law may not be as general or violent now as it was in the sixties, but it is fairly clear that we are still in an era of confrontation rather than negotiation, despite all the Presidential promises of the last few years.

Individuals and associations of individuals are acting on their own notions of what the laws should be, and, ironically, they all seem to feel the need to be loyal to something. Squeaky Fromme pulls a gun on the President in Sacramento apparently because she feels lost in her private life, has no family of her own, but is loyal to Manson's bizarre collection of defeated and frustrated souls.

Patty Hearst was either captured or captivated by the Symbionese mystique, and gives her clenched fist "loyalty" salute to what she calls "revolutionary feminism." It is all a little odd. She will not be a "prisoner" in her parents' home, she says, apparently forgetting that her parents have been prisoners of her own madness for the past year.

"Do your own thing" seems to be the motto of the contemporary counterculture, and it is not limited to the kooks. Not only Nixon's gang but other top officials of the Federal Government, we now know, have not only been following his illegal practices but even disobeying his legal authority—hiding the most lethal military poisons and weapons, even after he ordered their destruction.

So it is obviously not merely the human wreckage of our society that substitutes its own selfish interests for the law. The record has been laid out on Capitol Hill in the last few days and even admitted that big American corporations made illegal and concealed political payments to political parties in the United

States and that they paid out millions to get contracts for planes and tanks and missiles overseas.

The United States is now both the foremost advocate of peace and disarmament in the world and the most successful peddler of the most sophisticated military weapons ever invented. In the Middle East alone, Henry Kissinger is the principal mediator for peace, but the Pentagon is the major arsenal for planes, tanks, and missiles not only for Israel but for the Arab world.

An argument can be made for all these seemingly contradictory decisions by the Ford Administration, but President Ford is not making it. He has his own confusion of loyalties. For almost twenty-five years, he has been a Capitol Hill man, a leader of the Republican Party, a member of the Armed Services Subcommittee of the Appropriations Committee, a philosopher and darling of the Republican conservatives at political rallies. But he has not convinced either the labor unions, or even the conservative business community, let alone the revolutionary crazies, that he has a program for America's problems.

So they all operate on their own. Lacking confidence in either the Republican or the Democratic leaders, they create their own associations to confront and even defy the authority of government. This is the central problem: Increasingly, individuals and associations are giving loyalty to themselves, and forgetting about the common problems of the nation.

8 A RETURN OF CONFIDENCE

WASHINGTON, Dec. 18, 1976—The signs of change now dominate the capital. The inauguration stands are going up on Capitol Hill. President Ford is sending his official papers to the National Archives. The book publishers are throwing money at Henry, and the new boys in town are whistling Dixie.

In the few short weeks since the election, the mood of Washington has been transformed. Somehow the town seems younger and livelier. All the old problems remain at home and abroad, but with the innocence of inexperience, the newcomers have revived the spirit of hope.

The transfer of power from one government to another has been turbulent in China, Japan, Spain, and Portugal in recent months, but here, after a bitter war, a constitutional crisis, and a very close election campaign, the political system has worked in good order and even with amiable good humor.

Much credit for this must go to President Ford. Here is a caretaker who has really taken care. Though he became increasingly eager for victory as the election campaign went on and though he lost by a whisker, he has not uttered a single grudging word of criticism or even regret.

Unlike Mr. Nixon, who is still fighting in the courts for personal control and exploitation of his Government papers, Mr. Ford handed over everything except his pipes, photographs, and a few other mementos. The first thing he said when he came into the White House was that "our long national nightmare is over," and if this is true, he can leave knowing that he helped lead us out of the tunnel.

The condition of the nation at the end of the old Administration and the old year is far from ideal but in relative terms it seems manageable. The economy still has the hiccups, with both unemployment and inflation higher than Governor Carter expected during the campaign, but more Americans are employed today than ever before, and the United States is leading the world out of the recession, and the economic indicators promise more progress for the coming year.

Elsewhere in the world, there are obvious problems. Beginning close to home, there is some anxiety here about the financial crisis in Mexico, which is exporting its unemployed to this country, and in Canada, whose unity is threatened once more by the separatist movement in Quebec. Accordingly, the outlook is for some anxious days along our two great borders in the Carter years.

Nevertheless, the worst fears of a few years ago have been avoided. The defeat in Vietnam did not destroy the world's confidence in the United States, as often predicted. Washington still has better relations with China and the Soviet Union than they have with one another. The Western alliance is a little shaky and the political weather is stormy in Japan, Britain, France, and even West Germany, but the calamitous predictions about the mounting cost of oil have not come to pass in the industrial world, and there is even new hope for another step toward peace in the Middle East.

There are, of course, fundamental differences here about the relative military strengths of the United States and the Soviet Union. Also, the big United States labor unions are increasingly worried about the importation of illegal foreign workers and the exportation of jobs by the multinational corporations, and these problems, along with the energy crisis, are likely to test the new Administration before its first one hundred days are over.

Still, Governor Carter's approach to his coming responsibilities has added to the growing confidence in Washington. He has not been as populist or as conservative as his opponents feared during the campaign. He is putting together a cabinet of energetic, pragmatic, nonideological problem-solvers, and recruiting under them the youngest and most enthusiastic team seen around here since the early days of the New Deal.

All this is contributing to the new sense of bustle and optimism, and of course it may be a temporary and deceptive phase, but the psychological and political atmosphere is obviously different, not only downtown in the big executive departments but in Congress as well.

The fight over the majority leadership in the House, resulting in the narrow victory of Representative James Wright of Texas, has left some open wounds. Also, it seems likely now that Senator Robert Byrd of West Virginia will defeat Hubert Humphrey for the majority leadership of the Senate, but in both houses it will be a new beginning under different men who are likely to give Governor Carter more support than they gave President Ford during the last two years.

One other point: The element of luck in this superstitious town is a big factor in politics, and the impression is getting around that Mr. Carter is not only a capable and confident but a lucky man, and his confidence is obviously infectious.

Thus, the mood has changed here for the better, not because the problems have changed, but because the new men believe they can change things, and the rest of the capital is eager for change. In general, things are seldom quite as good or as bad as they seem here in Washington, but for the moment, people seem to feel better, even if they don't quite know why.

---

9   HOW TO WIN THE PULITZER

WASHINGTON, April 7, 1979—This year's Pulitzer Prize for public service by a newspaper went to the *Point Reyes* (California) *Light*, a husband-and-wife weekly, with a circulation of 2,700. It beat all the big city dailies and syndicates with its reporting on Synanon, a drug-rehabilitation center in its neighborhood, which the editors believed had degenerated into an authoritarian cult.

It is one of those romantic Ben Hecht, Ring Lardner, or Horatio Alger stories: Young, struggling couple out of Stanford University, David and Catherine Mitchell, buy little rag of a paper, defy the powerful interests in the community, and win the big prize.

Well, it's all true—it's David and Goliath, small is beautiful, and all that. But this little personal and local triumph is a symbol of something much bigger in the history of the press and of democracy in the United States.

We are in the middle of a printing revolution in this country, maybe comparable to the invention of movable type. The developments of photocomposition and the offset press have transformed the communication of ideas.

It is no longer necessary to find professionals who can master the lovely but complicated techniques of the linotype machine in order to set metal slugs and arrange them in steel forms and read them upside down.

The same thing can be done now by modern photocomposition computers, far less expensive than linotypes, by anyone who can master a typewriter, and then, with a clear eye and a pair of scissors, paste up the column-wide rivulets of photocomposed type into pages for production into thin metal plates for the new, modern offset presses.

I talked to David Mitchell at the quaint Reyes *Light* newspaper in California about how he and his wife had managed to put all this together, with only one other reporter, and somehow had hit the jackpot. He said that they had gambled on the new technology. They sold their house and bought the paper for less than fifty thousand dollars, and they all typed and pasted up, and worked together on the news. They couldn't, he said, have afforded or survived under the old hot-metal technology—no way!

There may be an important point here about technology and democracy in America. The conventional wisdom is that our machines are destroying our liberty and that the tax structure and death duties are forcing privately owned newspapers to sell out to public combines and syndicates.

It is true that the number of daily newspapers in the United States is declining, but as people move from the cities to the suburbs and beyond that to the villages, especially along the seacoasts, the weekly or country newspapers are growing and attracting more and more young, intelligent people who are looking for a simpler refuge from city life.

Thus, the modern printing technology can be a liberating force. Any group of people, of whatever political, economic, social, or religious persuasion, can now, even with limited finances in these inflationary times, paste up a newspaper and have it printed by some local jobber.

This competition is going on now all over the United States. The big syndicates are challenging the major newspapers in the suburbs of the great cities. Even in the villages, new papers are using the new printing techniques to appeal to limited audiences, and this is a good thing. The Pulitzer Prize for the little paper in Point Reyes emphasizes and encourages this spirit of competition.

Obviously, the big daily newspapers and syndicates are not amused by the Pulitzer Prize awards in all cases. Many of them did good work in the last year and hoped for the public service Pulitzer award, and there will undoubtedly be endless controversy about why David and Catherine Mitchell got the gold medal rather than the big papers in New York, Philadelphia, Chicago, and Los Angeles.

But who is to say? For every prize recommended by the Pulitzer board, many others are disappointed and some are aggrieved and even angry. Life is unfair, said John Kennedy, who gained and lost everything in the end; but it has a way of sorting things out and remembering people who do their work—Herbert Block of *The Washington Post*, Ed Yoder of *The Washington Star*, Russell Baker of *The New York Times*, and many others, including David and Catherine Mitchell of the *Light*, in Point Reyes, California.

The theory is that we perpetuate what we reward, and this year's prize to the Mitchells dramatizes the point.

The only trouble with this is that the one Pulitzer Prize, the gold medal for the Mitchells, didn't include the usual thousand-dollar check. The Pulitzer board has always assumed that the winner of the public service award would probably be a big paper that didn't need the thousand dollars. But the Mitchells needed it more than anybody else, just to pay for the celebration of their neighbors in the city room when the news came to Point Reyes.

---

10 MARCH ON THE CAPITAL

WASHINGTON, Aug. 27, 1983—President Reagan was out of town when close to a quarter of a million people came calling here today for "jobs, peace, and freedom." And maybe he was wise to be absent. For he referred earlier in this week to the demonstrators against his nuclear arms policies as "the so-called peace movement," which they regarded as a slur comparable to calling him "the so-called President."

He tried to make amends by endorsing the objective of the march, and issued a statement in praise of their dreams as they gathered in the Mall to condemn his policies.

It's easy to understand why the President interrupted his vacation to address the American Legion convention in Seattle this week, and avoided the multitude gathered at the Lincoln Memorial on the twentieth anniversary of Martin Luther King, Jr.'s march on Washington. He is more comfortable with the old soldiers.

What is not easy to understand is why he insists on mocking the peace marchers. "Peace is a beautiful word," the President told the Legion. "The real peacemakers are people like you." Those who abuse the beautiful word "peace," he added—using two ugly words—are engaged in a campaign of "modern hype and theatrics"; and he should know, being a master of both.

There is clearly an honest difference of opinion in this country about how to get the nuclear arms race under control. The President and the Legion believe that the way to peace lies in more and more military arms, more MX missiles, B-1 bombers, and even the militarization of outer space. It would be a mistake to doubt their sincerity.

On the other hand, the marchers here in the Washington sunshine, with equal sincerity, believe that "the real and present danger" to the Republic is not the threat of a Soviet nuclear attack on the United States or its allies, but in economic and social disruption, unemployment, and moral chaos in the Western world.

Both sides have something important to say, and are worthy of respect, but there can be no honest debate if the President vilifies his opposition as a lot of misguided dreamers, and his opponents condemn him as a cold-war warrior who is not really interested in the control of nuclear weapons.

The facts are quite different. The President always sounds like "the boy on the burning deck" or "the terrible-tempered Mr. Bangs," but actually, he has proposed more compromises on nuclear arms control than the Russians have.

He has not cut down the budget for arms control under Ken-

neth Adelman, but has increased it, given the disarmament organization more staff in its relations with the State and Defense
Departments, and insisted that it make every effort possible to
reach a verifiable compromise with the Russians and the allies on
the control of nuclear weapons.

The puzzling thing about Mr. Reagan is that he says so many
outrageous, provocative things in public, but acts so cautiously in
private. He condemns the Soviet Union as an "evil empire" for its
invasion of Afghanistan, its pressure on Poland, and even for its
"godless philosophy," denounces his allies for selling gas-pipeline
facilities to the Soviet Union, and then lifts controls on the sale of
pipe-laying equipment to the Russians and signs an agreement to
supply them with nine million tons of grain a year for the next
five years, not knowing what will happen in the meanwhile.

Even Mr. Reagan's own officials complain about his inconsis-
tency. They observe that he's in trouble with the Russians on the
control of nuclear arms because he started out with one policy
and has switched three or four more times.

It's not that he has a clear intention, but that he has no intention at all; that he balances the books every day, addresses his
friends and avoids his opponents, and leaves everything to
chance, with the next Presidential election in mind.

What's surprising is that, coming out of a poor and church
background, Mr. Reagan seems so indifferent to the conscience of
the preachers and the plight of the unemployed workers. These
are the people he came from, and it's astonishing that he seems to
have forgotten their faith and longing.

The point about this weekend's march in Washington is to
remember Martin Luther King's crying out from the Lincoln
Memorial: "I have a dream!"

In many ways, his dream has been realized. Look around and
you can see how black people have achieved their pride in these
last twenty years, while not forgetting the many who have been
left behind.

But what is our dream now? What is President Reagan's
dream? What if he had stayed home in Washington this weekend
and faced the crowd? What would he have said in the shadow of

the Lincoln Memorial? Like Lincoln at the end of the War Between the States, would he have asked us to bind up our wounds
and try to get together? And to think, as Lincoln thought, that as
the world is new, we must think anew, respecting one another
and working together?

---

11 WHERE ARE WE GOING?

WASHINGTON, Dec. 22, 1979—This is a troubled city, at the end
of the 1970s, because it is leading a life of pretense. It is anxious,
not primarily because of its immediate problems at home and
abroad, but because of a growing conviction that it is dealing with
a world of divided national states that is out of control and that
the Government is not working effectively on the challenges of
the eighties.

Put more simply, what is bothering thoughtful people in both
parties here is that the world changed faster in the seventies than
we have been able to change ourselves; that the prevailing attitudes of our people and the assumptions of our institutions, including the divided responsibilities of the Federal Government,
are out of date.

There is a vague understanding here that some kind of major
transformation took place in the world of the seventies; that the
United States was no longer self-sufficient in the resources essential to sustain its industrial growth; that it was no longer the most
productive or most successful nation in the export markets of the
world; and maybe not even the undisputed military or moral
leader in the shifting balance of a rapidly changing world.

But Washington has not been able to adjust to these fundamental changes. It has been trying to deal with them as if they
were a passing phase which could be corrected by a larger defense
budget or by blaming Carter and substituting Kennedy or
Reagan or Connally or somebody else who would make the rest of
the globe shape up to our ideals and interests.

Meanwhile, as Congress scatters for the Christmas holidays, depriving us of its advice (which may not be an intolerable loss), we clearly need a little time at the turn of the year to sort out and redefine our problems and priorities. The OPEC nations and Ayatollah Khomeini are trying to tell us something: namely, that we are confronted not only by the growing power of Soviet missiles in Eastern Europe and by Moscow's naval power in the oceans of the world but by the economic power of the oil-producing nations and the philosophic challenge of Islam to the materialism of the West.

The political debates raging in the headlines of the world's press these days—in Iran and elsewhere—do not really deal with the deeper and more tragic tides running under the surface. The world is being changed, not primarily by the ayatollahs or even by the contemporary leaders of the principal industrial states. The world is being changed by the fertility of the human body and the mind; by ordinary people who produce more children than they can feed and educate; by science that preserves life at the beginning and prolongs it at the end, leaving to the politicians the problem of finding remedies for this deluge.

Where the politicians as well as the teachers and preachers and reporters and editors can be faulted is in failing to make this fundamental fact clear to the people as the central question for decision. Here in Washington, for example, at the end of the old year and decade, we are preoccupied, and understandably so, with the lives of some fifty American captives in Teheran. So, too, we confront the paradox of increasing the United States defense budget in order to control the arms race; and the struggle for the American Presidency among a group of men who have been talking about transitory issues, as if nothing had changed— and if it had, it was somebody else's fault.

But under the surface of these arguments, there are serious people with long experience in Washington and elsewhere who recognize structural defects in our Government that must be repaired if we are to deal with our present and coming problems.

This is not a partisan or ideological observation. For example,

Douglas Dillon, former Under Secretary of State and Secretary of the Treasury, called the other day before the National Institute of Social Services in New York for a reappraisal of our thought and government to deal with all these changing problems:

> What we are suffering from today is not incompetence in our Foreign Service, or in our intelligence services, or in the office of the President. Unfortunately, our problem gives every sign of being much more serious than that. It is, in my view, the beginnings of a crisis in the operation of our basic system of government.
>
> We must learn to accustom ourselves to a new world, a world in which actions taken by others can have rapid and serious effects on our economy and on our standard of living, a world in which others have the military means to destroy our nation whenever they are prepared to accept the consequences. I very much doubt, that in such a world we can long continue to afford the luxury of the division of power and responsibility between our executive and legislative branches of government . . . . I have no pat answer. But I do know that until we are prepared to examine the basic structure of our Federal system and its functioning in today's world rather than indulging ourselves in continuous personal and political recriminations, our problems will remain with us and, in all probability, increase in severity.

12   CHANGING OF THE GUARD

WASHINGTON, Jan. 13, 1981—The changing of the guard in Washington is much more than a switch of power and policy. For those going out and those coming in, it is a deeply moving personal experience.

For while it is popular to blame Washington for all our anxieties these days, it has a kind of magical attraction for those who wish to serve their country. It may tear up their private lives when they come here, yet most of them hate to leave, for despite all their regrets and disappointments, they usually remember their work here, successful or not, as one of the most important chapters of their lives.

This is not a sentimental point about the people at the top in Government, except maybe for Jimmy Carter. The guess here is that he will wake in the night for the rest of his life, wondering what went wrong and why he was rejected. He will have no financial problems; the job of ex-President is the surest hedge against inflation in America today. He will have everything, like Richard Nixon, except the work he loved and lost.

Carter's Cabinet and his White House staff will disappear from here in a few days, and will probably have nothing to worry about except their income taxes. It's an amusing paradox in this country that the big corporations rail against the leaders of the Democratic Party in Congress and the Cabinet, then hire them at preposterous salaries when the Democrats are defeated.

What's particularly interesting in this case is that so many prominent members of the defeated Carter Administration can't go home again, or have been here so long in exciting jobs that they don't want to go home and in many cases don't really know where home is. Their children are grown and scattered, their friends of middle age are here, their political careers are over. Secretary of State Muskie and Secretary of Defense Brown, for example, will not go back to Maine or California, but will settle here in some useful and lucrative jobs on the fringe of politics.

The changing of the guard in Washington is not merely changing offices. It is changing houses, changing schools, leaving old friends, changing relationships between husband and wife and children, taking on new responsibilities, abandoning old clichés and comrades.

Perhaps the hardest of this transition, for men coming in and men going out, is for their women. They are the ones, while the old man is posing for his picture on arrival or departure, who have to get ready for the movers, console the children, give the farewell or welcoming parties for the staff in just the right dress, pretty and smiling—and then clean up the mess.

This is a hard town on women. Politics is more dangerous than booze or sex, being excessively vulnerable to both. The subject is beyond journalism, and it's a mystery why no great novelist or biographer has failed to concentrate on the glories and contributions the women of this town have made to the history of the Republic.

There is another aspect of this transition from Carter to Reagan that has scarcely been mentioned. This is the role of the many young people in their twenties and early thirties who were recruited by Jack Watson, Hamilton Jordan, Jody Powell, and others to serve at the lower political levels of the Carter Administration. Some of them were, to put the point gently, less than adequate, but many of them were very good indeed, and these are the people who are the real losers of the departing crowd here— unknown, unrecognized, and out of work.

It is not as hard on them because they are younger than the defeated Democratic Senators such as George McGovern, Frank Church, and Birch Bayh, who were defeated in middle age, just when they expected to enjoy the advantages of seniority after their long years in the Senate.

For the work in Washington is very special for those who have had even a small part in serving the nation. No amount of work or money quite equals it. No other city is so maddening, frustrating, or, paradoxically, so satisfying.

Al Haig has achieved more in his thirty-eight years as a military man than anybody else except maybe Dwight Eisenhower or General George Marshall. He has had a triple heart bypass and has no knowledge how long he can endure. He is not a rich man, yet he has given up the security of a nine-million-dollar private job to accept his appointment as Secretary of State.

Why? Because, as with so many others who are coming here with Reagan or leaving here with Carter, Washington has all the attractions of a love affair, with all the potential dangers and glories that suggests.

This is why the Reagan people are coming in with such enthusiasm and the Carter people are leaving with such regret. Some town! the big shots say, going through the revolving door. But it is their women who have to suffer their fleeting successes and console their losses.

13   YOU *CAN* GO HOME AGAIN

URBANA, Ill., Sept. 15, 1984—Many old folks in this gypsy country would probably agree with Thomas Wolfe that "you can't go home again," but after coming back here to the University of Illinois for a fiftieth class reunion, I disagree.

Nothing makes the nation seem larger or the individual smaller than returning to the campus half a century after they turned you loose. Sometimes you *have to* go home again—if you can remember where it is—to understand the meaning of time and the power of ideas.

It was here in Illinois that Justin Smith Morrill, former Senator from Vermont, convinced President Lincoln to take time out during the Civil War to provide Federal land for the creation of "seats of learning" for the education of the children of the poor.

You should see these land-grant colleges now: in Chapel Hill, North Carolina, where Thomas Wolfe and two of my own sons went to college, or in Champaign-Urbana, where I met my wife, who assumed the formidable task of educating me.

This place is now jumping with life. According to Chuck Flynn, another old scribbler on the Champaign-Urbana *News-Gazette*, there were 10,892 "students" here fifty years ago, and there are now over 32,000. The budget of the university that year was $6.5 million; it's now $491.6 million. Today, everything is bigger, noisier, and dirtier, but by some magic, while everything looks different to the old generation, it probably seems the same to the new generation.

The Big Prairie and the Big Sky still dominate the growing towns of Champaign-Urbana. The big student body is composed of young men and women who, as usual, are still more interested in one another and in biology than in any other subject.

Some things are different. Back yonder, we were instructed by Tommy Arkle Clark, the dean of men, to "keep off the grass" in the lovely quadrangle between the colleges. And the dean of women, Maria Leonard, warned the young women not to wear red dresses on the theory that this might arouse the passions of young men.

Now the grass is a coeducational picnic and mating ground. The boys in their jockstrap shorts and the girls in their cutoff jeans leave little to the imagination, which may explain why they are more interested in having fun than in having children.

Football is different, too. They've put the "foot" back into the game since the drop-kicking days of "Frosty" Peters here. Red Grange is still vaguely remembered as the runner who left Michigan in the dust, but now there is no dust on these plastic gridirons and the runners have been replaced by passers.

Yet the other day, when we watched Illinois beat Missouri with the help of a running clock and a driving rainstorm, almost eighty thousand spectators—the largest crowd in Illinois football history—wandered across the campus through the mist, and one wondered what they thought.

They were clearly drenched but happy. In these indecisive days of politics, sports are at least decisive. They have rules and referees, and everybody knows at the end who won. And there were symbols on the fringe of this campus that would probably have pleased Senator Morrill and President Lincoln.

There was, first, the vast crowd in Memorial Stadium, one of the few noble sports arenas in the land, with its columns high above the field, dedicated to remembering the forgotten heroes of forgotten wars. And behind the stadium, in the rain, are the university's experimental agricultural plots, which probably few people notice.

But in looking back over the long history of this university, I think that it is probably on the land, rather than in the machine shops or even the scientific laboratories, that America has led and is still the envy of a hungry world. And the land-grant colleges were undoubtedly the seedbed of that agricultural revolution.

So it was good to go home again and see what institutions do for the continuity of ideas and life. I was a little sorry for the students on two counts: They have so many varied choices now. They cannot quite appreciate the simplicity of the adversity of the Depression days, when we expected so little and got so much.

Also, while the girls seemed recklessly smart and pretty, they didn't seem nearly as smart or pretty as the one I took away fifty years ago.

14 THE CLASS OF 1985

Washington, May 19, 1985—Most of the young men and women graduating from college this year were born in or around 1963, the year President John F. Kennedy was murdered.

They were five years old when President Nixon was elected, eleven when he resigned after Watergate, twelve at the end of the Vietnam War, and seventeen or eighteen when they entered college and Ronald Reagan entered the White House.

Dates are important. For this year's college graduates, the recent fortieth anniversary of the Second World War, with its flickering black-and-white television pictures of broken cities and broken lives, must have seemed almost as remote as the struggles of the pioneers on the prairies or the bread lines and the flight of the Okies during the Great Depression.

So it's no surprise that there's a gap, as usual, between the memories of the Class of 1985 and the perceptions of their parents and grandparents. But somehow, or so it seems in this corner, the gap is wider and deeper this year than usual.

It's not only that the graduates and their old folks have changed, but that the nation has changed faster than we can change ourselves. The population of the United States has increased by over fifty million since this year's graduates were born. The wheeled industries have moved into the computerized world, from coal and steel into laser beams on earth and even in the stars.

This is not the sort of thing, in the confusion of leaving college, most young graduates are thinking about. They probably think they're going into a world as dangerous and troublesome as any faced by any other generation. But I happen to think they're the lucky ones and are going into the most hopeful years of the twentieth century.

In the next fifteen years, despite all the present commercial conflicts, local wars, tribal brutalities, and philosophical confrontations backed by nuclear weapons, the chances are that the Class of 1985 will not have to face a third world war in this century; and if they do, in this nuclear age, they won't have to endure it for long.

Their problems are likely to be quite different and maybe more difficult: not how to deal with war that threatens the nation and brings people together; not even how to deal with adversity (the poor and uneducated, as usual, have to deal with that); but how to deal with prosperity and the new Four Freedoms of the modern age: the freedom of sex, the freedom of booze and other drugs, the freedom of divorce, and the freedom to run away from the consequences of their disbelief in anybody or anything.

This is a hard call for the Class of 1985. Most of the 960,000 college graduates this year will get jobs, including the 60,000 blacks among them—most in useful work far from the sooty industrial tunnels of the past. They'll work in the new, clean, antiseptic computerized service industries in the sun: jobs for both educated husbands and wives, bringing in enough money to hire other people to look after their children.

There are ways to escape from this opulent trap of material success, but the Class of 1985 has not had much help in trying to do so.

Since high-school days they have been encouraged to believe that college is not a means to an understanding of the history and poetry of life, but an employment agency, promising two careers in every family, and two cars in every garage.

The Wall Street Journal reported the other day that economics was now the favored subject among undergraduates, even at Harvard. In the early 1970s, economics at Harvard ranked sixth, after studies in history, English literature, government, philosophy, and something called the psychology of social responsibility. But no more. Even the *Journal*, no enemy of economics, didn't seem to think that this switch in priorities was a good idea.

The Class of 1985 has heard a great deal in these last four years about the "gross national product," the menace of the Russians, and the dangers of Federal budget and trade deficits—all important—but very little about the suffering of the human family at home or abroad.

In a period of spiritual bewilderment, this year's college graduates have been asked, often in the name of religion, to confuse selfishness with self-reliance, to regard their own government as an enemy, and to concentrate on their own material well-being. My kingdom come . . . My will be done . . . Hallowed be My name . . . .

It will take awhile for the Class of '85 to sort out the tinsel and hollow political cardboard characters and false values of the present day. Here's hoping they'll have somebody to hold their hand to keep it from trembling.

15 THE MISSOURI COMPROMISE

WASHINGTON, Oct. 23, 1985—Without taking sides between the Royalists of Kansas City and the Cardinals of St. Louis, it is clear that both are in violation of the spirit of compromise that brought the state of Missouri into the Federal Union on August 10, 1821. Not being satisfied to join the club, they decided, in 1985, to take the joint over.

As every attentive high-school student knows, the Missouri Compromise of 1821 stipulated that Missouri would not be given the status of a state until it agreed that nothing in its Constitution should be interpreted to abridge the privileges and immunities of any citizens of the United States.

The meaning of the Missouri Compromise was obvious. It was intended to limit the spread of slavery and preserve the rights of its black citizens. Missouri was chosen by Congress as the designated hitter for freedom and equality.

For 164 years, Missouri faithfully kept its place, but in the year 1985, from Kansas City in the West to St. Louis in the East,

it rebelled at being merely an equal state among many, and it
proclaimed its domination over all others.

In the long history of conflict between the states, nothing in
the outfield or the infield or the bullpen has matched Missouri's
imperious and aggressive claim to superiority. It has not even
shown pity for the immunities of the southern states, with which
it originally shared the Louisiana Purchase.

Infuriated by the charge that the coastal cities of New York
and Los Angeles, with all their money and computers, were the
pathfinders to the future and that the prairie states of the Middle
West were hopeless strike outs, Missouri swept the Yankees and
Dodgers from the field in the most dramatic agrarian uprising and
upset since Harry Truman in 1948.

Missouri did more than this. Originally it was established by
explorers, traders, and settlers from Canada, whose dreams out-
ran their energy and whose fastball was better than their control.

Still, these French Canadians got Missouri out of the bush
leagues into the big leagues and statehood. But when Toronto
ventured to seek a place in the final test for the championship of
the world, the Midwestern isolationist impulse put down the
rebellion, and Missouri stood alone.

This established the Second Missouri Compromise: Don't
show me, I'll show you. A fifty–fifty compromise: hits and runs
for us, errors and oblivion for you.

So what? So watch out, you fancy guys, the country boys are
on a roll not only in St. Louis and Kansas City. The Bears are
howling again in Chicago, and Iowa and Michigan are back on
top of the college football ratings. It was bound to happen. Folks
get soft in the Sun Belt eating quiche and drinking wine, while
the meat-and-potato boys in the mud belt are planting corn.

Abe Lincoln of Illinois figured all this out long ago. In the
darkest days of the Civil War, he insisted on the creation of the
land-grant colleges, giving Federal aid, of all things, for the education of the poor and instruction in the mechanical, agricultural,
and sporting arts of survival, especially in the ninth inning.

And so it came to pass that there arose a breed of men and
women under the Big Sky who grew tough by farming and by

fighting bankers to save their farms from bankruptcy. For a time they couldn't compete with the computer generation around Boston in Massachusetts and Silicon Valley in California, but they learned how to work, to block and tackle, to hit and run—boy, how they run the bases!—and how to produce more food for a hungry world than any other people on earth.

As time went on, knowledge spread across the world. Places like Japan and Germany began building autos and computers, and Korea and Hong Kong produced shirts and underwear cheaper than on Seventh Avenue in New York, creating the greatest trade crisis in the history of the Republic.

But try as they might, none of these workers in far-off lands even came close to matching the production of corn, wheat, and soybeans. Production rose to such an extent on the American prairies that the farmers had to work only half time to meet their quotas, so their sons spent the other half pitching screwballs and sliders, and hitting fungoes over the barn.

All this explains why Missouri conquered the East, the West, and the South, and ran the Canadian invaders out of town. But it doesn't explain how they lost the spirit of compromise and in a spirit of pride and revenge monopolized the glory for Missouri.

16 THANKS FOR WHAT?

WASHINGTON, Nov. 27, 1985—No thoughtful citizen of the United States can reflect on the sufferings of the world in the year 1985 without counting the blessings of America on Thanksgiving Day.

It was a year of natural disasters in Mexico and Colombia; of famine in Ethiopia and sub-Saharan Africa that could take more lives than the First World War; of calamitous wars along the Persian Gulf and in Southeast Asia; of racial violence in South Africa and terrorism in the skies and seas.

It was also a year of widespread unemployment in Western Europe (12.6 million in September), of millions of refugees scrambling from one country to another, often illegally, of political tension, and of an arms race costing over seven hundred billion dollars in this year alone.

Even though glimpses of this appalling human sorrow and carnage were more vivid on our television screens this year than ever before, the magnitude of the human tragedy and the cost of containing it is still almost beyond comprehension.

Yet it may be useful in this age of drift and hallucination to recall the foundations of the first Thanksgiving Day celebrations.

The Puritans were undoubtedly motivated primarily by gratitude for survival, but also by something more. They were rooted in the conviction that their prosperity had come from their industry, discipline, and virtue, and not their virtue from their prosperity.

More than that, they believed that they were their brothers' keepers and had survived by helping one another; that they were the trustees for future generations and were to set an example for a civilized world.

Later, the Jeffersonians argued that these principles were a practical guide to life, for if each citizen found contentment in a justly and richly rewarded toil, that citizen would not be disposed to take advantage of his neighbor.

Even this secular age would have to agree that this older spiritual shield is worth preserving while the scientists produce a nuclear shield for their own promised land.

For if, in our clash of philosophy with the Communist states, we say that the individual does not belong to the state, it is necessary to keep defining what the individual does belong to. The people are listening in the Communist empire and elsewhere.

The Puritans sensed it, but the Founding Fathers defined it better than anybody before or since. They said man belonged to his Creator, and since man was, therefore, an immortal soul, he possessed inalienable rights as a person and was honor bound under constitutional representative government to respect the rights of others and practice the courtesy of the spirit.

Walter Lippmann called this "the forgotten foundation of democracy," and wondered if democracy could endure at home or withstand its enemies abroad unless it remembered where it came from:

The decay of decency in the modern age, the rebellion against law and good faith, the treatment of human beings as things, as mere instruments of power and ambition, is without a doubt the consequence of the decay of the belief in man as something more than an animal animated by highly conditioned reflexes and chemical reactions. . . .

If you teach a people that the character of its government is not greatly important, that political success is for those who equivocate and evade; that acquisitiveness is the ideal, that Mammon is God, then you must not be astonished at the confusion in Washington. . . . You cannot set up false Gods to confuse the people and not pay the penalty.

Here endeth the lesson. It was not intended by Lippmann as a sermon—he died without religious faith—but it was meant as a warning that a secular society that forgets its roots is in danger of losing the spirit that holds a nation together.

There has been much evidence in recent years of confusion over what defends a nation. The overwhelming emphasis has been on military power, which was necessary, but at the expense of many other attributes of national security.

The nation has much to give thanks for this week: 107,867,000 employed, and perhaps the beginnings, but only the beginnings, of reduced tension with the Soviet Union.

But 8,291,000 unemployed; the largest debt in the history of the Republic; chaos on our southern borders; and, by the Reagan Administration's own figures, over thirty-three million Americans living below the official poverty line? And a hungry world that could soon be spending a trillion dollars a year on weapons?

We have a democratic system to be thankful for. But what about the forgotten foundation?

---

17 THE CURSE OF WAR

WASHINGTON, May 26, 1986—There is no more beautiful ceremony here in the flowering spring than the decoration of the

graves in Arlington National Cemetery on the banks of the Potomac.

It lies on a slope between Robert E. Lee's modest house at the
top of the graveyard and Abraham Lincoln's memorial on the
other side of the river—the symbols of reconciliation—with the
Pentagon a few thousand yards away, and a new commercial city
crowding it on the Virginia hill.

There is a quiet procession this weekend from Cathedral Hill
and Capitol Hill—the sacred and the profane—to honor the
dead. But there are some things we forget to remember, including
the causes and curse of war. We forget that fourteen wars are now
in process: in Afghanistan, Angola, Cambodia, Ethiopia-Soma-
lia, El Salvador, Guatemala, Iran-Iraq, Lebanon, Mozambique,
Nicaragua, Peru, Sri Lanka, Uganda, and the Western Sahara.
The human suffering of these struggles is beyond our knowledge
or belief.

The people who keep a record of these disasters don't count
the outrages of South Africa, or the wars of terror, or the hidden
massacres of tribal conflict. But adding it all up as best we can, it's
clear that this is the most violent century in human history, not
only between the nations, but in the murders in our streets.

Memorial Day, or Decoration Day as it was originally called,
was established in 1868. Since then there have been 271 wars,
accounting for the deaths of at least eighty-eight million people—
and God knows how many more.

In this century alone, there have been 207 wars, taking about
fifty million lives in the two world wars alone, more of them from
the Soviet Union than any other country.

This is the unresolved problem. President Woodrow Wilson
justified U.S. intervention in the First World War on the grounds
that it was "a war to end all wars." President Franklin Roosevelt,
confronted by isolationist sentiment, tried to evade Hitler's effort
to dominate the Western world until the Japanese destroyed the
American fleet at Pearl Harbor.

But the nations are still trying to deal with the strategy of
theoretical future wars in outer space rather than the practical
causes of present conflicts here on earth.

Consider the news here in the week before Memorial Day, the Pentagon was publishing its opposition to the Contadora proposals for peace in Central America; the State Department was condemning the Pentagon's opposition, and the White House was saying there was no conflict between them.

The Secretary of Defense was in Europe arguing for a new "family" of nerve-gas weapons; the President was saying that all was well abroad and that nobody need be hungry at home unless they weren't smart enough to know where to get a handout.

Give us this day our daily tranquilizer, and deliver us from evil, for mine is the kingdom and the power and the glory.

There is obviously a conflict here in this lovely swale by the Potomac about how to honor the dead, and it's an honest conflict among the mourners.

The White House calls on the men on National Cathedral Hill on Memorial Day to pray over the graves, but denounces them and other church leaders for their efforts to control the arms race. And the Administration's people are joined by men of equal sincerity who come down from Capitol Hill and the Pentagon believing not in the power of the spirit but in the power of missiles, called "peacekeepers."

Lincoln on one side of the river and General Lee on the Virginia hill, having tested military power in the Civil War, came finally to believe in the spirit of moderation and reconciliation, and the importance of compromise.

"I would save the Union," Lincoln wrote to Horace Greeley, in a famous letter we also forget to remember:

If there be those who would not save the Union unless at the same time save slavery, I do not agree with them.

If there be those who would not save the Union unless at the same time destroy slavery, I do not agree with them. . . .

If I could save the Union without freeing any slave, I would do it; and if I could save it by freeing all the slaves, I would do it; and if I could save it by freeing some and leaving others alone, I would also do that. . . .

I shall correct errors when shown to be errors, and I shall adopt new views so fast as they appear to be true views. I have here stated my purpose according to my view of official duty; and I intend no modification of my oftexpressed personal wish that all men everywhere could be free.

This is a theme and a clarity of purpose and modesty worthy of emulation on Memorial Day, and explains why Lincoln's memorial still shines along the river.

PART II

POWER
AND POLITICS

18 THE CONSOLATION OF THE ELECTION

FIERY RUN, Va., Nov. 5, 1966—Nobody can follow an American election without being appalled by all the noise and nonsense and yet impressed that the system works as well as it does.

The quality of the candidates for Congress this year, while no worse and probably a little better than a decade ago, is still mediocre. In very few cases do they compare favorably in knowledge or wisdom with the best brains in their own states or districts. The level of debate in this campaign, of rational discussion of the monumental issues before the nation, is not only poor, but in many ways worse than it was a generation ago. This country had the gift of speech, even of eloquence, in the nineteenth century, but we have now come to the end of the campaign without hearing a single memorable speech from any member of either party.

The Unifying Principle

Nevertheless, in some mysterious way, the principles of freedom and democracy still manage to work on a continental scale among people whose interests are different from one region to another. This is not true anywhere else in the world. The American system has worked in this election to reduce rather than exaggerate the fundamental differences between the parties and the candidates. They emphasize their differences, but outside of a few districts, the ideological fever of the 1964 elections has dropped and the general trend in the elections of 1966 has not been toward the extremes of right and left, but toward the center.

Even the war in Vietnam, which is the most puzzling, agonizing, and ambiguous question of the postwar period, has not been the major issue of the campaign mainly because the instinct for unity in the country is stronger than the conviction for any other course of action. Maybe this is not a good thing, for the present policy in Vietnam may very well be wrong and stronger Congressional candidates with a wider knowledge of the world might very well have made an issue of it, but the main fact is clear: When in doubt, most candidates in both parties, probably representing the feeling of the voters, have gone along with the President.

Most of the angry shouting in this campaign, the ridiculous and expensive political commercials on television, the emotional charges and counter charges between the Congressional candidates on the hustings are misleading. Since the last election of 1964, this country has had a kind of revolution of policy. It is not only that we are fighting a war with four hundred thousand men in Southeast Asia but that we are committing ourselves to keep the peace and raise the standard of living in all of free Asia, wipe out poverty in the American cities, distribute Federal funds to private and parochial as well as public schools, and transform the economic and social relations between the races.

Never in two short years have there been so many fundamental changes of American foreign, economic, financial, racial, and educational policy as in this period between 1964 and 1966, but in this election no major move has been made to reverse the trend. The conservative Republicans and the southern Democrats have complained about the *pace* of change, and there has been a lot of nostalgic muttering about the past, but on the whole, most of the candidates in both parties have avoided any fundamental challenge to the extraordinary and even revolutionary policies of the last twenty-four months.

The Political Decentralization

This is not because the power of the two national parties has dominated the election. The decline of partisanship and of central party control has never been more apparent than in the last few months. Paradoxically, the national Democratic Party, under the most political President of the century, has seldom been weaker than it has been in this campaign. To reduce its four-million-dollar deficit of 1964, President Johnson cut its staff and didn't even mount an effective national registration campaign. The black leaders, sympathetic to the Democratic Party, were so involved in their own intramural battles and so preoccupied with demonstrations in the cities that they did not even take advantage of the Voting Rights Act to register their people. And the Republican National Committee's control of the state parties was little better.

Thus, the election of 1966 was left mainly to the state and local political leaders in both parties. It has been a battle, not between two centralized party organizations directed from Washington, but between the hundred Democratic and Republican Parties in the cities, counties, and municipalities.

Remarkably United

Nevertheless, a remarkable degree of unity on most major policies—or at least an acquiescence in those revolutionary policies—has been maintained throughout the continental United States in this election. In Georgia and Maryland, segregationist candidates are running for the governorships—and having a hard time—but elsewhere, very few politicians are trying to reverse the Administration's Vietnam, poverty, education, or racist policies.

It is a curious thing. The candidates on the whole are unimpressive, the debates boring and stale, the verbal tricks and insincerity appalling, the apathy, defeatism, and fatalism of the electorate palpable. But somehow the idea of unity, despite all the disparity and argument, prevails, and most voters seem to feel, probably correctly, that the present tides of policy and politics are so strong that the results on Tuesday will not really change anything very much.

19 A NATION OF AMIABLE GRUMBLERS

SAN FRANCISCO, July 27, 1968—You cannot cross the continent these days without hearing a lot of amiable grumbling about every one of the Presidential candidates, and some of it not so amiable either.

They are a poor lot, according to the common talk of the people, and scarcely worth the trouble of going to the polls—except maybe to vote for somebody else.

Why the Gloom?

What explains this general peevishness? It cannot really be that Humphrey, McCarthy, Nixon, and Rockefeller give the voter a poorer choice than, say, Johnson versus Goldwater in 1964, so why all the unhappiness? The explanation seems to be that problems somehow seem larger and more intractable this year and therefore much bigger than the candidates.

The war and the cities were discussed in the last Presidential election campaign, and the voters were deceived about both; but a lot of Americans have died in Vietnam since then, and quite a few American cities have burned, and the people now have a more solemn vision of the tremendous scope and complexity of human reconstruction.

Thus, the more the voters face these problems, the less adequate the candidates appear, and the present crop has been made to seem even less satisfactory since the rise of the Kennedy personality cult in American politics.

The Kennedys revive the American thirst for dramatic heroes. Neither President John F. Kennedy nor his brother Robert ever came close to an adequate program for our major domestic and foreign policy problems, yet somehow they managed to convey the notion that they might really have changed things and solved things. And in the process, they left us an appetite for these things.

Feuds and Illusions

Now, with the last of the Kennedy brothers out of the 1968 race, we are left with a lot of the old Kennedy feuds and illusions. It is not at all clear that the leading candidates of 1968 are less capable of grappling with our present problems than Johnson or Kennedy in the past; we are merely looking at the problems and the candidates in a different way, and maybe with older and sadder eyes.

Another reason for the negativism of the moment is that the candidates are merely symbols and targets of our deeper national discontent. We are unhappy with the candidates at least partly because we are unhappy with ourselves.

The American Conscience

Nobody can cross this country without seeing and feeling once more the generosity, affection, and kindliness of the American people and their deep sense of family pride. And yet we are doing mean and brutish things to one another in the cities and in the war in Vietnam. The American conscience is not quiet these days. It would like to be eased by some political savior, but somehow nobody on the political stage quite fits the role.

All the symbolism of American politics is still evident in this campaign. Humphrey, the druggist, and Nixon, the grocery boy, are stock Horatio Alger types of the self-made man. Rockefeller is as good a symbol of responsible wealth as we have. McCarthy, the preacher and teacher, and Reagan and Wallace, the dissenters, are all recognizable characters out of our political folklore.

In fact, a good case could be made for the proposition that this year's Presidential candidates came from the very things we admire the most in American life: money (Rockefeller), techniques (Nixon and Humphrey), entertainment (Reagan), and nostalgia (Wallace).

Nevertheless, we are now a more solemn people. Vietnam has been a humbling experience. The Johnson promises of the last election are not forgotten or forgiven and Hubert Humphrey will

still be hearing about these things here in California in the next
few days.

A Political Symbol

Meanwhile, the defiant cries for equality among the blacks has
made the black community a political symbol and force much
more powerful in this election than ever before.

So the grumbling goes on, and the candidates are catching
hell, but maybe this is not all bad. The mood is sadder, but it
seems more sensible and realistic.

---

20 THE POLITICS OF VIOLENCE

WASHINGTON, Sept. 11, 1968—Men are resorting to violence
these days because, we are told, they have no peaceful and legal
remedies for their grievances. It is a common complaint heard all
the way from Chicago to Vietnam and from Moscow to Suez and
Nigeria, but violence doesn't seem to be working either. The
record of the past few years, in fact, is very bad indeed.

Nobody has found any remedy through violence in Vietnam.
The Arab armies tried it against Israel and were destroyed, and
even the violent counter-violence of the Israelis has left them in a
state of profound insecurity.

The Chinese Communists resorted to military force to achieve
their internal political objectives and are now in disarray. Moscow invaded Czechoslovakia to unify its empire in Eastern Europe, and now finds that empire more divided than before.

The Record at Home

Even in the United States, it would be hard to prove that the
protesters, once they crossed the line from peaceful dissent and
civil protest to violent confrontation, have helped their cause or
removed or diminished their grievances.

Pressure in politics works, up to a point. The peaceful demonstrations of American blacks did produce some legal remedies

in the fifties and in the first half of the sixties. Without them, who is to say that the indifference and legal inequality of the last hundred years would have been removed?

But violent pressure in politics, as in physics, tends to produce counterviolence and counterpressure. We saw it at the Bay of Pigs, in Vietnam, in the Sinai desert, in Biafra, in Chicago—and we are now seeing the reaction to all this violence and lawlessness in the Presidential campaign.

Reaction Buildup

The reaction has been building up for a long time. The violence abroad and at home has created an alarming sense of insecurity and a longing for order at almost any price. The grievances have not been removed but increased by the violence, which is being used now not only as an excuse for more violence but as an excuse for ignoring the grievances that produced the violence at home in the first place.

Vice President Humphrey and former Vice President Nixon almost seem irrelevant to the problem. Mr. Nixon is talking about the effects of the violence—the insecurity of the cities—while Mr. Humphrey is at least talking more about the causes of the violence—the economic and spiritual poverty of the underclass in the slums.

Neither of them, however, is generating much enthusiasm, for neither has yet put forward a convincing program for dealing with the scope of violence. Mr. Nixon is offering us more cops and more war. Mr. Humphrey is offering us more Lyndon Johnson, and George Wallace is getting more emotion from his audiences than anybody else because he is denouncing everything and everybody in sight.

It is going to take a whole lot more than George Wallace's verbal violence, however, to get us out of our present pickle. He no doubt appeals to the nothing's-good mood of the moment, but the more of this hot air we breathe in the next eight weeks, the less prepared we are likely to be for the solemn if unhappy choice that has to be made between Mr. Nixon and Mr. Humphrey on Election Day.

The overriding question is how to get at the causes of violence now loose in the world. In the short run, this means keeping the right of dissent and public protest short of physical violence for the rest of the campaign so that we can vote in a reasonable and rational way.

In the longer run, it means taking risks for peace so that the cost of military arms can be reduced and substantial sums of money can be diverted to the causes of poverty and violence. We are not likely to get any risks for peace from Mr. Nixon. He is a believer in the hard line toward the protesters and the Communists, and Moscow has helped him along with its invasion of Czechoslovakia.

This provides him with a sound platform for the campaign. Neither the violent protesters nor the aggressive Communists are popular, and many voters confuse the two. But it is a poor platform for governing the country, for it foreshadows more cold war abroad when we need peace and more division at home when we need reconciliation.

Humphrey's Dilemma

Humphrey's chance—maybe his only chance—is to break out of the cycle of violence, to risk a policy of ending the bombing in North Vietnam and recapture the peace issue. It is a hard and dangerous choice, surpassed only by the risks of going on as before, but it may be the only way to turn back from the violence that is dividing and wounding the human family.

21   THE LATEST FAD—WRONG-WAY POLITICS

WASHINGTON, April 30, 1970—If you're a little confused about what's going on around here these days, it may be because you haven't caught on to the new rule of politics. The new rule is that logic is out and reverse logic is in, and under this rule, everybody talks and acts against his own self-interest and in the interest of his opponent.

Take a small example. Kingman Brewster, the president of Yale, loves his university and the law. So he makes a statement that he is "skeptical of the ability of black revolutionaries to achieve a fair trial anywhere in this country."

This was supposed to help protect Yale from the wrath of the Black Panthers, but all it did was to hurt Brewster, Yale, and the law, and give Vice President Agnew a fit. But wait.

Spiro's 'Revenge'

The Vice President, in his anger, applied the same reverse logic. He called publicly for the dismissal of Mr. Brewster and thus provoked a massive demonstration in Mr. Brewster's support. It is an interesting new technique.

Another way to understand the new wrong-way politics is to remember that everybody's now his own worst enemy. Pat Moynihan at the White House thought a little less controversy about the race problem would be a good thing for the blacks and everybody else. So he used a fancy phrase to convey his idea— "benign neglect." Result: the opposite of what he intended; more controversy over race relations than before.

Nixon's Tactics

It is only when reverse logic is practiced at the very pinnacle of the Government that you see the possibilities of the new system. President Nixon wanted a Southerner on the Supreme Court and led the charge with such aggressive clumsiness that he had to settle for a pleasant man from Minnesota.

His formula for "bringing us together" is to tear us apart, and his latest experiment with the new technique is an attempt to end the war quicker in Vietnam by expanding it into Cambodia.

One has to wonder what ever happened to all the early talk about low profiles and lower voices and Nixon Doctrines to minimize American involvement in other people's wars. It was working fine for the President.

By bringing the boys home from Vietnam, cutting the military budget, sweet-talking the Congress, and crying peace to the world, he had the Democrats, the demonstrators, and even the press off balance or off-key, and then he began to overplay his hand.

Now there is a reaction to the backlash. There is more opposition in the Senate today to the President's move into Cambodia than to any other Presidential action in the foreign policy field in the last ten years. The President's challenge to the Senate's constitutional right of confirmation has aroused the upper chamber against him, and even the Democrats are beginning to think they may still be alive.

In short, the old rule of compensations is at work again. Every excessive pressure produces a counter pressure. This rule worked at first against the militants who resorted to violence. It worked against the press when it overplayed the violence and the negative. It worked against the excessive profit margins of business and the stock market, and it is working now against the Administration's policy in Cambodia.

The Bad Time

No doubt this will all settle down in time, but the mood of the moment is anxious and even irrational. Even if the President succeeds in his policies of clearing out the military sanctuaries in Cambodia and bringing the boys back home, there is clearly no assurance that the enemy will not drift back into Cambodia or create new and even more dangerous diversions elsewhere, as the Soviet fighter pilots and missile technicians are now doing in the Middle East.

It is a bad time in foreign relations, race relations, university relations, economic relations, and human relations, and the Administration seems to be developing an infallible instinct for doing the wrong thing. The unavoidable perplexities are understandable, but the avoidable stupidities are intolerable. Failure seems to have gone to their heads.

22 THE ENDLESS TRAGEDY

WASHINGTON, June 16, 1971—For the first time in the history of the Republic, the Attorney General of the United States has tried to suppress documents he hasn't read about a war that hasn't been declared. This is one of the final ironies of this tragic Vietnam War, but it won't work for long.

The constitutional issue can be left to the courts. They need time. The issue is complicated: There is clearly a conflict between the Government's desire to preserve the privacy of its internal communications, which everybody recognizes, and its attempt to extend this procedure to old historic documents, which analyze the blunders of the past.

But in practical terms, the documents will not be suppressed. *The New York Times* will abide by the final decision of the courts, but too many copies of the McNamara Papers are around, and too many fundamental issues are involved to suppose that this official record of the war can be censored for long.

It is easy to get lost in the legalities, ambiguities, and politics of this controversy, but the central issue is what former Secretary of Defense McNamara had in mind when he ordered this analysis of the war in the first place.

McNamara was a principal actor in the drama, deeply involved and even incriminated in the struggle, but near the end he insisted, on his own responsibility, that outside and objective minds should look at the record and try to find out what went wrong and why. This involved many people—around thirty—all of whom have knowledge of critical parts of the Pentagon investigation, some of whom have some of the documents, and a few of whom have copies or access to copies of most of the whole.

McNamara is clearly not alone in feeling that the basic questions—how did we really get involved? how did we lose our way?—should be made clear in order to avoid similar mistakes in the future. And at least some of these men are not going to be silenced by temporary or even permanent court injunctions against publications of the facts.

The Attorney General, by seeking for the first time a court injunction before publication, has dramatized the issue. He has transformed an academic monograph, with a very limited audience of politicians, bureaucrats, journalists, and scholars, into a world issue on the American war and the First Amendment of the American Constitution on the freedom of the press. And his efforts at suppression, while they may prevail for a short time, will almost certainly fail in the long run.

For the men who know most about these documents do not believe that publication involves national security or would cause, in the Attorney General's words, "irreparable injury to the defense interests of the United States."

In fact, many of them in possession of the facts, and a few of them in possession of the documents, believe that the security argument is being used to cover up the blunders and deceptions of the past in Vietnam, and would gladly go to jail rather than submit to the suppression of their information.

Mr. Mitchell, consciously or not, has raised a fundamental question: What causes "irreparable damage" to the Republic? Publication of documents that expose the weaknesses and deceptions of the Government on issues of war and peace? Or the censorship of these documents in the name of "national security"?

This is the central issue. The Attorney General and the Secretary of Defense have a respectable argument; they have the right to private communication. The Secretary of State, William Rogers, also has a point: Other nations cannot do business with Washington if their communications are going to end up in the headlines of the American press. But beyond that, and even above it, there is the question of the integrity of the American executive in its dealings with the American people and their representatives in the Congress.

These documents are in the possession of the principals. President Johnson has a copy; Clark Clifford and Robert McNamara are reported to have copies; and other interested parties have copies or access to parts of them—and all are writing their own versions of history. So the legal injunction, as it now stands, is only against making the main documents available to disinterested scholars and the general public.

This is the main point about these documents and why the documents themselves had to be published. For they demonstrate beyond question, not reporters' opinions or speculations about Presidential action, but obvious and even calculated deception in the words of the officials themselves.

It will be interesting to see how the courts, and even the principal personalities, react to this tangle of legal and philosophical questions. But however they react, the objective of the McNamara inquiry is going to be achieved. The basic facts of the American involvement in Vietnam, many of them idealistic and many of them tragic, are going to be revealed, no matter what the Attorney General says, and in the end, we may be a little nearer to the truth.

23   MR. NIXON'S HISTORIC ALIBI

WASHINGTON, May 24, 1973—President Nixon's latest explanation of his part in the Watergate scandal—which is quite different from his first two explanations—is that everything he did, or failed to do, was motivated by his concern for "national security."

In his mind, it is probably true, and this is precisely the problem. In fact, it is the main theme of his political life. Whenever he has been charged with dubious political or executive decisions, he has always justified them on the ground that, right or wrong, they were done in the name of "national security."

Does he have constitutional authority to bomb Cambodia in order to keep the Lon Nol Government in power, or carry out the nation's commitments under the Southeast Asia Treaty, or try to compel North Vietnam to abide by the cease-fire agreement in Indochina? The Congress questions that he does, but he bombs anyway, in the name of "national security."

Was he fair in his savage attacks on Harry Truman and Dean

Acheson in questioning their motives in the Korean war? In his mind, he did it for "national security."

It is a very old Nixon story. He came into politics vilifying Helen Gahagan Douglas and Jerry Voorhis as "pinkos," and he wanted the United States to intervene in the French Indochina war at Dienbienphu, and he fought everybody who thought it might be possible to arrange an accommodation with Peking and Moscow—all for the same reason. He thought he was fighting for "national security."

More than that, he still feels he can use any blunt instruments at his command to serve his own notion of national security today. His latest statement on the Watergate was not a satisfactory explanation, or even a credible alibi, but a confession of wrongdoing, of losing control over the F.B.I., of executive negligence, and even of Presidential knowledge and approval of bugging and burglary—all in the name of "national security."

It is very easy and dangerous to guess at his motives, for he has invited all kinds of dubious speculations, but his judgments are the main thing. Assuming the best of motives, he thought, by his own testimony, that in the name of "national security," he could tap telephones, even of his own staff, authorize burglaries, ignore the disclosures of the press and the questions of the Congress, urge his staff to defend the "national interest" against its enemies, and then pretend to be surprised if they bugged the Watergate or raided Dr. Ellsberg's psychiatric files.

He asked for loyalty from his staff and he got it. He had a chance to get campaign finance reform and he opposed it. After his spectacular victory last November, he had a chance for reconciliation with his old adversaries and he refused it. After the facts began to come out on the Watergate scandal and he announced that he wanted all the facts to come out and that he was going to get to the bottom of the whole thing, he ducked direct questioning and put out what can only be called a mystifying clarification, which raised more questions than it answered.

What the nation obviously wanted and needed was a plain and honest statement of the facts from the President. What it has had from the President is one statement last August and one in October that he didn't know anything about the Watergate and no-body on his staff was involved, and then, on April 17 of this year, that maybe he had been misled by his own loyal public servants, and now, in summary, that he really did know a lot about the cover up but that it was done in the name of "national security," which must still limit the investigation in the Senate and the courts.

"In citing these national security matters," he said, "it is not my intention to place a national security 'cover' on Watergate, but rather to separate them out from Watergate. . . ."

But he is in fact putting on a cover. He is limiting the inquest. By his own testimony, he has created an atmosphere of fear, suspicion, and hostility in the White House, which has infected not only the Haldemans and the Ehrlichmans and the Mitchells, but all the other minor characters in the tragedy.

"To the extent," the President said, "that I may in any way have contributed to the climate in which they [the illegal activi-ties] took place, I did not intend to; to the extent that I failed to prevent them, I should have been more vigilant."

This is probably the most candid confession he has made in this whole tragedy, but he did not rest his case on this confession. He rested it, as he has done throughout his long and remarkable political career, on the proposition that whatever he did was done for "national security."

And the tragedy is that more crimes and brutalities have been done in the name of "national security" in this country in the last quarter-century than in the name of anything else, and Mr. Nixon is still falling back on this excuse, as he has done through-out his long career.

---

24 CONGRESS ON TRIAL

WASHINGTON, July 28, 1974—After the Judiciary Committee's vote, the question is now up to the House, but one thing is clear. Somebody is obviously going to be impeached: the President, the

Congress, or the American ideal. The President, the courts, and the press have had their turn. Now: the Congress.

The closer President Nixon comes to impeachment, the louder his supporters proclaim his innocence and predict his coming victory on Capitol Hill.

This is understandable, but a consoling fantasy. It is a strategy of optimistic forecasts and dreadful foreboding: If you say he is innocent often enough, maybe you can make the people believe it. And if he is impeached and convicted, somehow mortal damage will be done to the stability of the American system of government. So the President's argument goes.

Even *The Wall Street Journal* has been lending support to this second point. "The extraordinary stability of the American political system is an invaluable asset to the nation and the world," it said the other day. "And surely this stability is at stake in any impeachment. Surely it is rooted in the principle of fixed terms and in the instinct that the verdict of the last election should not be lightly set aside. . . ."

Well, we have all had a tug of war in our minds about all this, but the stability of the American political system surely rests on something more than "fixed terms." It rests primarily on the fixed principles of the law, on the integrity of its people, and the examples of its leaders.

The outcome of this nightmare of lawlessness and hideous stupidities will break our hearts if we end by convicting Vice President Agnew for fiddling with his income tax and excuse President Nixon for trifling with our freedom and our ideals.

"What is it that has shaken the nerves of so many?" Walter Lippmann asked many years ago.

It is the doubt whether there exists among the people that trust in each other which is the first condition of intelligent leadership. That is the root of the matter. The particular projects which we debate so angrily are not so important, the fate of the nation does not hang upon any of them. But upon the power of the people to remain united for purposes which they respect, upon their capacity to have faith in themselves and in their objectives, much depends. It is not the facts of the crisis which we have to fear. They can be endured and dealt with. It is demoralization alone that is dangerous. . . .

Mr. Lippmann went on with a principle which might well be read on Capitol Hill these days:

> Those in high places are more than the administrators of government bureaus. They are more than the writers of laws. They are the custodians of a nation's ideals, of the beliefs it cherishes, of its permanent hopes, of the faith which makes a nation out of a mere aggregation of individuals. They are unfaithful to that trust when by word and example they promote a spirit that is complacent, evasive and acquisitive. . . .

We have been spending our days in Washington pawing over the intrigues of little men, and a lot of people are now thumbing through the law books looking for loopholes, but everybody is not trying to be so shrewd and clever and calculating. There are echoes of the moral foundations of the nation in the televised Judiciary Committee debates. At least some Republican Congressmen seem to remember that Mr. Nixon's appeal to the "silent majority" was essentially a cry for law and morality.

Besides, the Congress has to decide some precedent. It has to set the precedent of impeaching and/or convicting Mr. Nixon or the precedent of excusing his record and deciding that a President cannot be dismissed unless he is proved "beyond reasonable doubt" to be a crook.

There is some force to the argument that "fixed terms" of four years for an American President give stability to the system and that he cannot be sacked for frivolous reasons. But there is little danger that we will have another White House gang like this one, and it is probably no great danger to the Republic to establish the precedent of getting rid of them if we do.

Finally, the stability of the American system has survived, though Presidents do not always complete their "fixed terms." The system made provision for human frailty and death, even for murder, of which we have had more than our share, but the system goes on.

It is really a little hard to be asked by President Nixon and his supporters to believe that he is essential to the strength and integrity of the Presidency, since he has done so much to weaken it. But this is for the Congress now to decide, and it sounds as if it's beginning to get the point.

25 A SENSE OF NATIONAL RECONCILIATION

WASHINGTON, Aug. 8, 1974—The capital took the news with remarkable serenity, almost as if it had lost a President but found itself. And President Nixon, in his noble farewell, contributed to this sense of national reconciliation. Washington is looking forward gladly now, having looked back for so long, and Mr. Nixon joined in forgetting—almost insisted on forgetting—the facts of the past.

Indeed, he ignored all the crimes and lies that had forced his resignation, and talked generously about the future, as if the whole Watergate thing was sort of an awkward misunderstanding, which had somehow destroyed his authority and should be forgotten.

Capital Seeks to Forget

Washington has a somewhat different view of these past tragic years, but it is willing, and almost eager, to forget.

In the last eleven years, it has seen one President murdered, another choose, under attack, not to run again, and a third driven from office, so it was vaguely sad, but at the same time, it was almost unanimously relieved that the dark riddle of the Nixon Administration had finally passed.

The relief was tangible in the private comments even of the President's Cabinet and most loyal supporters in Congress, and in the faces of the people who gathered quietly outside the iron palings around the White House.

The fears of an uncertain result, of division, bitterness, and recrimination, and of a long trial of a paralyzed President, so menacing only a few short days ago, had been avoided. And the nation's political institutions, so long under skeptical attack, had held together and come out with a clear decision and a fairly united people.

In the end, Mr. Nixon did, as he had done so many times before, what he said he would not do. As he had switched on China, the Soviet Union, on economic policy, executive privilege, and many others things, he abandoned his threat to fight both impeachment and conviction.

"Leaders should guide as far as they can, and then vanish," H. G. Wells once wrote. "Their ashes should not choke the fires they have lit." Almost all Mr. Nixon's friends gave him this advice, and finally he took it.

What has been the effect of all this on the nation, its people, its political parties and other institutions, and its relations with the rest of the world? These were the questions that were being asked here even before Mr. Nixon resigned.

The practical and personal questions of leadership are unprecedented in the history of the Republic. There are 896 days to go before the end of the term Mr. Nixon was elected to fulfill by the largest popular majority in the history of American Presidential elections—two years and five and a half months.

The nation will be led in this period, including the two hundredth anniversary of the Declaration of Independence on July 4, 1976, by President Gerald Ford and a Vice President yet to be chosen, neither of whom will have been elected by the people of the United States—a situation that was not foreseen and probably would have startled the Founding Fathers.

Nevertheless, the outlook is that Mr. Ford will have the greatest support and sympathy, even if not elected by popular ballot, of any President since Lyndon Johnson took over the White House after the assassination of President Kennedy.

In Washington, there is already a marked change. Mr. Nixon was a secretive, furtive, and fundamentally intricate man, who regarded Congress and the press as his enemies. Mr. Ford is just the opposite: open, uncomplicated, and modest. He is conservative and partisan, but he has spent most of his mature life in the give-and-take of the House, and regards the majority Democratic leaders not only as powers that have to be dealt with but also as his personal friends.

Had Planned to Retire

At sixty-one years old, he has got beyond all ambition, in fact has achieved far beyond his dreams. He was planning to retire to private life, on a promise to his wife, even before Mr. Nixon picked him as Vice President.

In the nation, the spirit of the people may very well be going with Mr. Ford—at least for the time being. It has gone through a long period of division over Vietnam and Watergate, and is tired of contention, and is longing for a little peace and quiet.

There is a strong feeling here that Mr. Ford could be an ideal President in such a time. Just as Calvin Coolidge took over after the scandals of the Harding Administration and quietly calmed things down and created an atmosphere that kept the Republicans in power for another nine years, Mr. Ford has a chance to revive the fortunes of the Republicans in 1974 and 1976.

Meanwhile, Watergate has had its effects on the country as a whole, and Mr. Ford, with his simple moral approach to the Presidency, may be very much in touch with the mood of the country.

Though he is a party man, he is likely to support reform in campaign financing, preservation of personal privacy, and strict control over the integrity of the Internal Revenue Service, the Federal Bureau of Investigation, and the Central Intelligence Agency.

He will be cautious about change, and will probably keep most of the Nixon Cabinet for a while, particularly at the Departments of State, Defense, and the Treasury; but he is not overly enthusiastic about Attorney General William B. Saxbe, so there will be no political control of Justice soon, and like President Truman, he is likely to change most of his Cabinet before the end of the year.

One of the interesting things about Mr. Ford, though he is no intellectual, is that, unlike Presidents Johnson and Nixon, he does not feel uncomfortable or threatened by exceptional talent. In this he is more like President Truman, who could trust the sophisticated minds of Dean Acheson and Robert A. Lovett and bring into the Cabinet strong men such as General George C. Marshall.

Rockefeller Appears in Lead

This is really the main question in Washington now: How will Mr. Ford approach his new responsibilities? It is clear that he will keep Secretary Kissinger at State, but who will be his Vice President and his chief of staff in the White House? These are the questions now being asked in the capital.

The front-runner for Vice President, with the backing of Melvin Laird, is former New York Governor Nelson Rockefeller, but there is a lot of support for George Bush, the chairman of the Republican National Committee, who is young and attractive, and could be a candidate for the Presidency in 1976 if given a chance at the Vice Presidency now.

All this, however, is speculative. The main thing is that even the thought of a Ford Presidency has changed the mood here, and increased the hope for a more open, candid, and cooperative Presidency.

26 WHO WILL LOSE?

WASHINGTON, May 10, 1980—The real question about this Presidential election is not who will win it, but who will lose it. The game is likely to be lost on fumbles, and on this negative test, Jimmy Carter and Ronald Reagan are about even.

On the losing side, Mr. Carter may be a bit ahead, for he had more to lose. His economic record is the worst since Herbert Hoover's. His personal record in antagonizing the most influential members of his own party in the Congress has been unmatched in recent times by any President but Richard Nixon.

These things may have been unavoidable, but recently Mr. Carter has shown a gift for stumbling into avoidable disasters— by ignoring and then losing his Secretary of State, Cyrus Vance, over the rescue operation in Iran, and then by criticizing his old buddy, absent-mindedly, after he was gone.

For "losers," this is a formidable record, but nobody should underestimate Mr. Reagan's ability to match it or beat it. Reagan's best hope of election is the disastrous economic policy of the Carter Administration, but he has fiddled for months about defining his own economic policy. And he keeps talking nonsense about foreign policy.

He suggested in San Francisco this week that the United States should join with its allies in Western Europe and Japan to send a "warning" to the Soviet Union that the West would not tolerate the overthrow of the Government of Saudi Arabia, either by internal uprising or external aggression. And if we send such a warning, he added, we should send it only with the collaboration of our allies, "who are so dependent on OPEC oil."

What does this mean? Mr. Reagan must know that the allies, precisely because they are dependent on OPEC oil and have other economic interests with the Soviet Union, would never join the United States in such a "warning," and would want to know what we would do if both the Saudis and the Soviets ignored it.

But the former Governor of California keeps babbling on about "punishing" the Soviets by taking military action against their ally in Cuba, without saying what this means. He accused the Carter Administration, in San Francisco, of "hypocrisy at its worst in cozying up to the Soviets" precisely at the time when President Carter was so angry at the leaders in Moscow that he didn't even have the common sense or good manners to attend Marshall Tito's funeral in Belgrade.

It is not going to be easy for Ronald Reagan to lose this election, considering the economic slump and the divisions within the Democratic Party, but there are two ways in which he might be able to blow it.

One is to assume that the American people are so frustrated by the humiliation in Iran and so angry at the Soviet invasion of Afghanistan that they are in a mood to go back to the simpler anti-Soviet confrontations of the cold war, with all that that means in much higher defense budgets, more inflation, and less money for social services and the restoration of our cities. Mr. Reagan may be right on this, but it's not a good political bet.

The second is for Mr. Reagan, whose Presidential nomination seems sure enough, to assume that he can also win in November without fairly soon indicating who is going with him as Vice President, Secretary of State, and members of his Cabinet.

Mr. Carter and Mr. Reagan have at least one thing in common, aside from their ambition to reside in the White House. They both lack the confidence of a majority of the American people, and this circumstance is not likely to change, no matter who wins or loses, unless they come forward before the election with teams of men and women who can give the nation a sense of a new beginning.

President Carter has at least made a beginning with the appointment of Secretary of State Muskie, who has already demonstrated in a few days what one new man can do by speaking out on his own with courage and humor, even in amiable criticism of himself and his own President.

Carter will undoubtedly make more such moves. He knows that he's in serious trouble and will probably lose on his own, and he is looking to a new Administration with new people as a means of restoring confidence and assuring his reelection.

Reagan has not yet got to this point. He is concentrating so much on his own personal nomination that he is neglecting the problem of election in November. That may well depend on his decisions as to where he's going and who's going with him—the road taken and the road not taken, "which," as Robert Frost pointed out, "makes all the difference." Mr. Reagan has yet to answer these questions in any memorable speech.

The most thoughtful leaders of the Republican Party are not in disagreement on this matter. They are trying to tell Reagan that he has won the nomination but that he is forgetting what goes beyond: that Jimmy Carter may be a "loser" as a President but that he is a formidable politician and debater, that the real "loser" in this election may be the man who thinks he can go it alone.

27 DREAM AND REALITY

WASHINGTON, Jan. 28, 1984—If the Democrats had any doubts about the combined powers of the Presidency, Hollywood, and television, Ronald Reagan must have brought them to their senses with his State of the Union performance.

The man makes Johnny Carson sound like an amateur. Give Mr. Reagan a good script, a couple of invisible TV screens, and a half hour on prime time, and he'll convince the people they have nothing to fear but the facts.

President Franklin Roosevelt was a master of the political radio address, and John Kennedy almost made the Bay of Pigs calamity seem plausible on television, but President Reagan can make even the fact seem irrelevant.

The Democrats are trying to figure out why President Reagan goes up in the popularity polls when, as they believe, they are so much smarter and better informed than he is. This shows who's dumb. For in politics, as in Hollywood and on TV, the play is the thing, and the dream is often more alluring than the reality.

Are some people still hurting out there? Yes, says the President with an amiable duck of his head, but inflation, unemployment, and interest rates are down. The trend is the thing, and every day in every way things are getting better and better.

Are people a little anxious about the nuclear arms race and all this angry shouting between Washington and Moscow? U.S.– Soviet relations are more stable today than when he took office, Mr. Reagan assures them, because "America is back—standing tall, looking to the eighties with courage, confidence, and hope."

Isn't a budget deficit of $180 billion a year a little scary? Yes, he concedes, but he inherited the wreckage from the Democrats, and says he is willing to work with them to repair the damage and let them share the blame.

Washington hasn't seen such effective political vaudeville since "give 'em hell" Harry Truman beat Tom Dewey for the

Presidency in the election of 1948 by blaming all his blunders and troubles on the "do-nothing Republican Eightieth Congress."

But this is not all personal and theatrical magic. Mr. Reagan has challenged the welfare-state assumptions of the New Deal and Fair Deal days. He *has* improved the economy in the last year. He knows how to fight for his ideas, but he also knows when to switch and stop swallowing his own baloney.

He was mocked as a movie actor when he came in here, but all politicians are actors, and he learned at least one lesson from his Hollywood days: He pays attention to the reaction of the audience, and when they begin to jeer and toss chairs out of the second balcony, he changes his lines, and even his cast.

He toned down his Russian music when it began to rattle the rafters and scare the folk in the peanut gallery. He compromised with the Democrats on Social Security and nuclear policy. Under pressure from the Congress, he tossed Secretary of the Interior James Watt to the photographers, and relieved Secretary of State Shultz of the foreign policy wisdom of Judge Clark and Ed Meese.

This may be one of his greatest advantages over Walter Mondale. For Fritz is giving the impression that he'd rather go along with the old Roosevelt coalition than switch. Whereas Mr. Reagan, who is really backing into the future, is somehow getting across the notion that he knows how to tack with the wind while Mr. Mondale's rudder is stuck in the mud.

It's not true, of course, but that's the way it comes over so far on the tube. Mr. Mondale and John Glenn can complain, but the President of the United States can always act. If he thinks going to China is good politics, while Messrs. Mondale and Glenn are mushing through the snow in Iowa or New Hampshire, he will go to China, and come back through Israel, Italy, and Ireland if he likes.

If the crisis with Moscow seems to be getting out of hand, he can always set up a commission of U.S.–Soviet philosophers to define an agenda for some vague future dialogue with Yuri Andropov. And if the pressure to get the Marines out of Lebanon gets too strong, he can always move them around or even bring them home during the Democratic nominating convention in San Francisco.

In short, as is well known to the Democrats, who invented this political-foreign policy, partisan-nonpartisan game, Mr. Reagan is in the driver's seat. He may not have a road map, but he knows his destination, "upstairs above the store" as he says, at 1600 Pennsylvania Avenue.

And the people obviously seem to love it. It's the best show on television. Never mind the deficit, or who will appoint a majority of the members of the Supreme Court of the United States in the next five years. For now, the President is telling the people what they want to hear, and he assumes, probably rightly, that maybe they'll think about the consequences later.

28 A REVIVAL MEETING

SAN FRANCISCO, July 21, 1984—This year's Democratic Party convention was one of the best of the twenty-one I have seen in the last forty years. It almost brought the party together—almost, but not quite.

Something intensely human and emotional happened in this gathering of the warring Democratic tribes that is hard to define and harder to measure. It was a revival meeting in more ways than one, vaguely religious at times, and defiantly, even mockingly, political.

The main thing that happened here was a restoration of hope, if not confidence. There was a whiff of defeatism in the air at the start, but the delegates went away in a blaze of stars and stripes, believing they now had a shot, if a long shot, at the Presidency.

None of the things they feared the most came to pass in this convention. They didn't fall apart. Gary Hart and Jesse Jackson gave Mr. Mondale a hard time, but they didn't break away. The Hispanic delegates weren't happy, but they didn't take a walk.

The convention even swallowed Bert Lance, though it gagged in the process.

On the positive side, the Democrats found their voice in San Francisco. There has been a woeful decline of public political speech among the Democrats in recent years, but in a masterful address, Governor Mario Cuomo of New York gave them a key and just the right note, and Jesse Jackson gave them the old-time religion and had them singing arm in arm in the aisles. Equally important, they kept their bores off television.

Also, they went back to their old promise and applied it to the future: They vowed "to comfort the afflicted and afflict the comfortable," and they denounced President Reagan for doing the opposite.

Fairness and openness were their favorite words, and the old-time values their constant theme. They were clearly conscious of the Republican charges that the Democrats were soft on loafers, soft on communism, soft on homosexuals, easy on crooks, and short on military and economic security.

But here on the stage was Geraldine Ferraro, the daughter of Roman Catholic Italian immigrants, the first woman to be nominated for the Vice Presidency, talking about hard work and children and the future and how many criminals she had put in jail. And here were Mr. Mondale and his wife, the children of Protestant ministers, testifying to the virtues of faith and the family.

How all this struck the vast television audience of voters and nonvoters one does not know. But listening to Governor Cuomo honoring his parents and watching him and Mrs. Ferraro fight back the tears had a powerful effect on these delegates.

In the middle of Mrs. Ferraro's speech, women were standing in the aisles, their cheeks wet with tears, pleading softly: "Don't cry, please don't cry."

But it was not all emotion. For a long time, the Democrats hesitated to attack President Reagan, but here they did not hold back. Mr. Jackson said he'd rather have Franklin Roosevelt in a wheelchair than Ronald Reagan on a horse. Mr. Mondale said: "Let's tell the truth. Mr. Reagan will raise taxes and so will I. He won't tell you. I just did."

Gary Hart said: "Ronald Reagan and his gang of greedy polluters can no longer sing 'America the Beautiful' while they scar her face, poison her air, and corrupt her waters."

Senator Edward Kennedy, nodding his head in approval of his own wisecracks, said the President had never met an arms control agreement he didn't dislike, and he insisted that Mr. Reagan "shouldn't be the only senior citizen who doesn't have to worry about the cost of Social Security."

Senator Kennedy added that the President "intends to spend billions on 'Star Wars' in outer space, and that's why we should send him back to Hollywood, which is where both 'Star Wars' and Ronald Reagan belong."

And yet all this emotion and mockery about President Reagan's presiding over a Government "of the rich, by the rich, and for the rich" didn't quite bring all the leaders together except for a final photograph.

Many delegates from the South have their doubts about the success in their region of a ticket of two liberals from the North. Others wonder about the popularity of Mr. Mondale's suggestions of large defense cuts, of protectionism, and limiting the President's power to send troops abroad.

Gary Hart was not a generous but a grudging loser, and Jesse Jackson keeps asking Mr. Mondale, "What have you done for me lately?"

Also, there was some anxiety about the Democratic appeals to class conflict. Nevertheless, there was general agreement that this was an effective partisan convention, and there was also agreement with Mr. Mondale's strategy for the campaign.

"Let them [the Republicans] fight over the past," he said "we're fighting for the American future."

29 MON DIEU! MON DALE!

WASHINGTON, Sept. 23, 1984—Q. How does he do it?

A. How does who do what?

Q. How does President Reagan manage to fly so high with no visible means of support?

A. He travels light. It's all done with gas and mirrors. What's bothering you?

Q. Look, our guys get caught in Beirut three times in a row with their gates down, and the secretary of war, Mr. Weinberger, goes on television and says he's sorry about those gates and proud of those brave boys who are our first line of defense against the wicked, evil Communist empire. And the President says we won't be intimidated by these terrorists, and yet a lot of people run around the streets of the United States shouting "Four More Years" for Reagan. I'm confused.

A. No, you're raving. Mon Dieu! Mon Dale! Here are the Democrats at the White House gate. Here is the President defending Christian civilization, the free enterprise system, and the gates to outer space and above, and you want him to check license plates in Beirut!

Q. You've got me wrong. I expect gates to be off their hinges under this outfit. I just don't know how they get away with it. Every time they fumble they pick up ten yards.

A. You're fumbling yourself.

Q. Look. He's the first divorced President we've ever had and he lectures us about the values of the family. He wants prayer in the schools but seldom goes to church or sees his grandchildren. He wants to get the government off our backs but tells women the government has a right to interfere with the question of abortion. He has piled up more debt in four years than all the other Presidents combined, and people run around saying he's taller than the Washington monument. I don't get it.

A. Let me explain. First, they know the power of advertising. For these Republicans, everything is Miller Time: If you've got the time, they've got the cheer. They make money the old-fashioned way—they let the poor earn it. Understand?

Q. No, but I'm listening.

A. The President is the Marlboro Man. He has moved Madison Avenue to Pennsylvania Avenue and always stands tall in the saddle with the mountains in the background and the pretty girl back at the ranch. Right?

Q. I think I'm beginning to get it, but you think the people swallow this baloney?

A. People love baloney if they have nothing else. Also, they see those cigarette ads of the lovers by the lake, and the little notice in agate type at the bottom that says, "Warning: The Surgeon General has determined that cigarette smoking is dangerous to your health." But if you're young and the lake is golden in the autumn sun, nothing matters until after Election Day, unless you inhale it.

Q. You said advertising was his first technique. Was there another?

A. When he and I were young together in Illinois, back—I can't remember when—there was a popular fad called the Coué System. It was supposed to make you successful if you bounced out of bed at 7 A.M. proclaiming: "Every Day in Every Way I'm Growing Better and Better." I tried it for a while, but the better I tried the worse I got. But believe me, the President has not only put this system into the White House but with a wave and a smile convinced the American people to do the same.

Q. You are saying he's a fraud!

A. No, I'm saying he's a genius. He has figured out the American people, but they haven't figured him out. He's winning the religious argument and winning the election because television and not religion is the opium of the people. He even has old Andrei Gromyko soaring across from Moscow for a photo opportunity in the Rose Garden.

Q. You reporters don't really like Mr. Reagan, do you?

A. That's not quite true. We like him, but we really don't know him. It's a funny thing: He's always on television, but somehow we never see him.

Q. You better be careful. If you go on like this, you'll be questioning the principle of democracy, for he's giving the people precisely what they want.

A. That's precisely what worries me: Hollywood, television, and baloney.

PART III

SPORTS AND POLITICS

BALTIMORE, Oct. 8, 1966—The first week in October in the frosty latitudes of America is a solace to the human spirit. The World Series is on, taking our minds off the ugly facts. The kids are in school, providing a little peace in the house, and the natural world, carpeted in green and flecked with red and yellow in the upland woods, is spectacularly beautiful.

The harvest this year is something special. The summer drought has stunted the crops, but the law of compensations seems to be working. Maryland has produced one of the worst Democratic nominees for Governor in this century, but the Baltimore Orioles can hit, and they have a twenty-year-old kid, named Jim Palmer, who outpitched Sandy Koufax in what the sports writers call "the world classic." H. L. Mencken should have lived to see the day.

Mencken on Baltimore

Mencken loved Baltimore and hated Washington. He regarded the Federal capital as an abomination, run by scoundrels. His conclusion about Baltimore, however, was: "(a) that its indigenous victualary was unsurpassed in the Republic; (b) that its native Caucasian females of all ages up to thirty-five were of incomparable pulchritude, and as amiable as they were lovely; and (c) that its home-life was spacious, charming, full of creature

comforts, and highly conducive to the facile and orderly propaga-
tion of the species."

This was before Baltimore came up with Johnny Unitas, the
best quarterback since Franklin Roosevelt, and long before the
Baltimore baseball club acquired Frank Robinson from Cincin-
nati in the best deal since the Louisiana Purchase.

Sports in America, despite all the commercialization, are an
antidote to many of the trends of our time. The cities are growing
together. Even the states are losing some of their identity and
authority of the past. The sociologists complain that the technicians and managers have taken over our institutions and the
young generation has no heroes. And this is not all.

Increasingly, they complain, it is hard to identify the point of
decision in our national life. A foreign policy may be good or bad
and there is much contention about it, but you have to wait
twenty-five years to discover how the thing comes out and meanwhile, nobody knows who's ahead. Similarly, the arguments
about the war on poverty, like the arguments about the war in
Vietnam, have no beginning or middle or end.

Sports and TV

It is nobody's fault, but this is the way it is: no clear geographical
or political or philosophical boundary; no clear point of decision
on great issues; very few decisive occasions; no clear lines of
Presidential or Congressional or state or even parental authority;
almost no pageantry or symbols or ideology—nothing clear,
nothing decisive, and no heroes.

American sports events at least provide a contrast—maybe it
is an escape—from all this vague uncertainty, but useful nevertheless. They are definite and understandable. They have a beginning and an end, and you know who has won when it's over.
Washington and Baltimore may be growing together with their
expanding suburbs, but Washington is at the bottom of the
American League and Baltimore is in the World Series, and nobody is confused about the difference. We know what team won
today's game and how it won it, and there was a sense of pag-

eantry and beauty, on an Indian Summer day, and the whole nation was watching.

Ironically, it is hard on the players. For a brief moment, while they are at the peak of their physical skill, they are at the center of the national stage. Aparicio is our ballet. Koufax is the hero, defeated by the twenty-year-old Jim Palmer, who is Conrad's "Youth." But there is a problem. Ideally, life should be an ever-ascending line of achievement and satisfaction; but what is likely to compare with young Jim Palmer's victory over Koufax in the second game? This, however, is only the negative personal side of the story.

Overemphasis

The sociologists, who have been worried about the "overemphasis" of sports in America, may be right, but in national terms, they also may be a little out of date. Maryland is divided about the race issue, and the Democrats here may have nominated for Governor one of the worst racist bigots in the history of Maryland politics, but Maryland is not divided about Frank Robinson of the Orioles, and this superb black athlete may do more for sanity on the race question in Maryland than all the fair-minded politicians in the state.

Some Positive Results

Nobody in America has really analyzed the *positive* effects of sports on the remarkable growth and development of state university education in America. No doubt state university sport has been professionalized and corrupted, but it has done something else. It has produced football teams which have become symbols of state pride. It has kept the alumni in touch with the university. More important, it has held the interest and the allegiance of legislators in the state capitols, and has in the process helped produce educational appropriations for all these land-grant institutions on a scale that would never have been possible without the attraction and the pride engendered by these sporting events at the universities on autumn Saturday afternoons.

In this sense, sports in America are something more than a diversion. They are a unifying social force in the country and a counter to the confusion about the vagueness and complexities of our cities, our races, and, in this long-haired age, even the confusion between our sexes.

---

31   GOLF, WHISKY, AND MR. JOHNSON

WASHINGTON, Sept. 28, 1967—President Johnson told his guests at the White House the other night that he had given up alcohol and taken up golf. This is alarming, if true, for in the present state of the world and the Presidency, it really should be the other way around.

When the Scots invented both golf and whisky, they had a definite purpose in mind. They believed in original sin and in redemption through punishment. For this purpose they invented golf and called it "a humblin' game." Devout Calvinists, weighed down by the burden of conscience, took up golf as a form of self-torment. It was their penalty for wickedness and their way of saying that even when mortal man was playing he should be made to suffer.

Scotland's Consolation

Whisky, on the other hand, was Scotland's consolation. Life was a Vale of Tears. Men would quarrel and make war and despair of the human race, but every once in a while they should be permitted "a wee nip o' the strong stuff," and that would revive them to suffer some more.

President Johnson, however, has apparently been misled. The United States has had Presidents who drank but did not play golf (Jackson and the second Roosevelt). It has had Presidents who did both (Taft and Eisenhower). But diligent research turns up nobody before Johnson who tried to escape from his worries by giving up liquor and taking up golf at the same time.

In the present mood of Washington, the impulse to escape

from pressure is not only natural but essential. Every visitor to the White House wants some incurable misery stopped immediately. Every newspaper carries its melancholy freight of bad news. Every television newscast (and Mr. Johnson has three of them tuned to different networks in his office and three more in his bedroom) carries the story of some other old friend denouncing the policy in Vietnam. In this atmosphere, even the tinkle of the telephone sounds like an ambulance siren.

The need for diversion is obvious. Mr. Johnson's latest hero is Eric Hoffer, the old West Coast dockside philosopher, who praised Mr. Johnson on Eric Sevareid's show the other night as a great President; and Mr. Hoffer is the author of the idea that play comes before work and is even more practical.

"It is evident," writes Hoffer, "that play has been man's most useful occupation. . . . Man painted, engraved, carved, and modeled before he made a pot, wove cloth, worked metals, or domesticated an animal. Man as an artist is infinitely more ancient than man as a worker. Play came before work; art before production for use."

Never in recent history has an Administration needed time for play and relaxation as badly as this one or got so little of it. John Kennedy sailed. Herbert Hoover fished. Harry Truman played poker. Teddy Roosevelt shot lions, pretending they were Senators, but Johnson and company seldom play anything but politics, and those of them who do, like Secretary of Defense McNamara, go in for preposterous punishments like mountain-climbing.

The Fatal Combination

In the President's case, it is the combination of giving up drink for golf that is so menacing. The great achievement of this Administration was its domestic legislative program in the Eighty-ninth Congress, and this extraordinary catalog of education, housing, and civil rights bills literally floated into history on a torrent of whisky.

To substitute golf for "whisky's old prophetic aid" is a puzzle and could be a calamity. And to do it as an escape from agony is the worst miscalculation since the start of the Vietnam War. Golf is not an escape from anything. It is itself an agony. Occasionally, a statesman finds some solace in it. An English politician during the First World War thought his satisfaction so exceptional that he celebrated its virtues in verse:

I was playing golf the day the Germans landed.
All our men had run away and all our ships were stranded.
And the thought of England's shame
nearly put me off my game.

But he was an eccentric, and like Clark Clifford, who put Mr. Johnson up to this nonsense, he was a good player. Even Ike, who had two terms on the golf course, was tormented to the end by a disobedient putter, and Mr. Johnson is indescribably worse. He is, in fact, a spectacular dub. The traps and hazards and insoluble problems of golf he does not need. He gets enough of them in his regular work.

32   SPORTS AND POLITICS

WASHINGTON, Nov. 25, 1971—The connection between sports and politics in America is getting to be front-page news these days. President Nixon was out at the Washington Redskins' football practice the other day, and the Governors of Oklahoma and Nebraska were leading the cheers at the big Thanksgiving Day game in Norman, Oklahoma, between the first two college teams in the country.

It is an interesting switch. Politicians used to feel that they had to identify themselves with the church in order to pick up votes, and they quoted the Bible to prove their fidelity to the old faith. Now they telephone football coaches instead of bishops and issue pronouncements on the cunning confusion of the modern Texas wishbone offensive strategy, which is now the new holy trinity of football.

Who can blame them? Politicians go where the votes are. The

stadium is now more popular in America, or at least more exciting and more decisive, than the church. The game of football,
unlike the "great game of politics," is mathematical and understandable. Its rules are plain: four tries to make ten yards, meas-
urable by the sticks. The field is clearly marked with its sidelines
and goal lines. It has a kick off, a half-time, and an end marked to
the second by the clock, and referees and a head-linesman to call
the close ones and spot the dirty tricks, and instant-replay cameras to let the people judge the decisions.

In short, football is not a metaphysical exercise. It has pageantry and a sharp practical clash between the weak and the
strong, and at the end you know who has won. It is not like a
theological philosophy or a foreign policy, where you have to
wait for a generation and sometimes even a lifetime to discover
how it all comes out.

Maybe, then, since sports are so definite and popular and
politics on the whole are so vague and unpopular, we should
think about applying some of the rules of football campaigns to
our Presidential election campaigns. Politicians, for example, are
constantly off-side or out of bounds. They are forever stalling,
jumping the gun, grabbing face masks, clipping from the rear,
gouging in the clinches, and, to use Mr. Nixon's own phrase,
taking "cheap shots" at crippled opponents.

But in politics, there are few referees or head-linesmen, and
there is no instant replay. Think of the possibilities of instant-
replay cameras on the fumbles of our politicians. The television
cameras actually did it, not instantly but a little later on, in
Vietnam. They showed what the battle in the elephant grass was
all about, what "search and destroy" missions really meant in
human suffering, what the war did in the Vietnamese villages and
what it did to the G.I.'s with their guns and their PX's and their
Vietnamese women and their dope.

The exposure of the facts in Vietnam, primarily by the TV
cameras, is really what drove Mr. Nixon to question his former
hawkish policies and withdraw. But there's still very little instant
analysis of the Government's latest policies on inflation, unemployment, the balance of payments, money, trade, or labor.

There is a big flap here in Washington now, for example, about whether George Meany of the A.F.L.-C.I.O. was discourteous to President Nixon at the labor convention in Miami Beach or whether the President went there spoiling for a fight and trying to blame Mr. Meany for wrecking the new wages and prices policy.

All this took place in the open, with the television cameras recording the scene. So with an honest political replay process, we should to be able to judge what happened, but unlike the football instant replays, there has been no national rerun of what actually happened in Miami Beach. Everybody seems to have an opinion about the facts, but nobody has replayed the events so that the public can judge for itself.

The fight between George Meany and Secretary of the Treasury John Connally after Miami Beach dramatizes the point. Mr. Connally went on national television to scold Mr. Meany for being discourteous, arrogant, and boorish toward President Nixon at the labor convention. "In my humble opinion," said Mr. Connally, who is not noted for humility, "Mr. Meany was offside and out of bounds, but lacking a replay of the events, nobody can be quite sure about whose manners were the worst."

So maybe, if the politicians are so impressed by the techniques and popularity of sports, they should apply the model sporting devices to themselves. With a Presidential election coming up, we really do need some ground rules, some check on foul play and dirty tricks, some instant analysis of controversial moves, some political referees and head-linesmen.

President Nixon's admiration and enthusiasm for sports is fine, but he had better be careful. For if he dramatizes fair play, fair and precise rules, instant-replay judgments on controversial decisions, and even the right of the people to boo in the stands, these procedures could also be applied to Presidential politics, and that could make quite a difference.

PART IV

THE PRESS

33 FREEDOM AND SECURITY

"Here various news we tell, of love and strife,
Of peace and war, health, sickness, death and life . . .
Of turns of fortune, changes in the State,
The falls of favorites, projects of the great,
Of old mismanagements, taxations new,
All neither wholly false, nor wholly true."

—New London (Conn.) *Bee*
March 26, 1800

WASHINGTON, June 18, 1971—Great court cases are made by the clash of great principles, each formidable standing alone, but in conflict limited, "all neither wholly false nor wholly true."

The latest legal battle, *The United States* v. *The New York Times*, is such a case: The Government's principle of privacy, and the newspaper's principle of publishing without Government approval.

This is not essentially a fight between Attorney General Mitchell and Arthur Ochs Sulzberger, publisher of *The New York Times*. They are merely incidental figures in an ancient drama. This is the old cat-and-dog conflict between security and freedom.

It goes back to John Milton's pamphlet, *Areopagitica*, in the seventeenth century against Government censorship or, as he called it: "for the liberty of unlicenc'd printing." That is still the heart of it: the Government's claim to prevent, in effect to license, what is published ahead of publication, rather than merely to exercise its right to prosecute after publication.

Put another way, even the title of this case in the U.S. District Court is misleading, for the real issue is not *The New York Times* versus the United States, but whether publishing the Government's own analysis of the Vietnam tragedy or suppressing that story is a service to the Republic.

It is an awkward thing for a reporter to comment on the battles of his own newspaper, and the reader will make his own allowances for the reporter's bias, but after all allowances are made, it is hard to believe that publishing these historical documents is a greater threat to the security of the United States than suppressing them or, on the record, as the Government implies, that the *Times* is a frivolous or reckless paper.

The usual charge against *The New York Times*, not without some validity, is that it is a tedious bore, always saying on the one hand and the other and defending, like *The Times* of London in the thirties, "the Government and commercial establishment."

During the last decade, it has been attacked vigorously for "playing the Government game." It refused to print a story that the Cuban freedom fighters were going to land at the Bay of Pigs "tomorrow morning." It agreed with President Kennedy during the Cuban missile crisis that reporting the Soviet missiles on that island while Kennedy was deploying the fleet to blockade the Russians was not in the national interest.

Beyond that, it was condemned for not printing what it knew about the U.S. U-2 flights over the Soviet Union and, paradoxically, for printing the Yalta Papers and the Dumbarton Oaks Papers on the organization of the United Nations.

All of which suggests that there is no general principle which governs all specific cases and that, in the world of newspapering, where men have to read almost two million words a day and select a hundred thousand to print, it comes down to human judgments where "all [is] neither wholly false nor wholly true."

So a judgment has to be made when the Government argues for security, even over historical documents, and the *Times* argues for freedom to publish. That is what is before the court today. It is not a black-and-white case—as it was in the Cuban missile crisis when the Soviet ships were approaching President Kennedy's blockade in the Caribbean.

It is a conflict between printing or suppressing, not military information affecting the lives of men on the battlefield, but historical documents about a tragic and controversial war; not between what is right and what is wrong, but between two honest but violently conflicting views about what best serves the national interest and the enduring principles of the First Amendment.

34   WHO ELECTED THE *TIMES?*

WASHINGTON, June 23, 1971—The public reaction to the publication of the Pentagon Papers has been overwhelmingly on the side of the newspapers, but there is a strong and vehement view that it is wrong, dangerous, and even criminal for a newspaper to assume responsibility for publishing private official documents without the consent of the Government.

Who, it is asked, elected *The New York Times?* How can outsiders judge better than the official insiders what damage may be done by publication of secret documents? By what right do newspapers presume to print official information which may embarrass the Government and give comfort to the enemy?

These are serious questions which deserve serious answers, for it is clear that the publication of the Pentagon Papers *has* embarrassed the Government, disclosed evidence of official deception, and in the process provided Hanoi, Moscow, and Peking with material for anti-American propaganda.

At first glance, it is a devastating indictment, but should documents not be published because they embarrass the Government? Nobody is arguing that newspapers have the right to publish the nation's war plans or troop movements, or anything else that would endanger the lives of the men in the American expeditionary force. But historical documents? Evidence that the Congress and the people were misled years ago—even if this embarrasses the Government and provides propaganda for the enemy? This is clearly another matter.

After all, every time Mike Mansfield, the opposition leader in the Senate, calls on the Government to end the war by a date certain, or any newspaper or preacher or group of citizens condemns the bombing or questions the loss of life or the diversion of resources or what the war is doing to divide and weaken the nation—all this is picked up by our adversaries and used against the United States.

Should we then suppress the documents because they "embarrass" the Government? Deceive the people about the record of the war? Submit to the Government's argument that publication will cause "irreparable injury" to the national defense rather than "irreparable injury" to the nation's reputation for fair dealing and plain and honest speaking to the Congress and the people? Confuse "embarrassment" to the Government and its officials with the security of the Republic?

In the absence of clear evidence that publication of these old documents is truly a threat to the defenses of the nation—which the Government has not provided—these are good political but bad philosophical and historical questions. Still, they are being raised by influential men and they come closer to the Marxist view of the press—that it should be a servant of the government—than to the American view of the press as defined in the First Amendment.

It is not good enough to suppress facts relating to the past, as distinguished from dangerous military information affecting the present or future, on the ground that this may be awkward. This resembles Nikolai Lenin's view of the press.

"Why should freedom of speech and freedom of press be allowed?" he asked in 1920. "Why should a government which is doing what it believes to be right allow itself to be criticized? It would not allow opposition by lethal weapons. Ideas are much more lethal than guns. Why should any man be allowed to buy a printing press and disseminate pernicious opinions calculated to embarrass the government?"

Well, many men who oppose publication of the Pentagon Papers don't go this far, but the violent opponents of publication, like Herbert Rainwater, the national commander of the Veterans of Foreign Wars, who is crying "treason," come very close to the Lenin thesis that opposition to the Government is unpatriotic or worse.

It is true that newspaper editors, raised in the American tradition of "publish and be damned," do not always know what damage they may do to the diplomatic process by publishing official documents. Their information is limited, and no doubt the official insiders know more than the outsiders, but even this is a dubious argument.

As Walter Lippmann wrote many years ago, you had better be careful not to go too far with the "insiders" argument. "For if you go on," he told the National Press Club in Washington on his seventieth birthday in 1960,

. . . you will be showing how ridiculous it is that we live in a republic under a democratic system, and that anyone should be allowed to vote.

You will be denouncing the principle of democracy itself, which asserts that the outsiders shall be sovereign over the insiders. For you will be showing that the people, since they are ignoramuses, because they are outsiders, are therefore incapable of governing themselves.

If the country is to be governed with the consent of the governed, then the governed must arrive at opinions about what their governors want them to consent to. . . . Here we correspondents perform an essential service. In some field of interest, we make it our business to find out what is going on under the surface and beyond the horizon. . . .

In this we do what every sovereign citizen is supposed to do, but has not the time or the interest to do for himself. This is our job. It is no mean calling. We have a right to be proud of it, and to be glad that it is our work.

---

35   A TROUBLED FRIEND

WASHINGTON, June 26, 1971—A troubled friend wants to know why the newspapers don't leave the questions of secret documents and national security to the President. Let us suppose that we did.

Presidential power is now greater than at any other time in the history of the Republic. Ever since the invention of atomic weapons and intercontinental ballistic missiles, it is clear that the nation could be mortally wounded before the Congress could ever be assembled on Capitol Hill.

Accordingly, the balance of decisive power in the foreign field—but not over internal policy—has passed from the Congress, where it lay before the two world wars, to the White House. This may or may not have been what we wanted, but it was clearly what we had to do.

Other inventions tipped the balance of political power toward the President, especially nationwide television. It is at his disposal whenever he likes, with a studio in the White House. He has instant communications with the people and the world, all of which is necessary. The Congress cannot compete with him in the use of these modern instruments in the conduct of public policy.

But these unavoidable facts raise serious questions. Should such power not be subject to review by the representatives of the people? Should the Congress not know what is going on? Should the executive be free to use the power it needs to deal with the threat of nuclear war in undeclared wars like Vietnam? Should the press shut its eyes to any documents, even old historical documents, the executive chooses to mark top secret?

The fuss over the Pentagon Papers is only a symbol of a much larger problem. It is true that these papers raise questions of "national security," but the greatest threat to national security in this time is the division of the people over a war they have had to fight in accordance with decisions of governments that didn't tell them the truth. The nation is seething with distrust, not only of the Government but of the press, and the issue of the Pentagon Papers is merely whether we should get at the facts and try to correct our mistakes or suppress the whole painful story.

Fundamentally, this is not a fight between the Government

and the press. It is not even a fight over the President's decisive power to defend the nation in an age of nuclear missiles. Congress has submitted to the scientific facts on the ultimate questions of nuclear war.

But now it has been asked, in the name of "security," not even to look at a historical analysis of a war it has financed but not declared, not to question the unelected members of the White House staff, who had access to the papers Congress could not see, and to respect the Administration's right to stamp "secret" on any documents it likes, and to keep them secret years after the event, when officials long out of office are writing their own versions of history out of the "secret documents."

My "troubled friend" has good cause for anxiety. He is right to wonder whether the press knows enough and is responsible enough to publish things the Attorney General wants suppressed. He is right to concern himself with the security of the nation.

But what is being exposed here is not primarily some Government documents that might cause "irreparable damage" to the defense of the nation, but a system of secrecy, of Presidential presumption, of influential staff advice by men who cannot be questioned, of concealment and manipulation, all no doubt with the best motives, but nevertheless, a system which has got out of hand and could really cause "irreparable damage" to the Republic.

No doubt the press itself is often poorly informed and clumsy in its efforts to expose the dangers of this system, but the greater the power in the hands of the executive, the greater the need for information and skepticism on the part of the Congress and the press.

My anxious friend might be careful about weakening the instruments of information and review at such a time. No doubt they are blunt instruments, often misused, but in this case of the Pentagon Papers, or so it seems here, the greater danger is the system of executive secrecy; and the greater danger to the security of the nation is the mistrust this system of secrecy and contrived television propaganda has caused.

James Madison summed up the problem at the beginning of the Republic:

Among these principles deemed sacred in America, among those sacred rights considered as forming the bulwark of their liberty, which the Government contemplates with awful reverence and would approach only with the most cautious circumspection, there is no one of which the importance is more deeply impressed on the public mind than the liberty of the press.

That this liberty is often carried to excess; that it has sometimes degenerated into licentiousness, is seen and lamented, but the remedy has not yet been discovered.

Perhaps it is an evil inseparable from the good with which it is allied; perhaps it is a shoot which cannot be stripped from the stock without wounding vitally the plant from which it is torn. However desirable those measures might be which correct without enslaving the press, they have never yet been devised in America.

---

36 REAGAN BEATS THE PRESS

WASHINGTON, Nov. 4, 1984—Among the losers in this Presidential election campaign you will have to include the nosy scribblers of the press. Not since the days of H. L. Mencken have so many reporters written so much or so well about the shortcomings of the President and influenced so few voters.

Mr. Reagan beat the newspapers by ignoring them. From his nomination in Dallas to election weekend, he has not held a single national news conference. He gave one or two interviews to sympathetic writers and allowed a few small-time high-school and college audiences to toss him some questions, but he dismissed the White House press corps with a wave and a smile.

In a switch from Jefferson's famous remark, the President said in effect: Were it left to me to decide whether to have a government without newspapers or newspapers without a government, I should not hesitate to choose TV every time.

Some editorial writers and columnists and most Washington reporters were on to his evasive tactics, easy cheerfulness, and unsteady grasp of the facts.

They did not hesitate to point out his deficits, personal and fiscal, condemn his windy theorizing, and mock his zigzag contortions, but Mr. Reagan had the photographers and television cameramen for allies and proved that one picture on the nightly news can be worth a million votes.

Was his advanced age an issue? He disproved it by bouncing up to the stage like a gymnast. Did he promise to balance the budget in his first term but wind up with the deepest recession in forty years? It was all the fault of Congress, which wouldn't pass his program or a constitutional amendment to balance the budget. What about those two-hundred-billion-dollar-a-year deficits? Just wait, he says, we'll grow our way out of them. That's like hoping to grow your way out of cancer.

So what? Nothing in the Constitution requires the President to hold press conferences or debate his opponent. If he wants to mobilize the preachers and turn their churches into political registration booths, nothing can stop him.

Jim Baker and the rest of his political and advertising managers can do anything they like within the law and are protected by executive privilege from giving an account of their activities to Congress or anybody else. Increasingly, the Government is run by an army of unelected political appointees.

For winning elections, Mr. Reagan's technique is as easy as playing tennis with the net down. And since winning is everything these days, you can't blame the President for trying. What's wrong with this is not that it cheats the press but that it cheats the people, and the surprising thing is that the press complains so little and the people not at all.

That quotation from Jefferson starts with this statement: "The basis of our government being the opinion of the people, the very first object should be to keep that right." But this is precisely what the modern Presidential campaigns do not do, and the danger is that Mr. Reagan's artful dodging is so successful that it is likely to set a precedent for more such shenanigans in the future.

It was only in the debates that the people had an opportunity to form an opinion about the statements of the President and Mr. Mondale together. The rest of the time, the candidates were like ships passing in the night, broadcasting whatever charges they liked without fear of immediate challenge or contradiction.

In the present mood of the country, most people couldn't care less. The President is telling them what they like to hear, and the papers are raising questions and doubts about his snappy judgments that the people don't want to hear.

Meanwhile, Mr. Mondale has been suggesting that the majority of the people, now in the upper- and middle-income brackets, should share the wealth more generously with the people who have been left behind. This, like reading, is not a popular pastime.

Nevertheless, the modern Presidential campaign is a good show in which the appearance of things seems more important than the reality of things. On the tube, everything seems clearer than the truth. There are shrill hosannas bordering on blasphemy on the side. Nothing is lost but the honest cut and thrust of democracy.

It is said that the people get the government they deserve, which is undoubtedly true, and also that what they see is what they get, which is not true. For the world of television is the world of illusion, and what they see and hear—all those promises of peace and prosperity—are precisely what they are not likely to get in the next four years.

---

37 POLITICS AND THE PRESS

WASHINGTON, April 9, 1986—The American Society of Newspaper Editors met here this week, which tempts me to butt in with an observation and a suggestion about politics and the press.

The observation is that from Roosevelt to Reagan, the arts of public relations and political advertising have not only tended increasingly to dominate our politics but also to diminish the influence of the printed word and distort the facts of our national life. In short, the hucksters are getting out of hand.

Managing the news, of course, is the oldest game in town.

Franklin Roosevelt was a master at it. The leaders of all institutions try to manage the news in the sense of emphasizing their virtues and minimizing or suppressing their failures. Even newspaper owners have been known to fiddle with the facts.

What is new, however, is that in the conduct of the public's business, the power of the unelected and largely unknown "specialists," or manipulators, who write the speeches for the executives downtown and frame the questions for the legislators on The Hill, has increased to such a point that while we know who is speaking, we don't know where the words come from.

We are seeing more than ever before, or so I believe, a distortion of the theory of representative government. Increasingly, the executive branch, with its dominance of television, tends to evade the doubts of Congress by theatrical appeals to the people on the theory that what's popular is right.

This is not a partisan or ideological argument. President Truman counted in advance on public support rather than on considered discussion with Congress when he dropped the atom bombs on Hiroshima and Nagasaki.

So did President Johnson, for a time, in his manipulations of public opinion on Vietnam, and President Kennedy in his covert disaster at the Bay of Pigs, not forgetting F.D.R's efforts to pack the Supreme Court.

The main difference now is that Ronald Reagan is better than any of them at reading speeches other people write and at using television to argue that Nicaragua and Libya are major threats to our security and that a permanent ban on the testing of nuclear weapons, which all other Presidents since Eisenhower have publicly supported, is just another Soviet trap.

Also, what was merely a cunning p.r. talent on the part of Roosevelt has now become a Deaverish industry under Mr. Reagan. The editors can check it for themselves: The publicity budget in Washington has soared, and the number of news conferences has declined. Publicity is not merely an instrument of government here these days: It is government.

The Founding Fathers didn't imagine that the great conflicts between nations, let alone the mysteries of outer space, could be decided by public opinion, except at election time. But that's the current trend and the question for the editors is what, if anything, they can do about it.

The short answer is not much, but at the opening of the baseball season, my suggestion is that they might get a tip by looking at their sports pages and their business pages.

Every day, editors devote two or three pages of newsprint, which is not cheap, to keeping the precise figures on Wall Street, who's up, who's down, and who's chiseling on the side.

Likewise on the sports pages. They keep the record: runs, hits, errors, stolen bases, beanballs, and other achievements and misdemeanors. But not on the political pages.

Sure, we catch the pols off base from time to time, but in over forty years in Washington I can't remember a period when so much obvious nonsense, even so many distortions of fact, have gone by unchallenged or been dismissed with scarcely more than a whisper by the public.

Roosevelt, in his cynical way, used to say: Just let me make the headlines on the front pages and I don't care what they say on the editorial pages.

Now the theme is: Give me half an hour on television and I'll prove the "freedom fighters" of Nicaragua and the "Peacekeeper" missile are essential to the security of the nation and that Colonel Qadaffi is masterminding the terror of the world.

Well, as the President says, it may not make sense but it makes news and it gets votes. You could say that Mr. Reagan is the most popular President since the last war and that the press is more unpopular than ever for questioning his statements and policies.

But there is a difference between the President and the press. He's in the popularity business and we're not, and never have been since the old pamphleteers raised hell against the British and the abolitionist editors fought against slavery, which was popular for almost a hundred years.

PART V

THE PRESIDENTS

Johnson

38 JOHNSON FROM ANOTHER ANGLE

FIERY RUN, Va., Sept. 1, 1966—One of the oddities of the Johnson Administration is that it looks so different from far away. Distance may not lend enchantment, but it lends detachment. From afar, the President's yearnings and purposes come across much clearer than his politics and his tactics, which dominate the capital in Washington.

I have been chasing salmon up the north and west Pabos rivers of the Gaspé Peninsula in Canada, and tramping through the fishing villages of Nova Scotia, and listening by shortwave radio in the evening to the news out of Washington and the struggle for the National League pennant out of Pittsburgh, San Francisco, and Los Angeles.

No Vacation for L.B.J.

This puts a different color on the world. Everybody seems to have had a vacation except Lyndon Johnson. He is all over the dial. One night, he is pleading for peace between labor and management. The next, he is crying for patience on Vietnam. After that, he is asking for self-discipline in New England, and appealing for racial tolerance in Chicago. He is talking about his life and his dreams and his disappointments out of Texas on his birthday and marrying off a daughter in Washington.

Incidentally, somebody is going to have to say a good word

for the Voice of America. With due respect for the commercial radio and television networks in the United States, this Government news service to the world must be the most detailed and accurate account of American and world news out of the United States today.

America's Voice

It is not peddling political propaganda. It is telling not only what the President and his associates say but what the opposition says. It is carrying the critical comments of the American press, and the protest of the American blacks out of Chicago, and the accounts of crime in the cities, as well as the stories of American universities, novelists, and poets. Meanwhile, it is broadcasting the news and comments of the political and editorial world, including all their sharp criticisms of American policy in Vietnam and elsewhere.

What comes out of all this is not that the United States is failing so often, but that it is attempting so much; not that it has failed to eliminate poverty or create a Great Society, but that it is aiming at these high ideals; not merely that it is experimenting with a planned economy and the welfare state, but that, despite these adventures in collectivism and socialism, it is still trying to preserve the best aspects of individualism of the Reformation and the freedom of personal initiative and responsibility.

The Canadian newspapers and radio and television networks seem provincial by comparison. They are much more preoccupied, even in the great cities of Montreal, Ottawa, and Toronto, with their own domestic concerns. Their railroad unions, now demanding a 30 percent wage rise, make our airline mechanics, or even Jimmy Hoffa, look like statesmen, and their insistence on states' rights or province rights make Mississippi or Alabama seem almost subservient to the central Government in Washington.

Everything in politics is relative, and Johnson's problems look different when observed out of Washington. Up here in the Virginia hills, for example, the talk is not about Vietnam but about the drought and inflation. Up here, the temperature has been around 90 degrees for over sixty days, and the stream beds are dusty and the fields parched and brown.

There is some talk of Vietnam among the farmers here, but the lack of rain and the cost of living are the main topics of conversation, and when people talk politics, they talk about the state, and Harry Byrd, and the defeat of Judge Smith, and the price of cattle, rather than the personality or politics of Lyndon Johnson, or the bombing of oil depots around Hanoi or Haiphong.

The angle of vision makes a difference. Nobody here in the foothills of the Blue Ridge talks much about who is going to replace George Ball or Alexis Johnson at the State Department, or whether Bill Martin, or the Secretary of the Treasury, Joe Foster, or the Council on Economic Advisers was right about a tax rise, or whether General de Gaulle's ideas on the neutralization of Southeast Asia made any sense, or about any of the other topics that concern the official crowd in Washington.

Just Plain Folk

It is noticed, along these hilly roads, that the Secretary of Defense, Robert McNamara, and his wife had a wedding in the family today, and that the same sort of thing has been going on in the President's family and the Vice President's family and the Secretary of Labor's family too, and this seems to reassure them that officials have family problems like everybody else, but they are not particularly concerned about whether the Secretary of Defense, or the Secretary of Labor, or the Vice President is really doing a good job.

What they notice and comment on is that the President is on the job. "He works hard," they say, and so long as there is prosperity, even with inflation, this seems to be about all they ask.

---

39   L.B.J.—"I HAVE SO LITTLE TIME"

WASHINGTON, Nov. 26, 1966—When colleagues ask President Johnson why he tries to achieve so many things so fast, he invariably replies: "I have so little time."

This is an intriguing comment, verified separately by at least three responsible men on different occasions, but what does it mean? Is it merely the reaction of a serious and ambitious man who wants to be a very great President? Or is it an observation on his declining Congressional majorities, or an indication that he may not run or win in 1968, or even some vague troubling presentiment about his health?

If he had not surprised and even startled so many different people with this remark, it would not be worth speculating about, but he has made it a topic of discussion in Washington either on purpose or by accident.

Johnson's Habits

Probably nobody knows the answer to these questions, but at least they are not new. Lyndon Johnson has talked for years in this mysterious and melodramatic idiom. When depressed over personal criticism in the press, he even talked, in 1964, about retiring from the Presidency then. Nobody took him seriously, of course, but it is a fact that he raised the possibility of not running less than a year after he entered the White House.

The most remarkable explanation of this remark is that he was referring to the mood and mathematics of the Congress. He knows more about this than any man alive. He has often said that Congress tends to be generous to a President at the beginning of a new administration and increasingly critical and grudging as time goes on.

This, of course, is true not only of strong Presidents but of strong Cabinet members like Secretary of Defense McNamara as well. The harder they press the Congress, the more they increase the counterpressure: The law of politics is almost as certain as the law of physics. Power creates its own resistance, and the rule of diminishing returns usually gets stronger for Presidents with every passing year.

The Johnson Record

Knowing this, President Johnson used all the power, sympathy, and sentiment at his command after the death of President Kennedy. As a result, he started a cataract of social and economic legislation unmatched in this century. But the second part of the Eighty-ninth Congress was far less productive than the first part, and with a stronger Republican opposition in the forthcoming Ninetieth Congress, the legislative progress is likely to slow down even more.

The chances are that President Johnson, who is a Capitol Hill man thinking in Congressional terms, probably makes too much of this tendency of the legislature to oppose. The rule of diminishing returns does not really apply to the field of foreign policy, which is where he is most likely to be judged.

If he never gets another major new social or economic program through the Congress, his domestic record in education, civil rights, and medical security will compare favorably even with the most successful chapters of Roosevelt's New Deal. It is in the foreign field where he needs both time and success, and in this field the Congress will let the President be as big a man, as creative and innovative, as he can be.

For this, however, he needs time. The North Vietnamese, according to General Westmoreland, are still sending about seven thousand troops a month into South Vietnam. The bombing undoubtedly has made this a more difficult exercise, but it is still going on. The disintegration of the Atlantic alliance continues, and only now, with fresh ideas from the new men at the State Department—Nicholas deB. Katzenbach, Robert Bowle, Eugene Rostow, and Zbigniew K. Brzezinski—is the Administration beginning to sound relevant again to the European situation.

The truth is that Lyndon Johnson probably has a great deal of time to deal with these questions, provided he really deals with them. Regardless of the election returns and the current polls which make the G.O.P. seem, temporarily, stronger than it actually is, nobody would like to bet a great deal of money on Governor Romney or Richard Nixon defeating Lyndon Johnson in 1968.

Nor is it likely that the President would refuse to run again in 1968, no matter what he says in his moods of depression, unless he could settle the war and retire in triumph. To quit with the war going on and the alliance still in a mess would probably mean writing himself down in history as a political accident between the two Kennedy Administrations, and this is not the sort of thing Lyndon Johnson is likely to dream happily about in the night.

The Danger of Speed

The danger is that, wanting to do too much too fast, he might try to hurry things faster than life will bear. He is an impatient and moody man. "I want to do only one thing as President," he once said. "I want to unify this country, and if I can't do that, I cannot succeed."

Well, the chances are that neither he nor anybody else can get the kind of unity and affection he expects. Even John F. Kennedy couldn't do it, except in death. Johnson has enough unity and enough time to deal with his main foreign policy problems, and worrying about time is only likely to make the task of dealing with them more difficult than it need be.

40 JOHNSON'S PERSONAL APPROACH TO HISTORY

WASHINGTON, Sept. 30, 1967—In the tragic week when President Kennedy was murdered, there was a crisis in Vietnam. The arrangements at that time were for President Kennedy to go from Dallas to Vice President Johnson's ranch in Texas to get a report on the war from Ambassador Henry Cabot Lodge, but after the assassination all plans were, of course, changed.

A few days later, however, Ambassador Lodge put the solemn facts before the new President. The South Vietnamese Army was in danger of being overwhelmed. Either the United States must take a much more active part in the fighting or the war might be lost. The problem, said Mr. Lodge, must be carefully studied and a decision taken. President Johnson's reaction was decisive and personal. He is reported to have responded as follows: "I am not going to be the first President of the United States to lose a war."

Johnson's Consolation

This personal approach to the terrible dilemmas of the war helps explain what has happened ever since. Mr. Johnson apparently sees himself as the defender of the faith. He is now very conscious of the past. The heroes of the last generations were the Cassandras who feared the worst and defied the public opinion of their day. Mr. Lincoln, Teddy Roosevelt, Woodrow Wilson, Franklin Roosevelt were vilified, but perceived the coming age and were finally redeemed and venerated by the historians. In fact, Mr. Johnson now carries around a piece of paper, which he recites, on the similarity between his problems and the problems of past war Presidents.

Historical Perspective

Never mind, say his aides in the White House, about the rising criticism of Senators Case of New Jersey, Morton of Kentucky, and the rest. Other great men have passed this way before. Look at Churchill, rejected until the evening of his days, but steadfast and defiant, and triumphant in the end—the great man of the age. What does it matter if you are defeated? So was Churchill at the end of the Second World War.

This sort of thing is going on around the White House today; make no mistake about it. The President is being told by his shrinking company of intimates that the Communist aggression in Vietnam is the same as the Nazi aggression in the Rhineland, Austria, and Czechoslovakia, and he is holding the line; as Churchill defended freedom in Europe, so Johnson is holding the bridge in Asia until Japan and India, the two potential anchors of free Asia, finally take over responsibility for creating order in that part of the world.

The trouble is that Lyndon Johnson not only wants to defend the principle of opposing aggression in Vietnam but that he wants to win the election of 1968 as well. His speech in San Antonio this weekend illustrates the point. He didn't say that it was important to oppose Communist aggression with an American expeditionary force of half a million men and that Eisenhower and Kennedy had refused to do so and therefore had underestimated the problem. This would have been a defensible policy. But instead, Mr. Johnson tried to give the impression that he was merely carrying on the same policy as Eisenhower and Kennedy, which is manifestly untrue.

Mr. Johnson's proposition at San Antonio this weekend was that committing American power and prestige to holding Vietnam, no matter what the cost in men and money, was essential to the security of Southeast Asia and even to the security of the United States. This is precisely the proposition that President Eisenhower rejected when the French and his own Secretary of State, John Foster Dulles, and his own Chairman of the Joint Chiefs of Staff, Admiral Radford, proposed it during the crisis of Dienbienphu.

Johnson's Problem

President Johnson is trying to have it both ways. He presented himself at San Antonio as both the bold Churchill, defending Western civilization, and the cautious Eisenhower, who refused to plunge an American expeditionary force into a war on the continent of Asia. He argued that the failure to do so would not only lose South Vietnam, but might lose all of Southeast Asia and lead to a World War, which is precisely the proposition Eisenhower rejected when he refused to follow Johnson's policy of intervention and escalation.

Widening Opposition

This is why the opposition to Johnson's policy is now both deep and wide. It is not that the opposition is sure he is wrong, because the opposition is not sure it is right. But there is a growing feeling here that he is thinking about the problem in personal and partisan ways, that as usual he is not dealing with the problem but merely with the politics of the problem.

Nobody in Washington is sure about what should be done in

Vietnam. But everybody is sure that there should be some trust in the people who make the decisions, and this is precisely what is lacking. In fact, the criticism of the President and his Vietnam policy is now so deep and wide that serious men here, including many of the President's own friends, are beginning to ask whether he can ever recover the confidence essential to the effective conduct of the Presidency.

Nixon

41   THE NEW NIXON REVISITED

WASHINGTON, Sept. 15, 1966—The man who is raising the most money, addressing the most meetings, and scoring the most points for the Republican Party in this year's Congressional elections is none other than that familiar figure, Richard Milhous Nixon.

At fifty-three, he is now a little heavier, a little more relaxed, a little wiser, and a lot richer than the tense and painfully suspicious young man who served two terms as Vice President of the United States, and at this point, he must be at least an even bet against any other Republican for his party's Presidential nomination in 1968.

The Early Bird Technique

Apparently this same thought has occurred to him, for he is flying through the Middle West and the border states this week at the start of an ambitious speaking schedule that will take him into half the states of the Union, raise more than one million dollars for the G.O.P., and enliven the races in the see-saw Congressional districts.

This was the technique that won the Republican nomination for Barry Goldwater in 1964. Over the previous four years he put more G.O.P. candidates, state and county chairmen in his debt than all the other Presidential hopefuls combined, and it paid off in the end. Nixon has been doing the same thing ever since 1964, and by his own estimate has already added between four and five million dollars to the party treasury.

Despite his humiliating defeat and bad-tempered exit in the California Governor election of 1962, also despite his temporary eclipse when he moved to New York, time has not been bad to him. The elders of the party, led by President Eisenhower, who stood in his light in 1964, have now faded from the scene, and the only prominent young Republican of the new generation, Mayor John Lindsay of New York City, is unacceptable to the conservative wing of the G.O.P.

Meanwhile, the only other Republican politicians of Nixon's own generation with experience in the field of foreign affairs—Governors Nelson Rockefeller of New York and William Scranton of Pennsylvania—have retired from Presidential politics, leaving Nixon with the argument that he alone in the G.O.P. can both unify the party and challenge President Johnson's experience in the vital field of foreign policy.

It is a strange thing that a party which has held the allegiance of most of the lawyers and business executives of the United States for the last two generations should not have produced any more young political leaders, but Mr. Nixon has benefited by this failure, and we will soon be hearing the argument that anyone who came within 113,000 votes of beating John F. Kennedy in 1960 surely deserves another chance.

How to Rope Johnson

Mr. Nixon, of course, is not making this argument. He is working the hustings, and traveling the world, and exploiting the troubles of President Johnson and the Democratic Administration. He is not talking about 1968, just aiming at it, and he is just enough of a pro to know that the outcome of the Congressional and gubernatorial elections this November will greatly influence the party's political foundation in the Presidential test two years later.

His main theme has some appeal and validity. It is that the

American political system is now out of balance, dominated not only by one party in the Congress and the state houses but by one man in Washington, who is in deep trouble abroad and getting into more trouble with the economy at home.

"The leadership gap we have in Washington now in foreign policy and in dealing with inflation at home," he emphasized in his speeches in Ohio and Kentucky this week, "is because we have a one-party Congress that will go all the way with L.B.J."

Mr. Nixon, who has not yet learned the art of understatement, goes on to argue that "this year will determine the survival of the Republican Party and the two-party system in this country," and while this is even gloomier than the facts, there's just enough truth in it to scare the faithful to the polls.

Accent on Youth

What Barry Goldwater has put asunder, no man is likely to join together in a hurry, but this is just the point about Nixon. He is starting early. He is convinced that Lyndon Johnson is in trouble with the young, with the intellectuals, and with the women, all of whom did so much to destroy Nixon's own political ambitions, so he has started down the long road again, peddling not youth but experience and looking very much the successful Wall Street lawyer.

---

42   RICHARD NIXON'S CAMPAIGN

WASHINGTON, May 6, 1967—According to The Associated Press, Richard Milhous Nixon is in Lima, Peru, this weekend. Last month, he was in Asia—or was it Europe?—and his schedule for the rest of the year reads like a Pan American timetable. So what is he trying to prove? He is trying to prove the new theories of American politics: (a) that motion is progress; (b) that the road to the White House runs through all the other capitals of the world; and (c) that distance lends enchantment.

Moreover—and it is quite an achievement—he is not only trying to prove these things, but he is actually proving that they work. Right now, the pros in Washington tend to agree that he will get the Republican Presidential nomination primarily because the competition is not very stiff and also because he not only knows all the Republican county chairmen of the United States but all the prime ministers of the world as well.

Nixon's Achievements

In personal terms, the Nixon story of the last few years is remarkable. Whatever else he does, he endures. The fact that anybody is even talking about him for the Presidency now is not only a sad commentary on the state of the Republican Party but a tribute to his persistence. He has defied every rule in the political book. He not only lost the Presidency in 1960 and the governorship of California in 1962, but he lost his political base as well. He moved to New York where he was supposed to be shut in by a successful Republican Governor and a young and attractive New York City Mayor. Yet he has not only survived these political and geographical difficulties but has made steady progress toward the Presidential nomination, without an organization, without much money, and without making a single speech anybody can remember.

Of What Significance?

As an exercise in political tactics and personal perseverance, this is a triumph, but what does it mean? There is absolutely no evidence that travel has given him any new or deeper visions of America's problems in the world.

He is saying, almost in the same words, what he said about Vietnam when he was Vice President: That is, that power, military power, is the answer. This is the straight cold-war dialogue. We are good, he says, and the Communists are bad. We must oppose them now or fight a world war with them later on. If we have our troubles in Vietnam, it is not that we have used too much military power, but that we have used too little.

A World in Flux

It is hard to believe he still feels, after all his troubles, that the world of today fits the same arguments he was making five years ago. Europe and Asia are dramatically different. The Communist world is much more divided. The world is confused and rebellious. The problems of population and food, of de Gaulle and Europe, of Britain and the Common Market, Latin America and Washington—all have changed.

Meanwhile, at home, the problems of the races and the cities and the parties are much more complicated and serious than they were when Mr. Nixon ran for the Presidency against John F. Kennedy, but the former Vice President has said nothing new about any of these things.

It is very odd. The theory of being out of office, enjoying the prosperity and leisure of modern big-city legal practice, is that you have time to think about the old problems in a different way and put new policies before the people, but this he has not done.

He has dealt with the tactics, but not the substance of the country's political problems. He is going abroad. He is getting headlines that show he has been in more foreign capitals than George Romney or Lyndon Johnson, but few candidates have ever seen so many new things or had so little new to say about them.

The Strategy Works

Mr. Nixon's rise toward the top of the Republican Presidential candidates list indicates that his strategy is working, but fairly soon now, he is going to have to speak out seriously on what all this travel means.

He has made a brilliant comeback and deserves credit for it. He is now obviously back in the center of the Republican Presidential arena, but to date, he has said nothing about Vietnam policy or trade policy or monetary policy, and he has not even had time to deal with the problems of the cities or the races at home.

43　THE PRESIDENT AT SIXTY

WASHINGTON, Jan. 2, 1973—President Nixon, who will be sixty on January 9, is now at the very pinnacle of his political power, and yet, coming into his second term and his seventh decade, he is still in trouble.

He is not in trouble with his own party: He is its unquestioned master. The divided Democrats cannot challenge him, and despite his savage bombing of Vietnam, he is undoubtedly more popular at the end of his first term than he was at the beginning.

Still, he has used his power since the election not to unite but to divide the nation, and has misjudged the deepest longings of the people for peace and reconciliation.

In the reorganization of his Administration for the second term, he let go the Cabinet members like George Romney and Peter Peterson who had ventured to express independent judgments on his policies or, what's worse, to associate with his political critics.

In the name of increasing the power of the Cabinet, he decreased its power, put his own deputies into the State and Defense Departments, and centralized even more authority in the White House staff.

He announced the resignation of Erwin N. Griswold as Solicitor General without a public word of thanks, and even replaced some of the new Assistant Attorneys General brought into the Government only a few months before the election by the new Attorney General, Richard G. Kleindienst.

When he ordered the most severe bombing of the war in Vietnam, he did so without consultation with the leaders of Congress and without any personal explanation of its purpose. His White House press secretary, Ronald Ziegler, linked the bombing to another North Vietnamese offensive in South Vietnam, though no evidence of this has ever been offered by Mr. Ziegler or anybody else.

And when the Swedish Premier compared the U.S. bombing

to Nazi atrocities in the last world war, the President had the State Department tongue-lash a Swedish diplomat and asked Sweden not to send an ambassador to the United States.

Has *The Washington Post* been criticizing the Republicans for bugging and burglarizing the Democratic headquarters at the Watergate? Suddenly, the *Post's* society columnist is not invited to cover social events open to other reporters at the White House.

When the Congress returned and Chairman William Fulbright of the Senate Foreign Relations Committee invited Secretary of State Rogers and Henry Kissinger to explain the breakdown in the peace negotiations and the bombing of Hanoi, they were not available to testify.

After the President's spectacular victory over George McGovern in November, there was a pause in the party strife, and even Senators Kennedy and Humphrey, who presumably read the election returns, were calling for cooperation with the victorious President; but the events since then, particularly in Vietnam, have changed the mood, and even Speaker Albert, who normally supports the President on foreign policy questions, is now predicting that unless there is peace in Vietnam, Congress will probably cut off funds for the war.

How to explain the President's approach to his second term is now a topic of constant conversation in the capital. He is entering into a critical phase of domestic legislation in which he needs the support of the Democratic majority in Congress to win consent for his announced reforms.

He is approaching new realignments of the nations in both Europe and Asia, but has been roundly condemned by allies and adversaries both places for his diplomatic bombing of Vietnam.

Beyond this, he talked endlessly in the campaign about creating, not a stronger party of loyal Republicans, but a "new majority" drawn from the ranks of both major parties and the growing body of independents.

His second term was not to be a period of strife and confrontation, but of negotiation abroad leading to a "generation of peace" and a period of moderation and reform, bringing the people together at home.

The period between the election and the inauguration, however, has been precisely the opposite—more war without either Presidential consultation or explanation; more confrontation between the executive and legislative branches; more vindictive reaction to dissent.

It is almost as if the President, coming up on sixty, was determined not to heal old sores but to settle old scores, and the odd thing about it is that his privately expressed ambition has been to preside over a unified nation on its two hundredth anniversary in 1976, at the end of his last term in office.

44 MR. NIXON'S LAST THOUSAND DAYS

Washington, Jan. 8, 1974—Among many who long at the beginning of the new year for a new Government and a new spirit in America, there is still a reluctance to call for the resignation or impeachment of the President, something that holds them back, probably some fear that somehow this would weaken the Presidency and harm the nation.

There is something to this notion, but not much. The President is not the Government. The security and continuity of the Republic do not rest on any one man, not even on a Lincoln, let alone a Nixon. The system is strong and resilient, and could not only survive Mr. Nixon's departure but might even endure his presence for three more years.

But if he were to go quietly, the Administration would remain in place with the Congress and the courts, the market would probably jump up after a startled hiccup, and the nation would rally around the new President, as it did after the deaths of Presidents Roosevelt and Kennedy.

The popular argument for tolerating three more years of Mr. Nixon is that his achievements in the field of foreign affairs, particularly with the Soviets and the Chinese, might be lost if he resigned and that Vice President Ford is not as experienced in the foreign arena as Mr. Nixon, which is obviously true.

But if the American people sometimes confuse the power of

America with the personality or character of the President, foreign governments do not. The danger now is not that powerful foreign governments might try to take advantage of a new President but that they might try to take advantage of a distrusted President presiding over a divided America.

Also, in the next three years, the critical foreign questions are not likely to depend on Mr. Nixon's personal relations with Leonid Brezhnev or Chou En-lai but on U.S. relations with Western Europe, Japan, and the Middle East, where Mr. Nixon's achievements in the last five years have not been spectacular.

These are the coming areas. In strategic terms, the Middle East is the key. It is the fundamental political question in the world, for the oil blockade, protected by Soviet power, threatens the industrial security of Europe, Japan, and, in a more limited sense, of the United States.

But the American answer to these questions depends more on a united nation than on Mr. Nixon. Already, the informing mind in all these diplomatic tangles is not the President's, but Mr. Kissinger's, and while all the courtesies of Presidential power are respected, the foreign embassies in Washington and their governments are more concerned about the internal unity of America than about anything else.

Another popular argument against the resignation of the President is that it might set a bad precedent and hurt the institution of the Presidency. But why?

Nothing is likely to hurt the Presidency more than tolerating a man who has been unfaithful to the spirit of the Constitution, who has put a gang of twisters and moral cripples in high office, and lost the trust of the people.

This trust is the first article in the political contract and essential to the moral authority of the Presidency. The question is not what Mr. Nixon's mandate was in the last election, but what it is now. Once a President has lost the confidence of the electorate, resignation is not a bad but a good precedent, and if it were established by any party that a President could be called on by its leaders to resign, future Presidents might be more careful about fiddling with the freedom of the people.

After all, resignation or dismissal is what happens in all other

American institutions or parliamentary democracies when the chief executive fails. They don't ask whether he meant to fail, or hire burglars, or turn over his authority to dunderheads or crooks, but merely whether he presided over the disaster, and if so, they get themselves a new chief executive officer, coach, or prime minister.

Maybe the silliest argument against the resignation of Mr. Nixon is that it would hurt the Republican Party. Quite the opposite is the case. Nothing could hurt it more than to keep him in place for three long years at the center of an endless controversy over Watergate and all its related horrors.

This is a political nightmare, whereas the alternative gives the Democrats the shakes. With Mr. Ford in the White House, backed by a Rockefeller or an Elliot Richardson as Vice President, all the intractable policy problems would of course remain, but the poisonous atmosphere of the country would be swept away, and the chances of a Republican victory in 1976 infinitely improved.

In human terms, it is easy to understand the reluctance of the people to insist on resignation or impeachment. They have too many regrets. It seems too cruel and humiliating, and would obviously be bad for Richard Nixon; but to argue that it would be bad for America in Mr. Nixon's last thousand days is palpable nonsense.

Ford

45 THE DECLINE OF PRETENSE

WASHINGTON, Jan. 11, 1975—At the beginning of the new year, the most hopeful sign in Washington is the general decline of pretense. There are still a few windbags around pretending that everything will turn out rosy, but on the whole, the mood here is serious, and there is a greater willingness to face the economic and political facts.

Suddenly, all the big shots have been cut down to human size. The President doesn't pretend he has all the answers. One day, he is fighting inflation with budget cuts and bigger taxes, then, he changes with the facts and proposes tax cuts and a bigger deficit to fight the recession—and doesn't grieve much over the switch.

Even the President's wife, who is expected by tradition to strike an adoring pose, treats her guy in public like any other fallible husband. Watching him on television celebrate International Women's Year the other day, she took him by the hand and laughed and told him he had "come a long, long way."

Things are so bad now that even the Vice President is given work to do. Unlike his predecessors, Nelson Rockefeller is spending most of his time downtown on the second floor of the Executive Office Building, across the street from the White House, making coffee for a stream of visitors. He hasn't had time to move into the new Vice President's house on Observatory Hill, or move his family to town, or organize his staff; but already he is deeply involved in domestic and foreign policy, not to mention the C.I.A. controversy, and is getting almost more assignments than he has time to handle.

The mood is different on Capitol Hill, too. Freshmen members of the House of Representatives are supposed to slip quietly into town and tip their hats to the elders of the establishment.

This year, the seventy-five new Democratic members arrived and demanded the right to question the Democratic chairmen of the committees, and their demand was granted. In the next few days, they will also be questioning Mr. Kissinger.

The balance of power is shifting in the Congress. The authority of the autocratic chairmen of the committees is waning. The tragic collapse of Wilbur Mills is merely a symbol of a much wider dispersal of power. The chairman of Ways and Means will no longer have a veto over tax policy. It will, for good or bad, be determined by a much larger and more liberal Ways and Means Committee. And even the leaders of the House, Speaker Albert of Oklahoma and Tip O'Neill of Massachusetts, are no longer as secure in their jobs as they were a year or so ago.

The reduction of personal authority in both the legislative and executive branches of the Government extends even to men like

Henry Kissinger, the Secretary of State, and to institutions like the Central Intelligence Agency, which have been relatively free of Congressional control in the past.

Now Mr. Kissinger is complaining, with some justification, that the Congress is not only performing its duty to set the broad lines of foreign policy but is trying to dictate the day-to-day negotiations. And the C.I.A. is protesting that it cannot run a secret intelligence operation if all its secrets are subject to public disclosure.

So the new mood around the White House and the Congress raises some new questions. Both places, the procedures are more open and liberal.

Hugh Sidey of *Time* magazine, for example, notes that Richard Nixon's sliding door in the Oval Office, the secret entrance for secret guests, has been removed and plastered over by Mr. Ford. The fifteen eagles and 307 battle streamers in the Nixon Oval Office have disappeared, along with the tape-recording system, and the President of the United States is now available to members of the Cabinet, the Congress, and the press for candid discussion of the nation's problems.

All this is to the good, but the question now is how this new freedom will be used. Nothing in recent history has prepared Washington for the shared responsibility President Ford is now offering to the Cabinet, the Congress, the press, and the people. They have all been complaining in recent years that the President and his staff were doing too much and were too remote, and now they are complaining that President Ford is doing too little, not being decisive enough, not coming up with a program that will solve all our problems in a hurry.

Even the press is slightly baffled by the President's informal and disarming ways. He gives interviews whenever he likes. Some of them are on the record, some of them are off the record, and usually he talks as frankly and casually as he did when he had the boys in for a drink on Capitol Hill.

In the process he exposes his problems and admits his dilemmas, uncertainties, and weaknesses. In other words, he is an honest man, limited in many ways and looking for help, insisting that the remedies lie not with him alone or even with the Government as a whole, but with the cooperation of the whole nation—business, labor, and all the rest. In short, no pretense; and the problem is that Washington hasn't yet adjusted to a President who admits honestly that he doesn't have all the answers.

Carter

46 THE PAUSE THAT DEPRESSES

WASHINGTON, Sept. 28, 1976—Looking back over the first quarter of the election campaign since the conventions, Governor Carter must be aware not only of the rising opposition of the Republicans but of the puzzlement and disenchantment of his own Democratic supporters. For the Governor, this is the pause that depresses.

He is still ahead. Nothing has been irretrievably lost, but his long lead has melted away, and all his dreams of a month ago now seem threatened.

It is not that he has been overwhelmed by events. The unemployment figures keep going up, and the Ford Administration's own Census Bureau has just announced that people below the poverty level increased by two and a half million in 1975, the largest rise in a single year since the Government began keeping poverty statistics in 1959.

The Governor's troubles likewise cannot be blamed on the brilliance of his opponent. President Ford is campaigning as usual as if he were running for Congress from Grand Rapids, avoiding questions most of the time and then promising in the South to stamp out crime and oppose effective gun-control! Accordingly, the nation is confronted by a choice between a mediocrity and a mystery.

What, then, is Governor Carter's problem? It is, I think, that he has forgotten why he was nominated in the first place, and has failed to organize the party he represents. He was nominated because he seemed to have a vision of the American future related to the ideals of the American past; yet since the conventions, he has not defined that future but merely expressed his longings, without any new facts or eloquence.

He called his campaign biography *Why Not the Best?*, and this personal factual account of a life in the South must be the most honest and moving political biography of our time. But in the organization of his campaign, he has not defined "the best" and he has not recruited "the best."

Probably, he didn't plan it this way, but he has been so busy flying around the country that he hasn't had anything new to say, and hasn't had time to talk to the people who might help him.

John Kennedy in 1960, like Mr. Carter now, had his own "inner circle" of advisers, but he reached out to his party for people who could nourish his speeches, give him themes, historical themes, analogies, slogans, or even amiable jokes that might keep the voters from going to sleep.

Mr. Carter has done none of this. He has been alone. He has kept his headquarters in Atlanta. There, he has the best team I have seen around a Presidential candidate in forty years. They are intelligent and fiercely loyal to Carter. They are available to the rest of the party, elaborately courteous and respectful to the old writers of the Kennedy and Johnson days, but nothing happens.

Mr. Carter doesn't get them together. He is on the road most of the time, scalding Mr. Ford. Meanwhile, his staff in Atlanta is working hard, but fending off old Democratic loyalists like Kenneth Galbraith with mimeographed rejections of offers to help.

All this is at present being reviewed in Atlanta. Mr. Carter is now leaving some time to reconsider, and maybe he will at least get his foreign affairs advisers together before the second Presidential debate in San Francisco on October 6.

He has many experts at his command: Paul Nitze on strategic nuclear arms talks with the Soviets, Clark Clifford on defense policy, and all the old State and Defense Department establishment in Washington and elsewhere, but he has yet to have a serious conversation with any of them about the foreign and defense policies he will have to debate with the President.

This is why so many of Governor Carter's supporters are wondering what he is doing. They want to help, but find him spending his time with the press: giving interviews with *Playboy*, talking to the New York *News* about "ethnic purity" and to the Associated Press, vaguely, on taxes.

So Mr. Carter is in trouble now, not mainly with the Ford people who oppose him, but with the Democrats who support him. He put his own people in charge of the state Democratic Party organizations. He put his own people in charge of advertising, public relations, and his television commercials.

The result is that there is now a kind of sad revolt against him within the Democratic Party: The old-timers want to help but feel that they are being shoved aside, and Carter is at least conscious enough of this revolt now to take time out for a review.

This is the paradox about Carter: He talks about teamwork, but works on his own. He presents himself as the successor to Roosevelt, Truman, Kennedy, and Johnson, but ignores their advisers. The result is that he is getting into serious trouble—so serious that he is finally beginning to question his own assumptions.

---

47 CARTER AND THE CONGRESS

WASHINGTON, Jan. 17, 1978—In his "Calendar of Great Americans," Woodrow Wilson made an observation about Mr. Lincoln which still stands as a fairly good test of American Presidents at the end of their first year in the White House. Wilson wrote:

The most significant thing about the career of the man [Lincoln] is the way in which he grew steadily into a national stature . . . as he grew, everything formed, informed, transformed him. The process was slow but unbroken. He was not fit to be President until he actually became President. He was fit then, because learning everything as he went, he had found out how much there was to learn. . . .

This is a startling observation from Wilson, who lost so much of his dream of a League of Nations because he learned so little about how to get on with the Congress. And this is the question now being asked about President Carter, as Congress returns to a snowy Washington: What have they learned about one another in this first year, and how will they get on together in the second?

They didn't get on very well in 1977 for many reasons, most of which are blamed on the President. The main charge against Mr. Carter is that he tried to do too much too soon, with too little advance consultation with the leaders of Congress.

Arthur Schlesinger, Jr., who has not been excessively critical of the Democratic President, takes a different view. He argues in *The Wall Street Journal* that Jimmy Carter is doing too little too late; that he is really a Republican in Democratic clothes; and that he is not really an "activist" President but a compromiser with the Congress, a "stand-patter."

There is obviously something to this argument, but I don't think it's quite fair. You can argue against the "imperial Presidency" or against the "stand-pattism" of Jimmy Carter, but it's a little awkward to do both. Nevertheless, Mr. Carter is clearly in the middle between the people who think he's being too dogmatic too fast and the people who think he's being too easy and too slow.

Which brings us back to Woodrow Wilson's question, which is whether new Presidents are "learners" or, as he put it at another time, "whether they grow or merely swell. The Democratic leaders, who met with the President today, say Mr. Carter has learned a lot in his first year that will be useful in his second.

For one thing, he has learned that it is wiser to discuss his policies in private and in advance with the legislative leaders than to announce them publicly and fight over them later. He has also learned that the Congress of the United States is not just a bigger Georgia Legislature and that it is much younger, much more independent and combative than in the days of Franklin Roosevelt, Speaker Rayburn, and Majority Leader Johnson.

Mr. Carter was probably quite wrong to assume, as he did in

the Presidential election campaign of 1976, that a Democratic President and a Democratic majority in the House and Senate would somehow produce party unity. He has learned since then that there is very little party loyalty, that most Democratic members of Congress ran ahead of him in the last election, and that the party leaders in the House and Senate can no longer command votes for his policies.

Two important things have happened since the war crisis in Vietnam and the constitutional crisis over Watergate:

First, the President has lost his power to invoke "executive privilege" in the name of "national security"; and second, power in the Congress has been dispersed from the leaders and the committee chairmen to the subcommittees and the party caucuses. So everybody is more equal, and nobody is in charge. This was President Carter's problem as he outlined his State of the Union Message and his budget to the so-called party leaders this week.

Under these circumstances, what the Democratic leaders are hoping for is that the President, in his second year, will be more flexible than in his first. They respect his intellectual gifts and his moral values, but not his political techniques. They think he has been too remote, rigid, self-assured, and even self-righteous; but they seem to agree that he is learning and will change in the coming year.

As one of the President's most loyal supporters puts it, Mr. Carter has been thinking like a prime minister instead of like a President. He sends up a complicated energy bill and says the freedom of the Republic depends on it without really serious consultation with Congressional leaders in advance.

But there are signs that this is changing now in the new year, for good or ill, depending on your point of view. The President has gone over his messages to the Congress very carefully with the Congressional leaders this week, and this is taken by Speaker O'Neill and by Robert Byrd, the majority leader in the Senate, as a sign that there will be a better partnership between the White House and the Congress in 1978.

48 WHO WILL TELL JIMMY?

WASHINGTON, April 15, 1978—President Carter has been calling his closest advisers together for what is billed as a "hard reappraisal" of his Administration's troubles, but who will tell him the truth? You can almost put it down as a general rule in this town that Presidents often invite "honest criticism" from their aides but seldom get it, and usually don't follow it when they do.

The reasons for this are not obscure. The Oval Office is the most intimidating room in America. It imposes a kind of chivalrous respect on most visitors, and even those legislative lions who roar against the President on Capitol Hill tend to usually lower their voices and swallow their prepared speeches when they walk in.

President Nixon was the most painful example of this conspiracy of silence. Even Henry Kissinger, who is not an excessively modest or silent man, hesitated to face Nixon with the disasters Kissinger knew lay ahead. Ehrlichman and Haldeman apparently saved their doubts for their memoirs, and the few Nixon White House aides who betrayed their fears were regarded as enemies or worse.

President Carter is a different and more complicated case. He is not a majestic personal figure like Roosevelt, and he doesn't inspire fear like Johnson.

He is elaborately patient and courteous with his visitors. In his first year in office, he has given all men and creeds, no matter how preposterous, a respectful hearing. He has listened to more bores, suffered more fools, made more speeches, and held more press conferences than any President since Roosevelt. And he has a kind of swinging-door relationship with Hamilton Jordan and Jody Powell, who are invited to blow in and blow off to the President whenever they want his attention.

So the problem is not that Mr. Carter is isolated, like Nixon, or overbearing, like Johnson, or mentally lazy, insensitive, indifferent, or dogmatic. He reads more and sees more people than most of his White House predecessors in this century, and is sympathetic to all their arguments and problems.

This may be precisely why he is now in trouble. For the main charge against him is not that he doesn't listen to anybody, but that he listens to everybody and cannot make up his mind—or maybe, that he makes it up too often: One day, that unemployment is the major problem and then, that inflation is the major problem; one day, that the Soviets are a threat in the Middle East and in Africa, and the next, that he must send Secretary of State Vance to Moscow to get Brezhnev to bring the arms race under control, etc.

The Cabinet and Mr. Carter's White House staff, when they meet with him at Camp David to review all these problems, probably don't tell him the "truth" or what he should do because they all have a little bit of the problem and don't really know what the larger "truth" is or what they would do if they were in his position.

Mr. Carter has another odd problem. Not since Eisenhower has there been a Cabinet or a White House staff who had more personal affection or intellectual respect for their skipper than this Cabinet and staff have for Carter, so they hesitate to criticize him to his face or tell him that part of his problem lies with himself.

For example, he has not made clear to the American people the complexities and ambiguities that have to be resolved. His speeches are wooden and statistical, his priorities confused.

Despite all our problems and blunders in the United States, there are few, if any, nations in the world today in which personal life is more decent or secure, or where people can have more hope for their children. The surprising thing about Jimmy Carter is that while these things are probably closer to his heart than anything else, he has not been able to articulate the wider humanistic problems or to reduce all this complexity to identity so that the people can understand just how difficult it is to choose.

This is probably the central question that was evaded at Camp David. For only the President, and not the Congress, or the Cabinet, or the White House staff, can clarify the problems for decision, and the difficulty of deciding them. Jimmy Carter cannot by himself decide what to do about problems at home or abroad. But he can give a clearer lead on how to attack these problems, and in what order.

For the moment, his popularity is sliding, but the stock market is reviving, and he will undoubtedly get his Panama treaties and probably a strategic arms agreement with the Soviet Union later in the year. Accordingly, it may be a little premature to conclude that he will be a one-term President, considering the alternatives. If he could parlay Plains, Georgia, into the White House, it may not be irrelevant to think what, despite all his troubles, he can do with the White House.

Reagan

49 GOVERNOR REAGAN ON EDUCATION

BERKELEY, Calif. Jan. 28, 1967—The balance of political power in California has now moved sharply to the right. The moderate establishment of Earl Warren's days is in disarray, and has been replaced by a conservative coalition under Governor Reagan. Dr. Clark Kerr believes this was the decisive factor in his dismissal as president of the University of California.

The question now is whether the Board of Regents of the university will try to implement Governor Reagan's philosophy about the university or whether, after all of the recent controversy, they will pause and pull back.

A University's Role

During the fight over Kerr, Governor Reagan developed two theses which are even more controversial on the Berkeley campus than his call for economy and higher university fees. The first was that the university was "competing" too much with Stanford and the other private universities. The latter, he suggested, should be concentrating on the very best students, and the public university system concentrating on the rest. In short, he seemed to think of the public university system as a sort of welfare agency to help those who couldn't make the prestigious private universities academically or economically.

The Governor's second theme was that university teachers had an obligation to deal not only with the intellectual but the moral development of their students, and should be judged on the basis of whether they did both.

How strongly the Governor holds these views is hard to determine because he is not available these days for questions, but it is clear that he will have trouble holding many members of the university's remarkable faculty and staff if he tries to transform the philosophy as well as the budget of the university.

The University of Michigan is already pressing Chancellor Roger W. Heyns of the Berkeley campus to accept the presidency of that university, and ever since the dismissal of Dr. Kerr, the offers to other distinguished teachers and administrators have been coming in from all over the country.

"Scholar" Wanted

Even some of the regents who voted to fire Dr. Kerr, however, are opposed to Governor Reagan's views on the way the university should go. It is known, for example, that Robert Finch has been advocating moderation on the Governor and that even Reagan himself has been talking lately about wanting a "scholar" to replace Kerr.

For the moment, an odd situation exists. The regents, who are specifically instructed to protect the university from political influences, have involved it in the most acrimonious political controversy in years, while the faculty, which endorsed Kerr strongly at all the university campuses, has been powerless to save him.

Even Dr. Kerr's opponents on the Board of Regents and elsewhere in the state are proud of the university's progress in recent years. Both in quality and quantity of education, the facts are impressive, and these may moderate Reagan's attack upon the present system.

Measurable Gains

Since Dr. Kerr became president in 1958, the University of California has moved up to first place as a center of graduate studies among the finest universities in the country. It is also first in membership of the National Academy of Sciences. It now has twelve Nobel laureates, as compared with the five it had when Dr. Kerr took over.

The expansion of the university in this period has been even more spectacular: from 43,000 students eight years ago to 88,000 in 1966; from a faculty of 4,125 to 7,429; and from two campuses to eight, with a physical plant now valued at over $1 billion. Meanwhile, the University of California's total budget has risen from $282 million in 1958 to $650 million in 1966; its endowments have almost doubled, and its Federal funds have gone up from $155 million to $360 million a year.

In the 1952 and 1956 elections, such was the atmosphere at Berkeley that even Adlai Stevenson was not permitted to speak on the campus. Since then, the university has been creating a much more free and liberal atmosphere, while the political temper of the state since the Goldwater defeat of Nelson Rockefeller in the primary election of 1964 has been moving to the right.

The New Left is not powerful in California, but in the last few years, with its provocative extremism, it has energized the conservative right and kept the university and Kerr in constant turmoil. In fact, the regents have been devoting so much of their time to these political and social crises on the Berkeley campus that they seem to have voted for change more than anything else.

Uniting the Opposition

What they have done, however, is to unify all factions on the campus against them; they have increased, rather than decreased, the atmosphere of tension, and raised the specter of tighter political and economic control.

This may not riddle their faculty, but it is bound to interfere with the university's recruitment program designed to deal with the seventeen thousand new students due in the university system later this year.

---

50 REAGAN'S DRAMATIC SUCCESS

WASHINGTON, Jan. 20, 1981—President Reagan has made a good beginning. His inaugural speech was a theatrical triumph, a cautious compromise between his supporters and opponents at home and abroad. And that is not all. He has something else more important going for him, which is that he is a lucky guy.

No brilliant Hollywood producer could have dared to imagine so reckless a script for Reagan on his Inauguration Day: a departing President Carter trying to liberate the American prisoners in Iran and handing them over to Reagan at precisely the hour when Carter was departing from the scene.

In his long years as an actor and a politician, Ronald Reagan never had such a perfect setting on the American stage, let alone the world stage. The drama critics would have loved it.

For the first time, a new President looked down from the West Wing of the Capitol toward the sunset, where he could see the memorials to Presidents Washington, Jefferson, and Lincoln, and beyond the Potomac to the grave of John Kennedy and the mansion of General Lee. There was a vast multitude at his feet, the largest at any Presidential inaugural ceremony, on the long swale below the Capitol.

Everything was planned to perfection for television. The new President's lady, beautiful as ever, had on a red or raspberry dress and hat, modestly spectacular, which dominated the eye of the color television cameras. The new President was amiably serious, and made one of the best inaugural speeches in recent memory.

It was flawlessly presented, and divided into three parts. First, he was courteous to President Carter, thanking him for the transition from one Administration to another, but ignoring Carter's successes while emphasizing his failures. Second, he blamed

Carter, among others, for the economic distress of the nation, which he said was threatening the future of our children.

"Government is not the solution, it is the problem," President Reagan said. "It is time to reawaken this industrial giant . . . to get Government back within its means, and to lighten our punitive tax burden. These will be our first priorities, and on these principles there will be no compromises."

He was very tough on this. No compromises? Yet in the last part of his speech, Mr. Reagan was not only generous but wise and even compassionate. He talked about making amends both at home and abroad, and was hopeful that we could revive our hope and make clear our will to defend our principles.

"How can we love our country and not love our countrymen? And loving them, not reach out a hand when they fall? Heal them when they are sick . . . ?" These were things right out of Franklin Roosevelt's oratory.

"And the enemies of freedom," Reagan added, "to those who are our potential adversaries, they will be reminded that peace is the highest aspiration of the American people. We will negotiate for it, sacrifice for it; we will not surrender it—now or forever!" This was, of course, John Kennedy's theme twenty years ago in his inaugural address. "Well," as Reagan is fond of saying with an amiable bob of his head, we shall see about all this later. The main thing now is that President Reagan, though he says he will never "compromise" on the conservative principles he insisted upon during his two Presidential campaigns, is now talking in gentler ways now that he has entered the White House.

It is a paradox that those who were most determined to elect Mr. Reagan now seem more worried about what he will do as President than those who opposed him.

What is clear, however, and agreed upon on all sides, is that Reagan has some personal qualities that may be very important and may be in the end decisive. First, he has demonstrated in his inaugural address, unlike most politicians these days, that he has the gift of speech. The question here, therefore, is maybe not so much who will be in his Cabinet or on his White House staff, but who will help him address the nation and who will help the new

President in the devilish problem of handling the daily press and television?

Reagan is clearly not an expert on the mystifying problems of inflation, unemployment, prices, or in handling the dangerous conflicts of money and other economic and political agonies abroad. But he does know how to read an English sentence, and he has the gift of friendship. This was probably why he won in November, and what will now probably have to sustain him in the coming months.

We see Reagan now in Washington, with his easy smile and cheery wave, not mad at anybody, answering insistent questions from reporters that he should ignore, while getting in or out of limousines. He is the "nice guy" who has come to town, but now he is expected to take the town over and prove that what he said in the campaign makes sense. But that's for another day. So far, like the fireworks, he has been spectacular.

51   THE AGE ISSUE

WASHINGTON, Oct. 10, 1984—In the wake of the Reagan-Mondale debate, the leading front-page story in *The Wall Street Journal*, no enemy of the President, dealt on Tuesday with the question of President Reagan's age.

The headline read: "Fitness Issue—New Question in Race: Is Oldest U.S. President Now Showing His Age? Reagan Debate Performance Invites Open Speculation on His Ability to Serve." David S. Broder also observed in *The Washington Post* that Mr. Reagan's performance in Louisville "let the age issue emerge as it had not done in any of his previous campaigns."

This is a sensitive subject, but it is not a "new question." In fact, the President's age was discussed more in the 1980 campaign, when Mr. Reagan was still in his late sixties, than it has been in this campaign, where if reelected for "four more years," he would serve into his late seventies.

Much has been made of the fact that the President seemed to lose his way in Louisville, got his figures mixed up, and didn't seem to be mentally alert in dealing with Mr. Mondale's arguments. This is being attributed by some to his advancing years.

Maybe that is the case, but Ronald Reagan has always lost his way in protracted debate on complicated issues, even when he was Governor of California; always got his figures mixed up, not because of his age or any physical disability, but because that's the way he is.

What Louisville did was not to expose his age, which everybody knew, but to expose his mind, which the voters didn't know. This is what has been covered up in the last four years by his amiable personality and his superb reading of speeches from invisible mirrors, written and contrived by the best public-relations team ever to enter the White House.

Nobody knows this better than his most intimate advisers. This is why they keep him out of press conferences as much as possible, didn't want him to debate Mr. Mondale, fight among themselves about policies, including arms control, that he has not mastered, and are less than enthusiastic about getting him into summit meetings with the Russians.

Age may have been a factor in his faltering performance in Louisville. Usually he is at his best onstage, and the bigger the audience the better. But he forgot his lines, even in his memorized closing speech, and that did surprise and trouble even his most devoted aides.

Public debating is not a good test for Presidents, but mastering the facts and details of complicated issues is, and this is what Mr. Reagan has not done, and this is what has been covered up. He has a brilliant intuitive gift of analyzing and appealing to the dreams and longings of the people, and this may very well carry him through in November. But an election is a bet on the future, not a popularity test of the past.

There is general agreement here that the next four years are going to require the most meticulous thought and judgment, for the world is changing faster than we can change ourselves or our institutions.

There is no relationship today—whether nation to nation, church to state, region to region, management to labor, parents and teachers to children—that is not under stress. These things are not likely to be handled effectively by old slogans of either party, or by old minds.

As our world is new, Mr. Lincoln said during the War Between the States, we must think anew.

This is the challenge of the 1984 election, and it's not merely a choice between Mr. Reagan and Mr. Mondale. The problems are so complicated that no one person can possibly comprehend or master them all. We need to know not merely where Messrs. Reagan and Mondale think they're going, but who's going with them in the Cabinet, the Federal agencies, and the embassies in the next four years.

This is what we'd like to know or at least get some hint of before the election. The age of the President is an important question, and his physical condition should not be left entirely to the White House physician. We were assured about that by Franklin Roosevelt's doctor in the campaign of 1944 when even the photographs of F.D.R. showed that his health was failing.

So there are a lot of questions to be asked before November. Louisville was a tip, but not an answer. What Louisville did was to give the voters a new look at the President and Mr. Mondale, and make them wonder whether their assumptions of the past about both men were right.

In this sense, the so-called debate was useful, and will probably produce a more alert electorate in the last month of the campaign.

52 THE LIE DETECTORS

WASHINGTON, March 5, 1986—We need some lie detectors around here.

The most prominent advertising agency in Washington these

days is the firm of Reagan, Weinberger, Shultz and Speakes, situated at 1600 Pennsylvania Avenue.

These guys, with the aid of Pat Buchanan inside and Mike Deaver outside, think they can sell refrigerators to the Eskimos, but sometimes they go too far.

Having sold "Star Wars" and dumped their old buddies in Haiti and the Philippines, they are now engaged in a major campaign to convince Congress and the American people that Nicaragua is a menace to the United States, and that unless they get one hundred million dollars for the "freedom fighters" on the border, Mikhail Gorbachev in Moscow and Fidel Castro in Havana will threaten the security and democracy of the Western Hemisphere.

It's the boldest advertising campaign since the Ford Motor Company tried to sell the Edsel.

Suddenly, the Administration has aimed all its big guns on Nicaragua—and let's agree, Nicaragua is a problem.

The President proclaimed that failure by the Congress to vote that hundred million for the Nicaraguan rebels, or "freedom fighters," would be a "strategic disaster" that could "well deliver Nicaragua permanently to the Communist bloc."

He gathered a few commentators into the theater of the White House the other day to emphasize the point, along with Secretary of Defense Weinberger and Secretary of State Shultz, who not only supported the President but indicated that he was minimizing the problem.

Then Mr. Shultz and other members of the Administration went on to veterans' groups and other so-called press conferences to pick up the theme of the coming "disaster" if they didn't get that hundred million.

At first they suggested that it might be un-American to oppose such an investment in Nicaragua, but when challenged on this point, they agreed that maybe it was all right, but wrong-minded, to disagree.

Nevertheless, the President has charged so hard on this hundred million for Nicaragua, and overstated his case so obviously, that he has challenged the judgment of Congress and vilified the press—some of whose members, when trying to question him, were denounced as "sons of bitches."

Well, as the President is always saying with an amiable nod of his head, we have to be careful. It's a hard call what to do about Nicaragua. The Secretary of State has said that the Russians have put about half a billion in there in the last five years, and he testifies that the Cubans have been engaged in military operations on gunships from the Soviet Union against the opponents of the Nicaraguan Government and therefore that Congress must act, and act quickly, to vote that hundred million.

But the Administration's pressure on Congress and on public opinion has been so sharp and accusative that a reaction has set in.

It's interesting what the White House has tried to do about Nicaragua. It has stated the menace in such harsh terms that its proposal for another hundred million dollars seems almost modest. If there is a threat to the security of the United States, as the President and the Secretaries of State and Defense say, why a mere hundred million? Why not a decision to intervene with our own troops to remove the threat they say is posed by the Sandinista Government?

This, of course, is precisely the decision the President is unwilling to face. He thinks he can deal with the problem by financing the rebels to fight the battle he insists is vital to the security of the Republic.

But Congress has its doubts, and so does the press. They have been told so many lies about the Nicaragua problem by the Administration that they are no longer willing to be overwhelmed by this latest propaganda campaign out of the White House.

Pat Buchanan's advertising campaign really has gone too far. His fastball is better than his control, and Congress and the press are on to it.

He has been trying to use the press and television to put over this latest vote on financing Nicaragua in Congress, but there have been so many deceptions and lies about Nicaragua that Congress and the press are beginning to rebel.

They admire Mr. Reagan's television techniques, but are increasingly skeptical about his policy on Nicaragua. They would welcome an honest discussion of the problem, but have become the lie detectors of the Administration's argument.

PART VI

THE COMMUNIST POWERS

The Soviet Union and Eastern Europe

53 WHERE ARE THE REVOLUTIONARIES?

Moscow, Nov. 19, 1968—The late November days in Moscow, halfway between the autumn rains and the winter snows, are brisk and brittle. Down the straight, wide streets this week, every branch and twig of every tree was white with frozen fog, and the capital has a rhythm and a unison quite different from the clattering diversity and disunity of New York or Washington.

All the promises and war cries of the American Presidential election somehow seem to have settled here. Moscow has its own "law and order." If justice is "incidental" to order, as J. Edgar Hoover is reported to have said the other day, he would be happy in Moscow. This is a policeman's paradise, and "crime in the streets" is manageable.

And yet, and yet. To a temporary refugee from the vigorous arguments and open conflicts of American life, the Soviet Union suddenly seems conservative and almost Victorian, while America, in contrast, seems young and pugnacious and even revolutionary.

In the Soviet Union, the old are lecturing the young and challenging them to live by the principles of the Soviet revolution, which even the old seem to be deserting. In America, the young are lecturing the old and urging them to live by the precepts of the American Revolution, which they never mention.

Come to Moscow

Americans who are troubled by the spectacular stupidities and accidents of our politics, by the uncertainties and ambiguities of our Presidential candidates, by the irreverent and often irresponsible defiance of our young people, by the lack of authority and manners, by strikes and demonstrations—in sum, by the violent clashes of husbands and wives, parents and child, employer and employee, teacher and student, church and state, and Government and individual could come here and wonder about the difference.

The difference, as it appears to a visitor in Moscow, is that the Americans are facing and really grappling with the most fundamental problems of human life, and the Soviets are either evading or suppressing them.

Both countries have comparable problems, and there is clearly no agreement about which of them is right. The Soviets, whatever they say, are terrified by freedom, and the Americans are skeptical of authority. And somehow both have to reconcile their systems and avoid a major war, which would destroy them both.

What is interesting and even reassuring here is that Soviet officials seem to understand this point as well as officials in Washington. They think we are mad to trust the people and tolerate all the strikes and demonstrations in America. Just as we think they are crazy and even wicked to suppress dissent in the Soviet Union. But, like Washington, Moscow has grasped the main point: That major war is death to everybody—and they seem to be agreeing with Washington on that central idea.

It is interesting here that Communist officials, who used to believe that capitalist economic ideas would certainly fail, are now more afraid of Western economic theory than of Western political theory.

Western Europe is being unified, not by the political philosophers, or the Western statesmen, but by the American scientists and businessmen with their computers and their capital. This is what is worrying officials in Moscow.

Officials here can deal with Dean Rusk, but not with I.B.M. They are not worried about Nelson Rockefeller as a politician, but about David Rockefeller as a banker at the Chase Manhattan Bank. The old revolution of politics and military power does not concern them—they are very good at both—but the new revolution of economics and capital and commercial technology not only worries them but makes them seem almost old-fashioned.

The Soviet Union, or so it seems to a visitor, is doing very well in preparing for the big military war which it dare not fight and could not win. But it is doing very badly with the new war of ideas and people and economics. It is betting on authority and on ideological monkey shines, on "right-thinkers" and disordered enthusiasts, and it may be right.

The Soviet Evasions

Certainly, it is getting more "law and order" than the United States, but it is getting these things by evading or suppressing its major problems. The difference is that America is taking the chance on freedom, and has deep troubles as a result, but it is moving and changing much faster than the Soviet Union, and in this sense, the modern revolution is taking place not in the Soviet Union but in the United States.

54 THE INVISIBLE BEAR AND HIS "FRATERNAL AID"

PRAGUE, Nov. 27, 1968—There is an eerie feeling in Prague thirteen weeks after the Soviet invasion. Nothing has been absolutely lost, but everything has been badly shaken, and the fear of the unknown and the unseen is very real.

What is particularly eerie about this is that the Red Army is practically invisible in the capital. Even flying in here from Moscow, not an identifiable Soviet official in sight; nothing but a plane full of beefy characters wolfing cold cuts and beer for breakfast.

It is almost easy to forget the main thing that happened here:

namely, that the Soviet Union invaded this allied country and kidnapped its Government. Prague is still a museum. It is full of music and spectacular spires and blinking lights on the great hill above the Vltava. It has been a capital here for a thousand years, and many of its ancient buildings are being redecorated, as if in celebration of some glorious liberation, and you have to hunt the city before you find a couple of Soviet weapons carriers in an obscure square in the old town.

But you have a feeling that a mischievous boy setting off a string of firecrackers down any dark alley would suddenly produce a forest of Soviet guns on every rooftop in sight.

This is nonsense, of course, but it says something about the intimidating influence of the Soviet Union upon its smaller neighbors—and the anxiety about the invisible and unknown here is not nonsense. The Czechs have awakened and angered the bear, and he is still prowling somewhere out of sight. What worries the Czechs and a lot of other people since the invasion is that the Soviet leaders now seem incalculable, and it is this uncertainty about what will happen next that is causing the uneasiness in Prague.

The Contradictions

The contrasts and contradictions here are startling. The newspapers and news broadcasts come in regularly from the West without official interference. The tenth-century Prague cathedral, standing high above the river in what must be the most beautiful silhouette of any capital of northern Europe, was alive with people of every age last Sunday and full of the glorious hymns of a more believing age.

The Western correspondents send their copy abroad uncensored and sit around in the snakepit of the Alcron Hotel trading rumors about what will happen next; and a lovely old man drives the Alcron elevator and has plastered its walls with pictures of Thomas Masaryk and Alexander Dubcek and the other Czech freedom fighters.

Still, a visitor is told that it is not wise to engage in critical political talk, even in a private car, unless the radio is going. And the correspondents, while uncensored, are not always unaccompanied on their private journeys around the city.

The Prague papers are neither quite free nor quite enslaved. A publication that was printed on a Government press was suspended the other day and got an apology when it threatened to take the Government into court. So there are still a lot of brave men around, and they are proving that all is certainly not lost.

But others have got into trouble for quoting Lenin against his present successors in the Kremlin, and a lot of them seem to sit around wondering what the next limitation of their freedom will be and who will give the order for the Russians and who will pass the order and convey it to the press with the sanction or acquiescence of the present Czech leaders.

Even certain words are important to this new relationship between the Slavic allies. The Russians did not "invade" Czechoslovakia, and this is certainly not an "occupation."

They are here, according to the approved hypocrisy, providing "fraternal aid," and the man who directs this "fraternal aid" is Soviet First Deputy Foreign Minister Vasily V. Kuznetzov, who is even more invisible than the Red Army.

The Naughty Children

Sometimes he is here, it is said, and sometimes he is in Moscow. The word is that he is more intelligent and reasonable than most, whatever that means. His job is to bring the Czechs back into Moscow's co-inefficiency sphere with the least possible trouble. Whom he talks to and what he says are not known, but his line apparently is that the Czechs were naughty children who, unfortunately, have to be punished for their own good.

With this invisible advice, backed by the invisible Red Army, Prague is naturally full of rumors, most of them bad. But it goes on playing its music and fixing up the Charles Bridge, which is sagging a little after six hundred years. The Czechs could do with some "fraternal aid" on this project, but the Russians apparently have other things in mind.

55 THE LAST OF THE GIANTS

BELGRADE, June 21, 1977—If you think you're confused about the politics of New York or Washington, you should come to Belgrade. It breaks every rule in the political book. It sounds like Moscow and works like Pittsburgh. Everything runs upstream in this bustling valley but the Sava and Danube rivers.

It has a controlled press, but you can buy not only Moscow's *Pravda* and *Izvestia* here every day but the Paris *Herald Tribune* and other papers of the capitalist West. Officially, it is militantly atheistic, but it is full of bell-ringing churches. It has at least its share of political prisoners, but its planes fly nonstop every day to all the other capitals East and West, and its citizens are more free to leave and return than in any other capital of the Communist world.

Accordingly, it is prudent to check your assumptions and prejudices at the airport when you come to Yugoslavia. This country is sort of a halfway house between the political East and West—defiantly independent, part Communist and part capitalist. The popular description is that of a country with seven frontiers, six republics, five nationalities, four languages, three religions, and two alphabets—all held together by one boss, Marshal Tito, now in his eighty-sixth year, who is around here somewhere, but nobody knows quite where.

There is a theory that Tito is not immortal, but little evidence to prove it. He is the last of the political giants of this century and has spent a good deal of time in recent years going to the funerals of former distinguished enemies who hoped to bury him.

It is interesting that after all these years, we know very little about the parents, friends, women, wives, teachers, comrades, or children who influenced his life and career. All we know is that somehow he survived, and is still one of the last of the phantoms of world politics.

His record is well known, but still unbelievable. He was conscripted into the Austrian Army in his early twenties, during the

First World War, deserted, and participated in the Russian Revolution sixty years ago. He led the partisan guerrillas against the Nazis in the Second World War, broke with Stalin in 1948, and has run this country for over thirty years.

He is an evenhanded sort: He takes from everybody and is beholden to nobody, and outlives them all. Like Mao Tse-tung, his only competitor for the twentieth-century political-endurance medal, he moves here in mysterious ways from his mansions in Belgrade to his retreat on the island of Brioni; and like Mao in his latter days, nobody quite knows whether his power is based on myth or reality.

In the early days of the Nazi invasion of this beautiful and pugnaciously independent country, the question was: Who is Tito? Later, as he made his way against his internal and external enemies in savage battles and brutal massacres, the question was: Where is Tito? And now the sixty-four-billion-dinar question is: What after Tito?

Everybody is guessing, nobody knows the answer, and it's a little ghoulish to press it too far, but it's easy to understand why so many people are asking. Geographically and strategically, Yugoslavia is either a highway or a barrier to the Soviet Union's ambitions to extend its Eastern European empire and growing naval power into the Adriatic and the Mediterranean. Tito has been the barrier to their southern thrust for more than a generation, but after him, what? This is what the other European powers and the Pentagon would like to know, for Yugoslavia could be the hinge in this sweep of Soviet power toward Africa and the West.

Politically, it may be more important. For Yugoslavia or Yugo-Communism is regarded by many observers in Europe as proof that a Communist state can be independent of Moscow and therefore a symbol and argument for Eurocommunism—for Communist influence and participation, if not domination, in the coming struggle for political power in France and Italy in next year's elections.

Tito is playing the middle game, listening to everybody and joining nobody, and getting what economic aid he can get from both sides. It is a remarkable political performance. He celebrates everything. His long life is now a succession of anniversaries: recently, his eighty-fifth birthday; soon, the anniversary of his break with Stalin; then, the sixtieth anniversary of the Russian Revolution and his coming visit to Moscow and Peking.

In short, he has mastered the politics of the middle. He is clearly not a man you would hand your hat to by mistake. In the coming struggle for power between left and right in Europe, and even in the larger world political battle, East and West, North and South, Tito will obviously have a major part to play even in the declining years of his long career.

56 POLAND'S ENDURING FAITH

WARSAW, June 18, 1983—It's not difficult to understand why the Polish Government was worried about inviting the Pope of Rome to come back to his native land. He may be more dangerous to the Communist philosophy than all the missiles of the West. For centuries, the Roman Catholic Church has been Poland's refuge from alien aggressions, and this particular Pope is a symbol of Poland's national identity and faith.

Nowhere else in this secular world today would it be possible to imagine the scenes this solitary man created in the streets and cathedrals of Poland. The people surround his various pulpits like the sands of the sea—hundreds of thousands of them—and listen to his message of hope with what can only be described as a kind of silent adoration.

It was not only that he repeated the ritual and "comfortable words" of his church. It was the way he talked about the sufferings of the past and the future of our children, and how he looked on the children and touched them with the utmost tenderness and attention.

When the Pope arrived in Warsaw and kissed the ground, he said: "I come to my homeland. It has a particular meaning for me. It is like a kiss placed on the hands of a Mother, for the homeland is our earthly Mother."

His confrontation with General Wojciech Jaruzelski was perhaps the most striking comparison between officials of church and state in our time.

The Pope argued for the freedom and sovereignty of Poland. He never mentioned the Soviet Union, but said Poland had paid for its right to freedom and sovereignty "with six million of its citizens, who sacrificed their lives on the various warfronts, in the prisons, and in the extermination camps." The Polish nation, he added, has confirmed at a very high price "its right to be the sovereign master that it inherited from the past."

This he said in a strong sad voice, and was followed by General Jaruzelski, whose speech was delivered with trembling hands, obviously hoping for reconciliation with the Pope on Communist terms, which he did not get.

"I ardently desire," the Pope said, "that Poland always have her proper place among the nations of Europe, between the East and the West. I ardently desire the re-creation of conditions of good cooperation with all the Western nations on our Continent, as well as in the Americas, above all with the United States of America. . . ."

The Pope even devoted long passages of respect for Stefan Cardinal Wyszynski, who was imprisoned here for many years, and added that "Divine Providence spared him [by death] the sad events associated with the date 13 December 1981" (when General Jaruzelski declared martial law).

A reporter was reminded here of Mr. Lincoln's lament for a nation "bereft of faith and terrified of freedom."

This applies to the present governors of Poland and their allies in Moscow, though it must be said of General Jaruzelski that he took the risk of inviting the Pope here, and still allows some freedom of religion and limited freedom of the press.

I mention the press because I came here, not to report on the Pope's visit, but to interview General Jaruzelski. After weeks of negotiation, the terms of the interview arranged in Washington and London were reversed by Polish officials once I got here.

They insisted on a commitment by *The New York Times* that: (1) the questions should be submitted in writing, which they redefined, and answered in writing; (2) the *Times* should agree in advance to print in full whatever the general said; and (3) our conversation about the questions and answers could not be quoted verbatim or even reported as given by the general.

I said I had no authority to give such a commitment; that it amounted to prior censorship. In the end, the *Times*, as in the Pentagon Papers case, refused to agree to such prior censorship.

This was merely an incident here, but it illustrates a significant fact: namely, that even in Poland, which is still probably the most liberal of the Soviet Eastern European allies, officials are terrified of freedom.

They risked it with the Pope here, to their credit, but they probably regret that they did so. For the Pope has dominated the life of this country these last few days with his faith, his patience, and his eloquence.

Even the old walls of Warsaw echo with the sound of his voice and the music of the church. You will know that Communism has finally prevailed in Poland when it reproduces the architecture, the painting, and the hymns inspired by Poland's nationalism and religious tradition.

The heroes of this week in Poland were certainly not the officials of the Government, or even the Pope, but the Polish people themselves. Somehow, despite all the death and suffering, they are now a million more than before the carnage of the last world war. Their beautiful children are here to be seen in the streets, and they were clearly the object of the Pope's message.

China

57 NOW, ABOUT MY OPERATION IN PEKING

PEKING, July 25, 1971—There is something a little absurd about a man publishing an obituary notice on his own appendix, but for the last ten days, this correspondent has had a chance to learn a little about the professional and political direction of a major Chinese hospital from the inside, and this is a report on how I got there and what I found.

In brief summary, the facts are that with the assistance of eleven of the leading medical specialists in Peking, who were asked by Premier Chou En-lai to cooperate on the case, Professor Wu Wei-jan of the Anti-Imperialist Hospital's surgical staff removed my appendix on July 17 after a normal injection of Xylocain and Benzocain, which anesthetized the middle of my body.

There were no complications, nausea, or vomiting. I was conscious throughout, followed the instructions of Professor Wu, as translated to me by Ma Yu-chen, of the Chinese Foreign Ministry, during the operation, and was back in my bedroom in the hospital in two and a half hours.

However, I was in considerable discomfort, if not pain, during the second night after the operation, and Li Chang-yuan, doctor of acupuncture at the hospital, with my approval, inserted three long, thin needles into the outer part of my right elbow and below my knees, and manipulated them in order to stimulate the intestine and relieve the pressure and distension of the stomach.

That sent ripples of pain racing through my limbs, and at least had the effect of diverting my attention from the distress in my stomach. Meanwhile, Doctor Li lit two pieces of an herb called *ai*, which looked like the burning stumps of a broken cheap cigar, and held them close to my abdomen while occasionally twirling the needles into action.

All this took about twenty minutes, during which I remember thinking that it was rather a complicated way to get rid of gas on the stomach, but there was a noticeable relaxation of the pressure and distension within an hour and no recurrence of the problem thereafter.

I will return to the theory and controversy over this needle and herbal medicine later. Meanwhile, a couple of disclaimers.

Judging from the cables reaching me here, recent reports and claims of remarkable cures of blindness, paralysis, and mental disorders by acupuncture have apparently led to considerable speculation in America about great new medical breakthroughs in the field of traditional Chinese needle and herbal medicine. I do not know whether this speculation is justified, and am not qualified to judge.

Hardly a Journalistic Trick

On the other side, it has been suggested that maybe this whole accidental experience of mine, or at least the acupuncture part of it, was a journalistic trick to learn something about needle anesthesia. This is not only untrue but greatly overrates my gifts of imagination, courage, and self-sacrifice. There are many things I will do for a good story, but getting slit open in the night or offering myself as an experimental porcupine is not among them.

Without a single shred of supporting medical evidence, I trace my attack of acute appendicitis to Henry A. Kissinger of the White House staff. He arrived in China on July 9. My wife and I arrived in South China the day before, just in time.

But when we reached Canton, we were told by our official guide that there had been a change in our plans. We were to remain in the Canton area for two days and proceed by rail to Peking on the evening of the tenth, arriving in the capital on the morning of the twelfth. We demurred and asked to fly to Peking at once, but we were told it was out of the question.

Three days later, at precisely 10:30 A.M., while I was describing to several Foreign Ministry officials at the Peking International Club the unquestionable advantages of my interviewing Chairman Mao Tse-tung, Premier Chou, and every other prominent official I could think of, Chen Chu, the head of the ministry's information service, interrupted to say that he had "a little news item."

Mr. Kissinger had been in Peking from July 9 to July 11, he said, and it was now being announced here and in the United States that President Nixon would visit Peking before May.

The First Stab of Pain

At that precise moment, or so it now seems, the first stab of pain went through my groin. By evening, I had a temperature of 103, and in my delirium I could see Mr. Kissinger floating across my bedroom ceiling, grinning at me out of the corner of a hooded rickshaw.

The next day, I checked into the Anti-Imperialist Hospital, a cluster of gray brick buildings with green-tiled roofs behind high walls in the middle of Peking.

The hospital had been established by the Rockefeller Foundation of New York in 1916 and supported by it, first as the Union Medical College in Peking and later as the Peking Union Medical College.

By coincidence, I had had a letter before leaving New York from Dr. Oliver McCoy, president of the China Medical Board of New York, explaining that his organization had been responsible for building and running the hospital with Rockefeller money until it was nationalized by the Communist Government in January 1951. Dr. McCoy said that if we should happen to notice "a large group of buildings with green-tiled roofs not far from the southeast corner of the Forbidden City, it might be interesting to inquire what these were." It was interesting indeed.

My wife and I were taken to Building No. 3, which is the wing used to serve the Western diplomatic corps and their families. On the right of the entrance was a large sign quoting Chairman Mao (it was removed during our stay): "The time will not be far off," it said, "when all the aggressors and their running dogs in the world will be buried. There is certainly no escape for them."

We were taken at once by elevator to the third floor and installed in a suite of plain but comfortable rooms with large light-blue-bordered scrolls of Chairman Mao's poems on the walls and tall windows overlooking a garden filled with cedars. It was a blazing hot and humid evening, with the temperature at 95, but a revolving fan at least stirred the air. I stripped and went to bed.

Tests and a Checkup

A few minutes later, the two doctors who had originally called on me at the Hsin Chiao Hotel came in and said they had arranged some tests. They were Professor Li Pang-chi, a calm and kindly man who was the "responsible person" for the case, and Chu Yu, a visiting surgeon and lecturer at the Anti-Imperialist Hospital.

Professor Li, who understood and spoke a little English, explained that other doctors would examine me later and that there would be consultations about what was to be done.

A parade of nurses and technicians then slipped quietly into the room. They bathed me with warm towels. They checked everything I had that moved or ticked. They took blood out of the lobe of my ear. They took my temperature constantly, measured pulse and blood pressure, and worried over a cardiogram showing a slightly irregular heartbeat. They were meticulous, calm, and unfailingly gentle and cheerful.

An hour later, the consultants summoned by Premier Chou arrived: surgeons, heart specialists, anesthetists, members of the hospital's revolutionary committee, or governing body. Each in turn listened to the offending heartbeat.

I felt like a beached white whale at a medical convention and was relieved when they finally retired for consultation and returned with the verdict: "Acute appendicitis. Should be operated on as soon as possible."

They sought my decision. It did not seem the time to ask for a raincheck.

Accordingly, at a little after eight-thirty in the evening, they rolled me through the dim, hot corridors to an air-conditioned operating theater, and Dr. Wu Wei-jan, a remarkably bright and lively man with a quick intelligence and a compelling smile, took over. He bound me tightly but comfortably on the operating table, put a small iron stand with a towel over my head, so that I could look backward to the interpreter but not forward, and then pumped the area anesthetic by needle into my back.

Everything Was Roses

Everything was roses after that. I was back in my room talking with my wife by eleven. The doctors came by to reassure me that all had gone well and show me the nasty little garbage bag they had removed. They asked my interpreter, Chin Kuel-hua, to remain at the hospital, gave me an injection to relieve the pain, and lit a little spiral of incense to perfume the room for the night.

Since then, I have lived with the rhythm of what must be the quietest city hospital in the world, constantly regaining strength and acquiring an intense curiosity about the politics and medical philosophy of the doctors in attendance.

They insist that the two cannot be separated, and they are quite frank in saying that the sole purpose of their profession since the Cultural Revolution of 1966–69 is to serve all the people of China, 80 percent of whom live on the land.

For this purpose, medical education and medical procedures have been transformed. The doctors at the Anti-Imperialist Hospital make an average of about 150 yuan, or sixty-five dollars, a month and take their turn for six months or more training barefoot doctors in rural farm and industrial communes. The aim is to prepare a medical army of young men and women for public-health service all over the People's Republic as fast as possible. Their training begins with political indoctrination in the thoughts of Chairman Mao.

The Anti-Imperialist Hospital is run by a four-man revolutionary committee—Tung Teo, chairman, and his deputies, Huang Chung-li, Shen Pao-hung, and Tsui Ching-yi—two of whom are qualified physicians and two of whom are not.

Discussion and Criticism

They meet with the professional staff of the hospital constantly for discussion of the philosophy of Chairman Mao and for common criticism of each other and their work, and they discuss the procedures with the zeal of religious fanatics, constantly repeating, as in a litany, the need to improve their work and their moral purpose in the service of the state.

To understand the urgency of China's medical problem and its emphasis on the quantity rather than the quality of medical training, it is necessary to understand the problem's scope. Edgar Snow quotes Dr. William Chen, a senior surgeon of the United States Public Health Service, as saying that before the Communists took over this country in 1949, four million people died every year from infectious and parasitic diseases and that 84 percent of the population in the rural areas were incapable of paying for private medical care, even when it was available from the twelve thousand scientifically trained doctors.

That helps explain the current emphasis on rapid expansion of the medical corps and the determination of the Government to increase the use of herbal medicine and acupuncture.

Dr. Li Chang-yuan, who used needle and herbal medicine on me, did not go to medical college. He is thirty-six years old and learned his craft as an apprentice to a veteran acupuncturist here at the hospital. Like most young apprentices in this field, thousands of whom are being trained, he practiced for years with the needles on his own body. "It is better to wound yourself a thousand times than to do a single harm to another person," he said solemnly.

Effects Were Observed

The other doctors watched him manipulate the needles in my body and then circle his burning herbs over my abdomen with obvious respect. Professor Li Pang-chi said later that he had not been a believer in the use of acupuncture techniques "but a fact is a fact—there are many things they can do."

Professor Chen Hsien-jiu, of the surgery department of the hospital, said that he had studied the effects of acupuncture in overcoming post-operative constipation by putting barium in a patient's stomach and observing on a fluoroscope how needle manipulation in the limbs produced movement and relief in the intestines.

Even the advocates of Western medicine believe that necessity has forced innovation and effective development of traditional techniques.

Mr. Snow quotes Dr. Hsu Hung-tu, a former deputy director of the hospital, as saying: "Diseases have inner and outer causes. The higher nervous system of the brain affects the general physiology."

Professor Li said that despite his reservations, he had come to believe in the theory that the body is an organic unity, that illnesses can be caused by imbalances between organs, and that stimulation from acupuncture can help restore balance by removing the causes of congestion or antagonism.

Dramatic Cures Reported

The controlled Chinese press is reporting on cases that go well beyond the relief of pain in the gastrointestinal tract and illnesses of the nervous system or those of neurological origin. It is reporting not only successes in treating paralysis and arthritis but spectacular results in curing blindness and deafness.

While I have no way of knowing the validity of the reports, the faith even of the professionally qualified doctors at the Anti-Imperialist Hospital is impressive. Maoism itself has obviously become an infectious disease, even among many of the well-educated urban citizens who had a hard time during the Cultural Revolution.

"We are just at the beginning of all this," Professor Li said as he prepared to unstitch me and set me free. "We have gone through great changes in this hospital. We are now treating between twenty-five hundred and three thousand patients here every day—over a hundred of them by acupuncture for everything from severe headaches to arthritis—and we are learning more about the possibilities all the time."

I leave with a sense of gratitude and regret. Despite its name and all the bitter political slogans on the walls, the hospital is an intensely human and vibrant institution. It is not exactly what the Rockefeller Foundation had in mind when it created the Peking Union Medical College, but like everything else in China these days, it is on its way toward some different combination of the very old and the very new.

---

58   LETTERS FROM CHINA: I

PEKING, July 27, 1971—The extraordinary thing about this oldest civilization in the world is that it seems so young. You do not have the feeling here—so depressing and oppressive in some other parts of the Orient—of weariness, sickness, and death, of old men and women, spent before their time, struggling against hopeless odds.

To an American visitor, China's most visible characteristics are the characteristics of youth: vigorous physical activity despite some serious health problems, a kind of lean muscular grace, relentless hard work, and an optimistic and even amiable outlook on the future.

In the vast expanses of the Soviet Union, you get the feeling that this is the way the world must have looked when it began, empty and untamed, all land and sky. China is not like that. It is alive with people. In the fifteen-hundred-mile train ride from Canton to Peking, my wife and I never once looked out the window and saw a vacant field, and the land is not untamed.

These people do not till the earth, they sculpture it, shape it with their own hands, bend and level it so that they can move the irrigating water from one level to another, not only on the level ground but up into the lovely terraced hills.

There are some machines around, heavy trucks on the tree-lined two-laned main roads, some twelve- and fourteen-horse-power garden tractors in the fields, a plague of bicycles in the cities, but everywhere the scenes are intensely human and alive—but everywhere.

This sense of youthful activity is not only physical but mental. In the twenty-one years since the Communist takeover, the people have not had time to settle into any stable routine, and even when they seemed to be doing so in 1966, the leadership convulsed them into new and dramatic patterns of life with the Cultural Revolution. This has now passed through its violent phase when the young were encouraged to challenge the leaders of the bureaucracy, and even some of the leaders of the Communist Party, but it is far from over yet.

Accordingly, China is still in a highly active state of transformation, where all workers, peasants, teachers, students, and even technicians and other professionals are challenged daily to self-criticism and self-improvement in the performance of their tasks. Thus, there is no time, even for older men and women, to settle down and relax. One is constantly reminded here of what American life must have been like on the frontier a century ago. The emphasis is on self-reliance and hard work, innovation and the spirit of cooperation in building something better and larger than anything they have known before.

Of course, they have desperate problems in trying to mobilize and feed between seven- and eight-hundred-million people—nobody knows how many. They have a problem of snail fever, a killer parasitic disease, prevalent in the Yangtse Valley. They have a shortage of fertilizer and an obvious shortage of machines.

We drove over a hundred kilometers out of Canton to see a pioneer agricultural community at a place called Lo Tung. All the way out and back, we never saw a single passenger car other than our own. We did see some garden tractors in the rice paddies, but mainly, the peasants were plowing the muddy fields behind water buffalo and, of course, planting the new rice seedlings by hand. On the way back to Canton, we came across a work brigade of what seemed to be over a thousand young men and women who were helping to build a section of highway in a gorge. So far as we could tell, they had no equipment other than long-handled picks and shovels, which they were using to dig the earth out of a hillside, and baskets, which they carried on long poles to transfer the earth to the bed of the new road.

This was, of course, draft labor by city youngsters who were living in makeshift straw huts and cooking their own food, but they were treating it like an escape from the city and an outing in the countryside.

Visitors, of course, go where they are taken. On this particular trip, we had to stop once at a police checkpoint beyond which foreigners are not allowed to go without a permit. Also, this was in the rich agricultural land of the south, which is quite different from many bleak areas in the west, and even here most of the houses we passed were poor by almost any standards except China's own in the past.

Accordingly, there is no way for a stranger to know whether China is likely to be the first major Communist country to solve its agricultural problems, but some things even a stranger can observe.

The people seem not only young but enthusiastic about their changing lives. There is no sense of intimidation in the relationship between the revolutionary committee leaders and the workers, and while the People's Liberation Army is undoubtedly the key to the future leadership of China, one is not really conscious of its pervasive influence.

Still, there is a second paradox: China is not only an ancient country that acts young, but its youthful energy is sternly controlled by a Government of old men. This is a question very much on the mind of the leaders here, but that is another story.

59 LETTERS FROM CHINA: II

PEKING, July 29, 1971—The Hsinhua News Bulletin, a mimeographed collection of state information in English, is delivered to your door at the Hsin Chiao Hotel here every morning, with a quotation from Chairman Mao Tse-tung printed in red at the top of the first page.

Usually this is some brisk and waspish denunciation of the wicked imperialists, but very often it is a McGuffy Reader moral maxim: "We must learn the spirit of absolute selflessness." "Diligence, frugality, and modesty: remember these three." "The eight points for attention are:

(1) speak politely; (2) pay fairly for what you buy; (3) return everything you borrow; (4) pay for anything you damage; (5) do not hit or swear at people; (6) do not damage crops; (7) do not take liberties with women; and (8) do not ill-treat captives.

Since you find the same sort of thing on each page of your calendar every morning or printed on top of any notebook you may buy, it is a bit of a shock to discover that your good Maoist not only believes in struggle and revolution but in plain living and high thinking. As somebody has said, "Communist China is a sink of morality," and in their glorification of the noble yeoman and puritanical righteousness, officials here make Spiro Agnew sound positively permissive.

It would be unwise to mock or minimize this side of the Chinese Communist doctrine. They would be the first to deny that there are any religious overtones to their propaganda and ideology, but the similarities with the dogmatism of the Protestant ethic are not only unmistakable but unavoidable.

Chairman Mao is not only presented as the savior of the nation but as the warrior poet and moral philosopher of a revivalist and evangelical movement, which has its own scriptural readings, its own Jerusalem (the Chingkang Mountains where Chairman Mao started his reformation in the wilderness), its own national revolutionary litany, its own heretics (Liu Shao-chi and Peng Teh-huai, for example), and even its own division of time and history (B.L. and A.L., before and after the Communist liberation in 1949).

Moreover, the influence of all this is pervasive. The education of a foreigner here illustrates the point and follows a simple pattern. It begins, whether you are taken to a model farm or table-tennis ball factory, in a common room dominated with a plaster or gilt bust of Chairman Mao. Here you are given cool wet towels, cups of delicious jasmine tea, and something like a military briefing on the purpose of the enterprise.

Here, says the chairman of the revolutionary committee, as the head man is invariably called whether he is the superintendent of a factory or the headmaster of a school, is what we do in this place.

Usually, he explains what was here before liberation, if anything, and it is a tale of unrelieved inefficiency and human misery, followed by an account of how, "with the help of Chairman

Mao's teachings," the people began to cooperate with one another, increase production or learning as the case may be, and
improve the general standard of life.

There then follows the inevitable disclaimer. The people have
worked hard, they have been inventive and faithful, but they
have not done as well as they might, not nearly as well as their
comrades in the model industrial and agricultural communes, or
even approached the goals they must meet if China is to become a
modern industrialized nation.

After this, the visitor is invited to tour and inspect the work,
and after the inspection, is brought back to the common room
for more cool towels and Pearl River orange squash and tea,
and invited, even urged, to question and to criticize what he has
seen.

No matter how often you go through this routine, you are
seldom tempted to be casual or lighthearted about the experience.
In the first place, there is something about these serious revolutionary committee chairmen that persuades you they are telling
the truth; and secondly, the atmosphere of intelligent and purposeful work is impressive.

More important, it is clear that you are in the presence not
merely of industrial or agricultural technicians but of true believ-
ers in the gospel according to Mao Tse-tung.

They don't only talk production but the Spartan philosophy
of Chairman Mao, and it is fairly obvious that they believe the
production will never be achieved without the philosophy.

All this, of course, raises many more questions than it answers. Can this philosophy of hard work, without the education
of a modern technocratic and scientific elite, really deal with the
vast complexities of organizing and administering an advanced
industrial society? Maybe not, but that, say officials here, is a
question for the future. The main thing is to get the purpose
straight, to mobilize the people even if they have to move mountains with teaspoons, and to find a common philosophy which the
people believe. And that they seem to be doing, ironically, by
adopting many aspects of the old faiths the West has dropped
along the way.

60 LETTERS FROM CHINA: III

PEKING, Aug. 3, 1971—The routine of life for an American visitor in China these days is full of paradox. For example, you live in an atmosphere of vicious and persistent anti-American propaganda, but are treated with unfailing personal courtesy and are free to cable your impressions without censorship from the lobby of your hotel.

There is not a word in the papers or on the radio here about the latest American moon landing, but you can call the desk at the Hsin Chiao Hotel for an excellent Chinese short wave radio and listen to the conversations of the astronauts on the moon via the Voice of America and the BBC.

Officials here are obviously pleased about President Nixon's coming visit to Peking, but his visit is not discussed in the press or on the radio, both of which relentlessly characterize the American Government as the "arch-criminal" of the world. The United States, they insist, has been "beaten black and blue" in Vietnam, but still goes on backing a "fascist clique" there, and is reviving "Japanese militarism" and plotting new wars of aggression in Korea and the rest of Asia.

When you ask who writes these editorials in *The Peking People's Daily* and *The Peking Review* (a weekly published in English, Russian, and many other languages) and ask to talk to them, you are told that your request will be "passed on." You are never told that any request is impossible. You are merely given the next day's schedule, which sometimes includes your requests but usually doesn't.

Still, things are obviously changing here, tactically and on the surface, at least. The Kissinger mission and the forthcoming visit of President Nixon are only the most dramatic evidence that the Chinese Government has decided to end its isolation from the rest of the world.

It sees Washington withdrawing from Vietnam, London joining a new Europe, Moscow and Washington talking about the control of strategic nuclear weapons, Japan emerging as a major industrial power, Moscow expanding its power in the Middle East and along the southern shore of the Mediterranean and building a navy for deployment in all the oceans of the world.

Peking obviously wants to be in on this new organization of the world beyond Vietnam, beyond the unification of Europe with Britain, beyond the present stalemate in the Middle East, and beyond the present talks on the control of nuclear strategic weapons.

So it is changing its attitudes and tactics. It is giving the diplomatic corps in Peking more leeway. It is allowing Western diplomats to travel more widely across China. It is inviting more journalists and scholars to come here. It is encouraging more nations to establish diplomatic relations with Peking, and for the moment, it is concentrating on getting into the United Nations.

Specifically, Peking is now negotiating with the British to establish embassies rather than lower-grade diplomatic missions in Peking and London. It has agreed to allow the Reuter News Agency of London to send off a full-time correspondent here, and it is now puzzling over the avalanche of appeals from Americans to visit or establish permanent offices in Peking. In a way, Peking's diplomacy with Mr. Kissinger and Mr. Nixon has outrun its capacity to deal with the practical problems of dealing with American scholars and the American press. The Foreign Office here now has over three hundred requests from Americans and American institutions to come here.

These range from appeals for visas from Senator Edward Kennedy of Massachusetts and Senator George McGovern of South Dakota, which puzzle them, to requests from news agencies to establish permanent bureaus in Peking and requests from the television networks to set up machinery for satellite broadcasts of the Nixon visit.

One has the impression that officials here don't quite know how they are to handle all these practical problems of their new diplomacy. They don't have enough Chinese-English translators on their staff to service so many visitors, and they seem a little vague about what the leaders of this Government want them to do with all these new requests.

So for the time being, there is a dilemma between Peking's strategy and its tactics. Its policy remains the same—indeed, Mr. Nixon's appeal to come here seems to have convinced Peking all the more that its policy has been right—and its more lenient attitudes and tactics seem designed merely to promote its policy of weakening American influence in this part of the world. In short, Peking is ready for normalizing relations with Washington, but on its own terms: total American withdrawal from Vietnam and Taiwan, and, what seems to interest officials here even more than anything else, a weakening rather than a strengthening of Japanese power in the Pacific.

61   LETTERS FROM CHINA: IV

TIENTSIN, China, Aug. 5, 1971—You hear a lot about the Chinese theory of "people's war" and "protracted war" these days, but what does it all mean?

Well, frankly, we don't know and the Chinese won't tell, but the 196th Infantry Division of the People's Liberation Army operates out of a flat agricultural plain at the village of Yang Chun, and for the first time since the Cultural Revolution of 1966–69, it is now open to inspection by invited guests. One thing is sure: That old country boy from Wisconsin, Secretary of Defense Melvin Laird, never saw a base like this. It does all the routine stuff: basic training, discipline, marksmanship, and particularly the techniques of guerrilla warfare; but in addition, it is a political school, a vast farm producing its own fodder, a pharmaceutical factory, and a machine shop making tools, spare parts, and repairing weapons and vehicles.

In short, it concentrates on political motivation, integration with the peasants and their work, simple weapons that can be carried quickly from one place to another, and self-reliance and self-sufficiency.

We were received at division headquarters by the deputy commander, Keng Yu-chi, who explained that the main purpose of his command was to help defend Peking. His division had been formed in 1937 during the early part of the anti-Japanese war, he said, and since that time, "under the guidance of Chairman Mao," had killed thirty-eight thousand Japanese, Chiang Kai-shek "traitors," and American imperialists in the Korean war. All this very politely.

His division, he explained, had three principles and three main tasks. The principles were to maintain unity between his officers and men, with each group teaching the other, to develop a common purpose between his division and the civilian population, and to disintegrate the enemy, undefined.

His three main tasks, he continued, were to develop his division into a fighting force, a work force in the fields and factories, and a production and political force. His division numbered "over ten thousand men," plus their dependents, who helped run the farms and factories, schools, and nurseries of his command.

He took us first to the barracks and club of Two Company of the 587th Regiment of the 196th Division. The club was a propaganda room, with maps of the company's battles, photos of its heroes, exhibits of its captured weapons and citations, and a Ping-Pong table.

The barracks in the plain red-brick buildings were immaculately clean, with bare double-decker bunks fitted with mosquito netting; at the end of each row of beds were neatly lettered company "newspapers" composed of letters of gratitude to Chairman Mao. Each man had his battle roll on his bed for instant action, and automatic rifles, carbines, and machine guns were racked neatly at a clear space beyond each double row of sixteen beds.

After a tour of the pig pens, rice paddies, and pharmaceutical sheds, we were shown how the pig bristles were used to make brushes to clean the rifle bores, taken to the machine shops, and then given or offered a lunch of wine, *mao tai* (a clear distillation of sorghum and dynamite), and enough food to paralyze a regiment.

In the afternoon, the division produced a concert and series of propaganda skits, remarkably good and even amusing, after which we were taken to a vast artillery range where Two Company put on a demonstration of marksmanship by rifle, automatic and machine-gun fire, antiaircraft, mortar, antitank, and rocket fire, and man-to-man combat and house-to-house guerrilla tactics. It was an impressive performance.

We were then invited to come back and discuss "the international situation." Asia, Africa, and Latin America, we were told, were fighting in unison against the American imperialists. Men, the deputy commander insisted, were more important than weapons. Any enemy invading China would be "drowned in oceans of people," he added, and did we have any comment?

We said we had come to China to report and not to argue, and suggested that things were changing in the world and America was looking now to the future and to peace and understanding in the Pacific. This proved to be a disastrous gesture.

The past could not be forgotten, the deputy commander insisted. The main trend in the world was against the U.S. imperialists and all their running dogs. All nations wanted independence and liberation, all peoples wanted revolution, and this was the irresistible trend of history.

China was friendly toward all peoples including the American people, he concluded, but imperialist and reactionary governments "never change," so the danger of a new world war still exists. Nixon, as he called the President, must get out of Taiwan and Vietnam and give China its rightful place in the United Nations.

He continued in this vein until an official of the Foreign Office intervened to say the sun was going down and we had to get back to Peking. The Chinese people and the American people were friends, he said, but the American Government was something else. It said it wanted to normalize relations with the People's Republic of China, but Secretary Rogers had suggested a two-China formula for the United Nations which was "a new brand with the same old stuff."

We went back to Peking a little sad, thinking about memory. Maybe we have to learn to forget, we said as we left. How could we forget the past, the Chief of Staff asked—forget the Japanese, forget Korea, forget Taiwan? We would like to ask Nixon to think about that.

62 LETTERS FROM CHINA: V

PEKING, Aug. 17, 1971—It is hard to see the Chinese people these days for the political billboards, but despite the ceaseless propaganda, it is easy to understand why so many Americans have had such a crush on them for so long.

For they demonstrate, among other things, that the human animal can endure anything but hanging. History has dealt them a rotten hand. They have been poorly governed, savaged by nature, plundered and dismembered for centuries by scoundrels foreign and domestic, yet they have not only survived but managed somehow to shinny up near the top of the greasy pole.

That is part of their appeal: They remind a doubting age of the immortality of the race, but there are other and simpler reasons why an American finds them so attractive, one of them being that they also remind us of our own simpler agrarian past, before the complexities of surtaxes and wage and price controls.

Whatever you think of their political system, they are consciously engaged these days in the common life of rebuilding the nation and even in reconstructing themselves. This country is engaged in one vast cooperative barnraising. They work at it night and day with a pride and persistence that are astonishing, and they do it against a background of sights and sounds that tend to make Americans outrageously nostalgic and even sentimental.

For an example, they have plain, old-fashioned steam engine railroad trains—what Tom Wicker would call the real thing—with big red wheels and red cowcatchers, and engines that pant and snort in the station and run with a red glow through the night, and dining cars where the cook comes back and negotiates your dinner, and compartments with fans and lace antimacassars on the seats, and long, lonely whistles that trouble your sleep.

Also, it is something of a relief to visit a country where they don't have so many things. The Chinese have few automobiles, for example. A "service station" here is a place where neighbors provide and deliver food or other necessities to the sick or to working couples who have no time to shop before dinner.

The bicycle is the principal instrument of transportation in the cities, and the dominant sound is not the automobile horn, but the tinkling of thousands of bicycle bells in the twilight passage home. There are, I suppose, two kinds of countries, or maybe it is only two different stages of development: one where the people take a great many things for granted, and the other where the people take even the smallest necessities with gratitude. The Chinese are in the second category. They are always telling you how much better things are now than they used to be, and they are almost childlike in their wonder and thankfulness for small mercies.

Over a hundred years ago, Bret Harte wrote that he thought he saw in the Chinese people "an abiding consciousness of degradation, a secret pain of self-humiliation in the lines of the mouth and eye . . . they seldom smile." He added, "and their laughter is of such an extraordinary and sardonic nature—so purely a mechanical spasm, quite independent of any mirthful attribute—that to this day I am doubtful whether I ever saw a Chinaman laugh."

He should have stuck around, for the corners of their mouths, like the corners of the roofs on their buildings, now turn up in a constant smile. Officials in Peking retain a noncommital and even skeptical reticence with foreigners, but such is the positive reaction of most nonofficial Chinese that they usually seem to be nodding their heads up and down in agreement before they have ever heard the translation of what you said.

There are, of course, some things on the other side. The glorification of Mao Tse-tung, though he undoubtedly deserves the credit for their present sense of unity and purpose, is more exaggerated than anything ever seen in the Soviet Union under

Stalin, and though they are struggling out of the world of the abacus into the world of the computer, they show very little curiosity about the scientific revolution that is shaking the world, ask few questions about it, and concentrate on China's problems, China's progress, and China's rights.

Still, leaving politics aside, which is hard to do in these parts, the people one meets seem remarkably simple, unspoiled, courteous, and appealingly modest.

Both sexes dress in plain blue pants and usually in white shirts, which somehow they manage to keep remarkably clean in the oppressive heat. The women wear absolutely no makeup, and while they have produced the largest population of any nation in the world, they have somehow managed to conceal if not obliterate the female bosom, turning China into the flattest-chested nation on earth.

Compared to the hairy costume party of the West these days, all this seems rather tame, uniform, and old-fashioned, but it has great beauty and charm. China is sort of a connecting link between a former period and the present generation. It is late in coming into the modern age, and that, paradoxically, with such an industrious and intelligent people, may be its great advantage.

PART VII

PORTRAITS

63 WALTER LIPPMANN GOES HOME

WASHINGTON, May 25, 1967—Walter Lippmann announced today that he is leaving Washington, but the reader should not be deceived. He is merely going away, as all men should, to the primary interests of his youth—back to New York, back to philosophy, back to Europe—but he is not really "leaving" Washington.

For he is the greatest journalist of the present age, and he will be around here much longer than he suspects. This is not because he was always right, but because he gave us a model of what newspaper political criticism should be, because he cut through the trivial to the important, because, as the title of his column—"Today and Tomorrow"—indicated, he put the day's events in the perspective of history, and because he was a gentleman who loved truth and reason and kept in touch with the coming age.

"Today and Tomorrow"

He came to us in the newspaper business from the world of Santayana and James, when journalism was skeptical of intellectuals and vice versa, and he gave us a higher and nobler vision of our craft. Now his old friends, the philosophers, the historians, and the diplomats, may criticize and even condemn him. We merely love him.

The reasons for this are fairly clear. It is not only that he showed us the way but that he lived the ideal of most thoughtful newspapermen. That is to say that he not only managed to avoid the tedious rubbish that occupies the time of so many reporters but that he managed to reconcile his personal and professional lives. He was not immune to the tyranny of the deadline—which is why he is now going away at seventy-seven—but in some mysterious way, he managed to do what few people achieve in this business—he found time to think, time to write, and still had enough time for his wife and his friends and anybody who needed his counsel.

W. L. & L.B.J.

All kinds of nonsense has been written about him leaving Washington because he wasn't getting on with President Johnson. He never expected that critics and Presidents should get along, or thought that they should. The personal relations between politicians and newspapermen, he wrote in 1936, when Lyndon Johnson was a rookie Congressman,

are invariably delicate and difficult. For obviously they must be close: correspondents must see much of the men they write about. Yet if they do, they soon find themselves compelled to choose between friendship and the ties of loyalty that come from companionship on the one hand, the stern embarrassing truth on the other.

This is the unpleasantest side of newspaper work and I have never heard of any way of avoiding it. When a personal friend becomes a public man, a predicament soon arrives in which friendship and professional duty are at odds.

Walter Lippmann's career is too important to be discussed in terms of Lyndon Johnson's vicious vendetta. He has been writing his column for thirty-five years. He wrote *A Preface to Politics* fifty-four years ago, *A Preface to Morals* thirty-six years ago. Since then, he has been vilified by experts; by Presidents who won wars and even Presidents who avoided them, so that the savage and cruel personal comments Johnson and others in the White House have made about him tell us more about them than they do about Lippmann.

The only significance in the Johnson-Lippmann feud is that it disproves one of Lippmann's ideals. As a young man, he set himself the task of avoiding personal criticism and sticking to principle, and he discovered in the Johnson Administration that it was impossible to be both relevant and impersonal because the news out of Washington and Vietnam was so often the reflection of President Johnson's mind and personality.

Thus he found himself writing of Johnson at the end:

The root of his troubles had been pride, a stubborn refusal to recognize the country's limitations or his own limitations. . . . Such pride goeth before destruction, and an haughty spirit before a fall.

This, however, is merely a disagreeable and probably inevitable incident in a glorious career. He has not only endured in a savagely competitive business for over half a century but forced officials all the way to deal with his ideas, right or wrong.

Not for Keeps

He is going away sad, for his belief in reason in the world is not prevailing, but what is silly is to think he is leaving for keeps. He tried it once before, thirty-three years ago, but he soon came back.

In vain [he wrote then] does a man imagine that he can go anywhere these days and shut himself away from the clamor of the front page. Even when the newspaper does not come, he is trying to imagine what is in the newspaper he has not seen. . . . The best one can do, I find, is to fret quietly for a few weeks instead of openly in public print.

64 EDWARD KENNEDY'S CHALLENGE TO PRESIDENT NIXON

WASHINGTON, May 21, 1969—The old pugnacious Kennedy spirit is beginning to be heard again in the Senate. Less than a year since the death of his brother Robert (June 6), Senator Edward M. Kennedy of Massachusetts is emerging as the most outspoken political critic of the Nixon Administration.

This new assertiveness has been coming on gradually ever since he sought and won the Democratic whip's job in the party leadership, but now he is clearly cracking the whip. He is no longer the quiet Kennedy, deferring to the conservative elders of the Senate and grieving over the past. He is now the head of the clan and aiming to be head of the party.

Early and Bold

All this was expected, but not quite so soon and not quite so direct and bold. He did not even wait for the end of the Apollo 10 moon probe to ask that "once the lunar landing and exploration are complete," the Administration divert a "substantial portion" of the space budget to the "pressing problems" of poverty, hunger, pollution, and housing down here below.

The next day, while most of his colleagues were celebrating the victory of our armed forces in a bloody ten-day battle for Hamburger Hill above the Ashau Valley in Vietnam, he condemned the whole operation as "both senseless and irresponsible" and asked why we were making such human sacrifices when President Nixon had already announced that he was not seeking a military victory.

The same day he took on the American oil industry—no modest antagonist—and demanded to know why oil imports couldn't be relaxed a bit since oil-import controls had cost American consumers between four and seven billion dollars a year.

The Kennedy Battleground

This is a fairly strenuous week's work, but it isn't until you go back through the files of his speeches since President Nixon's inauguration that you realize that his challenge to the Administration has been building up week by week.

It has not been a personal challenge to the President—though the political confrontation between the two is obvious. He has been courteous. He is less strident than his brother Robert and less elegant than his brother John, but he has clearly taken up a prominent position to the left of the Administration.

Primarily, he is challenging President Nixon's emphasis on foreign affairs and the defense budget, and arguing that the major threat to the security of the nation lies at home. The point is clear in an analysis of his speeches since President Nixon took the oath of office.

He has not only called for cutting the defense and space budgets but insisted on reducing the level of violence in Vietnam, concentrated on the human aspects of the war—casualties and refugees—opposed the antiballistic missile system, insisted on a more generous policy toward China and even the abolition of the American bases on Taiwan, and attacked the "brazenly practiced" corruption of the Saigon Government.

On the home front, he has not only defied the oil lobby but attacked racial discrimination in employment, demanded wage and price restraint, insisted on tax reform before the Administration took up the same cry, and even denounced the "demagoguery" of the Republican leader, Everett McKinley Dirksen.

This is about as far as a man can go in the first four months of a new Administration. He has picked his targets, and it is interesting that in the process, he has also condemned the young militants who have resorted to violence in the universities; but mainly, he seems to have established a political base to the left of the Administration—more in favor of the home front than the foreign front, more for taking risks for peace, more for social reconstruction at home than anything else.

The Party Strategy

Where he is moving, why he is moving now, and whether his decisions are wise are all subject to argument, but one thing is clear: Edward Kennedy has changed. The paralysis of last year is over. He is moving. He has taken up a position, and in the process, he is dominating the Democratic opposition.

No doubt events will decide whether he was wise to move so fast and so boldly. President Nixon is also moving under more difficult restraints toward a peace in Vietnam which will let him reallocate his budget toward home-front problems; and if he makes peace, he will blunt Senator Kennedy's arguments.

But meanwhile, the Senator from Massachusetts is establishing himself as the leading figure in the opposition party. His principal Democratic opponent four months ago was Senator Edmund Muskie of Maine, but in the last few weeks, Kennedy has clearly dominated the Democratic scene.

65 THE QUALITIES OF ROBERT KENNEDY

WASHINGTON, June 6, 1968—In many ways, the personal characteristics of Robert Kennedy were very much like the dominant characteristics of the American people. We are an ambitious, strenuous, combative, youthful, inconsistent, abrupt, moralistic, sports-loving, nonintellectual breed, and he was all these things. Yet paradoxically, he was running behind for the Presidency precisely because he exploited and personified these typical American traits of character.

The professional politicians, and much of Big Business and Big Labor, all of them ambitious, competitive, and abrupt men of action themselves, opposed him actively. The young, the blacks, and much of the rest of the poor backed him, all in both categories for the same reason: He was a passionate and pugnacious man who confronted the inevitable and sometimes the avoidable contradictions of life, and inspired great loyalty and great fear in the process.

He was not going to make it in this election—there were too many powerful forces against him—but this does not prove that he was either wrong or right. It merely proves that he was more willing than his party and the rest of the country to throw all his passion and energy into ending the war in Vietnam and transforming the life of the cities. He was an all-or-nothing man and he lost everything in the end, but he was determined to face the terrible dilemma of the war and the cities. He was prepared to choose between defeat at home and defeat in Vietnam and between Israel and the Arabs, as few politicians and few Americans are, and this cost him not only the leadership of his party but his life.

One of the many tragedies of his death is that it occurred just when he seemed to be regaining confidence in his own power. He lost it for a while during the agony of his brother's death. He went through a couple of bad years, when he seemed stunned, and stumbled into a couple of silly and unnecessary conflicts.

Spirits Revived

Even in the early primaries, when he was winning, he sounded strident and even immature, but typically, the defeat in Oregon revived his Irishness and he came out of the California struggle with a new sense of purpose and even serenity.

This was quite apparent in the last hours of his life. He had that fierce intensity under control. His voice was much calmer in the last week. He seemed, somehow, to regain both his sense of history and his sense of humor—and then he was gone.

Target of Irrationality

Somehow the Kennedys draw the lightning. They seem to be able to save everything but themselves. Having all the attributes of life most men desire—good looks, money, power, success, love, and even fame—they are the targets of envy, and, to twisted minds, the symbols of the inequality of life.

Killing Robert Kennedy to avenge the hatred of the Arab states for Israel—if that was the assassin's motive—was a wholly irrational act. He had nothing to do with Israel's spectacular victory in last year's war. He had no influence on President Johnson or Secretary of State Rusk on Middle Eastern policy—or any other policy, for that matter. He was not on his way to the Presidency, where he might have directed American foreign policy, and he was certainly not the favorite political darling of the Jews in New York or anywhere else. Yet he is gone.

Many men succeed in politics by using their worst qualities, and this applied to Robert Kennedy at the beginning of his legislative career; but in the end he failed while using his best qualities. It is all very strange, and for the moment repulsive.

"Politics!" exclaimed Paul Valéry:

At that word I am overcome with silence . . . . I regard the political necessity of exploiting all that is lowest in man's psyche as the greatest danger of the present time. . . . There [in politics], vibrant and buzzing, are the meddlers, the bores, the buffoons. . . .

Some roar, others whisper in your ear. Some know everything and are silent. Those who talk know nothing. By a trick of inverted lights, friends see each other as enemies, fools look impressive to the intelligent . . . . I could lose myself at this fantastic Fair, where even arithmetic—in fact, arithmetic especially—is subject to strange upsets.

66 McCARTHY'S ANTIWAR CRUSADE

WASHINGTON, June 28, 1968—The popularity of Senator Eugene McCarthy of Minnesota must be the most interesting political phenomenon in American politics since the rise of Wendell Willkie to the Presidential nomination in 1940.

He has been underestimated from the start by the press, the pollsters, the President, the Republicans, and even by himself. Hardly a day goes by without somebody explaining in great detail precisely why he will never be nominated, yet he came to New York this week and raised over nine hundred thousand dollars at a single rally and his standing keeps going up in the polls.

The Antiwar Tide

The main explanation of this seems to be that he is riding an antiwar tide that is much stronger than the professional politicians have estimated. The combination of the war in Vietnam and the troubles in the cities at home has undoubtedly uncovered some of the ancient American isolationism that still lies not too far below the surface. This may not be good for the country, but it's good for Gene.

Every published casualty list—and they are not as prominently publicized as in past American wars—seems to keep him going. This week's was the lowest in two months, 299 killed, but it brought the total for the first six months of the year to 9,370, just below the 9,419 Americans killed in the entire year of 1967.

McCarthy is cool on most issues, but while Humphrey, Nixon and Rockefeller have all been ambiguous about the war, McCarthy has been relatively clear. He has delivered the impression that if he were President, he would end it by withdrawing from Southeast Asia if necessary, and there seems to be enough support for this position to keep him in the race.

There are other reasons for his continuing challenge. He is so different in appearance and manner from the stock political types that even his own pros find him irritating, but after five years of President Johnson, a lot of people are obviously bored with the professional political types and therefore grateful for a quiet man.

The Antipoliticians

This contrast is obviously helping him, particularly with women, who are even more tired of violence and political trickery and blowhards than the rest of us. Watching McCarthy on the platform, and especially listening to him talk quietly in a room, it is easy to understand why he almost studied for the priesthood.

He meditates as he talks and even seems to think before he speaks, an astonishing trait in a politician, and it may be that this air of detachment, while irksome to passionate men who want him to howl the rascals down, is a relief to sensitive people who are affronted by the tumult of the age.

The leaders of the organized blocs of voters—the blacks and labor union members, for example—find this manner highly unsatisfactory. McCarthy does not react to their intense emotion. Like his friend Adlai Stevenson in the 1952 Presidential election, he refuses to adopt their prejudices in return for their votes. Even the shouts of his supporters seem to embarrass him, and he not only cools them off but almost seems to be saying that if he had known he was going to create all this noise and stir he would have stayed home.

Yet his campaign goes on, more like a seminar in political science than a battle for the Presidency. He is showered with speeches, which sometimes he reads, and with advice, which occasionally he takes. His aides brawl with one another over whether he should talk to the country or pander to the delegates, but he just goes his own way from city to city, stuffing his pocket with poems, most of them bad, written by his followers and brought to him as tokens of affection.

His Mistakes

Even his own mistakes don't seem to bother him. He had the silly idea the other day that he should go over to Paris and talk to the North Vietnamese delegates about peace. Most of his aides told him that this would be an interference in the President's negotiations and wouldn't do any good. He thought about that and conceded publicly that maybe he would be "meddling," but added that he would probably do it anyway.

All this suggests that Eugene McCarthy as President would at least be something different, and this may very well be what's holding him up. All the other candidates seem all too familiar, if not a little shopworn, but McCarthy is a change, and change from war and physical and verbal violence has its appeal.

Not to everybody, of course, and apparently not to the convention delegates, but to enough people with votes—and recently, to enough people with money—to keep the phenomenon in the headlines.

67   SOMETIMES NICE GUYS FINISH FIRST

WASHINGTON, March 30, 1969—The nation mourns the death of President Eisenhower almost as if it were grieving for the loss of its own youth. For Ike was a symbol of a simpler age, and he lived long enough to become part of all the old American legends of the frontier.

The sixties have enhanced his reputation. They have been years of solemn, clever, and calculating men, and in contrast the old soldier seems open, straight, natural, joyful, and trustworthy.

It takes these old-fashioned words straight out of the McGuffy Reader to describe General Eisenhower. He was forever quoting the old McGuffy maxims, and would probably like to be remembered as a symbol of them.

Ike's Caution

It was not so much what President Eisenhower did in the White House but what he didn't do that seems in retrospect so much more important than it did at the time. He did not misuse power. He did not allow his former colleagues on the Joint Chiefs of Staff to drag him into unnecessary military adventures, and while this native caution and conservatism limited his achievements on the home front, they also limited his risks and blunders overseas.

He talked a lot about "crusades"—the military "crusade" in Europe, the political "crusade" at home—but he was not really a crusader in action. In fact, he was almost too conservative in a convulsive world. He was a canny military commander. He was a traditionalist in politics and even conserved the domestic policies of his Democratic opponents, but he did know the value of what Kipling once called "the art of judicious leaving alone."

No doubt this kept him from innovating in many areas which needed social reconstruction, and permitted him to tolerate Joe McCarthy and other scoundrels who were destroying the liberties of the people in the fifties, but he did make peace in Korea, and he refused to get deeply involved in the conflict in Vietnam. After the past few years, this seems an even more important decision than it did in the fifties.

Principles and Personalities

Few men at the top of American politics in recent years have managed to make their way through the tangles and conflicts of Washington with so little personal rancor as President Eisenhower. There was nothing mean or petty about him, and he never allowed political differences to loiter down into personal animosity.

Senator Everett McKinley Dirksen tried to incite the Republican nominating convention to revolt against him in 1952, but after a brief spasm of anger, he forgot the incident and turned

Dirksen into a close personal friend. This script he followed with literally hundreds of other men.

Decentralized Leadership

He won the trust of his colleagues by trusting them—often with very odd results. Thus, he regarded the conservative George Humphrey at the Treasury as his theater commander for finance, and the much bolder John Foster Dulles at the State Department as his theater commander for foreign affairs; and while his money policy, his social policy, and his foreign policy were often wildly out of line with one another, that was his way of decentralized leadership.

The historians so far have not rated him among the great Presidents, but his contemporaries are certainly agreed that he was a remarkably warm, fair, and attractive human being. It was the personal Eisenhower rather than the political Eisenhower that triumphed, maybe because he was the living model for so many popular American myths.

He made Horatio Alger's ragamuffin heroes look like abject failures. He worked and smiled his way into West Point, up to the top of the Army, into the command of the great invasion, up to the presidency of Columbia University, and finally into the White House. To the present young generation, he may be a magnificent square, but in his own time he proved once more that the squares usually inherit the earth.

Now most of the towering figures of the last world war are gone. George Marshall and Douglas MacArthur, his most respected comrades, Roosevelt, Churchill, and Stalin, all made the long journey years ago, and only de Gaulle and Chiang Kai-shek are still in the battle from that distant period.

Ike will have his place in the story of this tremendous time. He proved that simple goodness can still be a power in the world and that luck helps. He didn't "fade away" like the rest of the old soldiers, but fought for life years after his obituary got dusty on the stone. This may be why even this cynical age has taken his death with such genuine regret and sorrow.

68 WHERE ARE YOU NOW, HENRY?

WASHINGTON, May 21, 1974—In the last three weeks, while Secretary of State Kissinger has been trying to arrange a cease-fire between Syria and Israel, India has set off a nuclear explosion, France has elected a new president, West Germany has a new chancellor, and some kind of political transition or upheaval is going on in China.

These are merely the symbols of new forces, new alignments, and powerful new personalities moving in the world, and while it is easy to admire Mr. Kissinger's achievements in the Middle East, the result of his restless diplomacy is that he unavoidably neglects other critical developments in his department, in the Congress, and in the world.

The control of nuclear arms, the avoidance of war between China and the Soviet Union, the battle against inflation, hunger, and soaring raw materials prices, and the stability and unity of new governments in Europe and the rest of the free world all rank along with peace in the Middle East as the presiding questions of world politics today. And in all of them, Washington has a critical role to play.

Washington cannot play that role, however, under present circumstances. The President is determined to give the impression that he is running the Government, but obviously he is trying to save his political life. For the time being, Judge Sirica is more important to him than Indira Gandhi in India, Valéry Giscard d'Estaing in France, Chancellor Helmut Schmidt in Bonn, or the political struggles in Israel and the Arab states.

Meanwhile, the operation of the Government here depends on members of the Cabinet and the civil service. And the reorganization and revival of confidence at the Department of State depends on Mr. Kissinger, who took over there last September 22.

Since then, he has been out of the country three days in October, eleven in November, fourteen in December, ten in Jan-

uary, fourteen in February, five in March, and forgetting time
out for a honeymoon in Mexico, he has been away since late April
and all of May, and will probably have to spend most of June in
Europe and Moscow, preparing for the President's visit to the
Soviet Union.

This is the life of a roving Presidential envoy rather than of a
Secretary of State. Mr. Kissinger makes John Foster Dulles, our
last State Department wanderer, look like a stick-in-the-mud.
And it is a practical problem for three reasons:

Mr. Kissinger hasn't had time to organize the State Department to deal with all these critical worldwide developments while
he's away in the Middle East; he delegates authority grudgingly
to Acting Secretary of State Rush; and he's not available to testify
in Congress on vital legislation such as defense funds and foreign
aid.

This does not mean that he's out of touch on his shuttle plane
between Damascus and Tel Aviv. The art of communication has
advanced since Mr. Dulles was flying around the world. He gets
between five and ten messages from the State Department every
day—and between fifteen and twenty from other departments—
asking what should we say about the Indian nuclear explosion or
how should we react to the change of governments in Portugal,
France, and Germany?

It leaves little time for reflection and definition on the really
major questions of nuclear arms control in Moscow next month.
It is certainly not the calm, thoughtful, orderly process of policy-
making he insisted he would bring to the Department of State
when he was appointed. The October war in the Middle East
blew him off course.

He won the trust of President Sadat and King Faisal and Mrs.
Meir and put his whole mind to getting a cease-fire in that part of
the world, but meanwhile, other fires are lighted.

The strength of the Kissinger system in the Middle East is its
weakness elsewhere. Where he concentrates—whether on Chou
En-lai in China, on Brezhnev in the Soviet Union, on Sadat or
Faisal or President Hafez al-Assad of Syria, on the political lead-

ers in Israel or the political leaders here on Capitol Hill—he has a remarkable gift of persuasion.

But strong as he is, physically and mentally, he cannot deal effectively with all this by himself, without organizing his department, unless he can invent the forty-eight-hour day. The way things are going, he is trying to do everything: set policy; advise the President as head of the National Security Council in the White House; organize and preside over the State Department; mediate the struggle in the Middle East; inform the press in his own name or as a "senior official"; be loyal to Mr. Nixon on Watergate without being disloyal to himself.

This is quite an assignment, but from here, it looks a little presumptuous, if not a little goofy, and at some point, he is probably going to have to decide whether he is a Secretary of State, a diplomat-negotiator-spokesman-scholar-philosopher, or a politician-apologist on Capitol Hill.

He can't go on doing all these things together. Maybe his new wife will have to tell him. Somebody is going to have to get him off that merry-go-round and bring him home to deal with the world as Secretary of State.

---

69 WHAT ABOUT MOYNIHAN?

WASHINGTON, Jan. 29, 1976—The Ford Administration is in a pickle about how to handle Daniel Patrick Moynihan, its Ambassador at the United Nations, but it has nobody to blame but itself.

He was sent to the U.N. to defend the United States against unfair attacks because he had argued as a private citizen that the time had come to "call a spade a spade," but when he got there, he called it a bloody shovel.

That's Pat. He didn't get where he is by using English understatement. He's an Irishman, a brilliant teacher, a vivid writer, and a nonstop talker: in short, a "character" and one of the last colorful personalities in American public life today. Precisely what we need in the Senate of the United States, where almost nobody is either eloquent or outrageously frank.

It seems a pity to waste Mr. Moynihan's talents for controversy at the United Nations, which was organized to compose the differences between nations. And it is ironic to hear him argue that it is a "basic foreign policy goal" of the United States to break up "the massive blocs of nations, mostly new nations, which for so long have been arrayed against us in international forums . . . ."

For while Pat was not around at San Francisco or at the skating rink in New York when the United Nations started, he is a good enough historian to know that the United States invented and organized the first "massive" voting bloc in the forties and fifties to support Washington's policies.

Moreover, his sense of humor must be as good as his sense of history, and he must remember that the men in charge of organizing the first bloc-voting in the United Nations, particularly in corralling the votes of the Latin Americans, were his old friends Nelson Rockefeller and Tom Finletter of New York, and Adlai Stevenson of Illinois.

So bloc-voting in the U.N. may be a bad thing but it is not a new thing, and not an invention of the new nations. They just happen now to be the majority in the U.N., and like the OPEC countries, who have learned the laws of supply and demand, they are using the old political tactics of the West against the nations that used them in the first place.

Mr. Moynihan was the first to dramatize the dangers of this latest outrage of bloc-voting in the U.N. and to insist that the United States defend itself against the unfair attacks of the "new majority." This is why he was appointed Ambassador, but he has turned his appointment and his principle into a crusade, and has lately been challenging not only the anti-American bloc in the United Nations but his own Government and colleagues in the State Department.

There was something elemental about India, when Mr.

Moynihan was Ambassador in New Delhi, that moderated his turbulence; but in his embassy in the Waldorf Towers and in the cockpit of the U.N. General Assembly and Security Council, he seems to have let himself go, and almost provoked his mission to challenge not only the opposition governments but his own President and Secretary of State. When he was in Washington, Moynihan recommended that there were times when problems needed a little "benign neglect," but when he got to the U.N., he forgot to remember his own principle.

His long diplomatic dispatch to Mr. Kissinger, complaining that the minor officials of the State Department, but not Kissinger, were opposing his outspoken attacks on the anti-American blocs, was a little too clever, and the Secretary's public support of his mission was misleading.

Mr. Kissinger agrees with Moynihan's defense of American interests, but not with his style, his provocative rhetoric, his rambling, off-the-cuff debating tactics, his self-concerning appeals to the rest of the U.S. Foreign Service, or his vicious attacks on the State Department bureaucracy.

But in the process of Mr. Moynihan's strictures, he has disclosed the sources of his information, particularly officials of the U.N. Secretariat, and spread his opinions so widely that, wise as he is in the ways of the press, he risked the almost certain chance that they would be made public.

Even so, Mr. Kissinger, who served with Mr. Moynihan at Harvard and knows him well, can scarcely be surprised. Pat's idea of confronting the U.N. was not only defensible but long overdue; however, leaving it to Pat himself almost certainly meant that it would be overdone, and that's what has happened.

Now Messrs. Ford and Kissinger support him in public and deplore him in private. Having put him in the job, they can neither tame nor repudiate him. He has always been the enemy of his best ideas, always used the most provocative phrases, but Mr. Kissinger knew all that before and is now having to deal with the consequences of his own regrets.

70   HUMPHREY'S LAST RACE

WASHINGTON, Jan. 1, 1977—Hubert Humphrey's service to his country has been so durable and faithful, his feelings for the poor and afflicted people of the world so sincere, and his spirit so full of bounce and mirth that even those who disagree with his policies hate to see him seek and lose the majority leadership of the Senate.

Why did he risk one last political defeat by challenging Senator Robert Byrd of West Virginia, who had the votes to win months ago? Why in his sixty-sixth year, just out of hospital after a serious cancer operation, did he not settle for the role of elder statesman?

Why do fish swim? Hubert can't help it. He has to run as dogs have to chase cats. He won't grieve if he loses, mind you, for he thought the cancer would kill him and he is grateful to be alive, but not to try for the leadership of the Senate he loves would in his mind be a kind of resignation of self-defeat.

Besides, even in his sixty-sixth year, and with half a gut, he has more to say about the squeaky and rickety progress of human affairs, and says it better, than any man in the Senate. In a stammering and stuttering tongue-tied world, he is the last of the great talkers and public speakers in this town.

This is one part of the majority leadership he could undoubtedly do better than anybody else. He would have a platform and position from which he could speak to the nation and, perhaps more important, speak to the new President in the weekly legislative meetings at the White House.

But this is only one part of the job. Another is to manage the complicated legislative calendar of the Senate, to keep in touch day by day with every member, to *know* the problems of their states, to serve them and trade with them for votes—and at this endlessly tiresome game, Senator Byrd knows every card in the deck and plays them with patience, cunning, and skill.

So the Democrats are torn both ways, between the old philosopher and the competent manager. Their hearts are with Hubert, but their minds and often their personal political interests are with Byrd.

It is important to most of them that they know precisely what the business of the Senate will be, say, between Thursday noon and Tuesday morning so that they can deal with their political problems in the states without missing anything, and on this point the industrious, meticulous, and punctual Byrd has picked up a lot of votes on Humphrey, whose reputation for punctuality and tidiness is a little thin.

Also, Hubert's sense of timing is slightly defective. He always seems to be starting too soon or coming in too late or going on too long. He was the prophet crying for human rights and voting rights in the forties, when the majority of our people weren't listening.

He broke with Lyndon Johnson's Vietnam policy too late in his Presidential campaign against Richard Nixon in 1968 and lost by a whisker. He fiddled around with running or not running against Jimmy Carter in 1976 just long enough to lose the edge to Byrd in the Senate race, but all his failings are so amiably human and forgivable that it seems odd that he has had so little effective help in his bid for the majority leadership from the people he worked for so long over so many years.

There is scarcely a labor union hall in this country he hasn't visited, or an old wobbly labor union song he hasn't memorized and belted out for twenty-five years, or a pro-labor bill he hasn't proposed or defended, but the labor union leaders haven't really come to his support in this fight, apparently because they think Byrd has the votes to win and will probably be around longer.

Even Fritz Mondale, Humphrey's Humphrey, has been neutral, maybe with good reason and maybe under orders from Carter not to get on the wrong side of Byrd, who will probably be directing Carter's legislative traffic in the Senate.

There is one view among some of Humphrey's friends in the Senate—maybe enough to make the difference in the vote—that they're doing him a favor by voting against him. He will not have to work himself to death, under this theory. He will have time to think and finally to rest. It is a kindly thought and there is something to it, but not much.

Hubert Humphrey is like a plane that takes off and soars only at high speed. Work and responsibility are what keep him at his best cruising altitude. He had plenty of time to reflect and rest after Nixon beat him in '68 when he was teaching at Macalester College in St. Paul, and he was in despair until some of his students called on him and told him to cut the gloom and get to work helping them.

He puts on a big act about being happy on the back benches and cutting wood in Minnesota, and finally spending time and making it up to Muriel, but nobody is fooled by this, especially Muriel. He wants to win this election in the Senate. He is running around and calling in his chips, and in a secret ballot, it is just possible that the bonds of affection and the remembrance of his long and successful career will put him over, but not likely.

Still, even defeat in his last race won't depress or silence him. Nothing can, for that's the way he is—the blithest spirit we've had in this town in the last quarter-century.

71 "JUST CALL ME ANATOL"

WASHINGTON, Jan. 15, 1980—The Soviet Ambassador in Washington, Anatoly Dobrynin, has been here since 1962 and is now the senior member or dean of the diplomatic corps. During these eighteen years, he has acquired a reputation for affability and influence. So it may be worthwhile to examine this in light of the invasion of Afghanistan.

As to his affability, there can be no doubt. No ambassador in town can match his ability to peddle outrageous nonsense with such a smiling face. His influence, however, is open to question, and so is Washington's preference for dealing with the Soviet Union through Dobrynin rather than through our own embassy in Moscow.

Dobrynin was undoubtedly consulted about the Soviet invasion. He left here suddenly on December 10, shortly before the Red Army crossed the Afghan border. He canceled a dinner in his honor at the Argentine Embassy on December 14 and another at the home of Lloyd Cutler, the White House counselor, on December 18, apologizing that he had to go home for a medical checkup.

The argument for dealing with him here is that he has been around Washington since the Kennedy Administration, knows the temper of this country, is well acquainted on Capitol Hill, reports accurately, and has easy access to the Soviet Politburo, of which he is a member. This at least is the theory.

Nobody here knows, of course, what he thought the reaction of this country would be to the invasion or whether he told his colleagues of the likely consequences on U.S.-Soviet relations. But in any event, he either misled them or had no influence on their decision.

This is not to suggest that Dobrynin or any other Soviet ambassador is responsible for the acts of his Government, but merely to question the wisdom of filtering our messages to Moscow through him. He is better than most Soviet ambassadors, but like the rest of them, he is suspected here of telling his bosses what they want to hear, and there can be no doubt that he is a dedicated advocate of a Soviet system that is out to do this country harm.

Former Secretary of State Henry Kissinger recalls in his book, *White House Years*, his first meeting with Dobrynin on February 14, 1969, in a bedroom of the Soviet Embassy on Sixteenth Street, when Dobrynin was not well:

Dobrynin greeted me with smiling watchful eyes and the bluff confident manner of one who has taken the measure of his share of senior American officials in his day. He suggested that since we would work together closely, we call each other by our first names. From then on, he was 'Anatol' and I was 'Henry'. . . .

He told me he had been in Washington since 1962 and had experienced many crises. Throughout, he had maintained a relationship of personal confidence with the senior official. He hoped to do the same with the new [Nixon] Administration, whatever the fluctuations of official relations. He mused that great opportunities had been lost in Soviet-American relations, especially between 1959 and 1963. . . .

I told Dobrynin that the Nixon Administration was prepared to relax tensions on the basis of reciprocity. But we did not believe these tensions were due to misunderstandings. They arose from real causes, which had to be dealt with if real progress were to be made.

Dobrynin's mention of the 1959–63 period as a lost opportunity, I pointed out, was bound to sound strange to American ears. That was, after all, the time of two Berlin ultimatums, Khrushchev's brutal behavior toward Kennedy in Vienna, the Cuban missile crisis, and the Soviet Union's unilateral breach of the moratorium on nuclear testing. . . . Dobrynin smiled and conceded that not all mistakes had been on the American side.

That's about as far as Dobrynin ever goes. No doubt he has been useful in stopping some impulsive and ill-informed actions by his Government, but there is something wrong with this buddy-buddy diplomacy, as Malcolm Toon, who recently retired as U.S. Ambassador in Moscow, complained ruefully and even bitterly.

We are told now that President Carter has learned an important lesson through the shock of Afghanistan and that we will be seeing many changes: higher defense budgets, new Mideast military installations, and a new "Carter Doctrine" to contain Soviet power.

All this will take a great deal of time and probably more cooperation from the allies and the neutrals than seems likely now, but a new diplomacy could be introduced without delay. It could begin on Sixteenth Street by getting our diplomacy out of the drawing rooms and into more traditional channels and by reviving that humane and tolerant skepticism which is the mark of a trained professional diplomat.

Dobrynin has been a master at the art of spotting differences between the President's principal foreign policy advisers. He played Kissinger off against Secretary of State William Rogers, and has not been unaware of the conflict between Secretary of State Vance and the President's national security adviser, Zbigniew Brzezinski.

It would be hard to overestimate the dangers of mixed signals going out of Washington to Moscow; of messages passed verbally instead of in writing; of imprecision and even friendliness; of jet diplomacy by ardent amateurs who increasingly displace the President's ambassadors on the scene.

So maybe Washington will leave a little air space between Sixteenth Street and the White House and the State Department when Dobrynin comes back, and get its policy straight before laughing along with "Anatol."

72   HENRY BEETLE HOUGH

MARTHA'S VINEYARD, Mass., June 9, 1985—One of the most interesting things about journalism in America is that so many of its memorable characters have been country editors. From Tom Paine to Mark Twain, William Allen White of Kansas and Elmer Davis of Indiana, and the Baltimore crowd from Henry Mencken to Russell Baker, it was, in a funny way, the hicks from the sticks who took over the big-city crowd.

The news heroes of recent years haven't been dominated by the city slickers or the Ivy League types, but by the country bumpkins—Cronkite out of the Midwest and Texas, Sevareid out of Minnesota, Tom Brokaw out of Dakota, and, among others, David Brinkley, Roger Mudd, and Tom Wicker out of North Carolina.

I mention this merely to pay respect to Henry Beetle Hough, who died the other day on Martha's Vineyard at the age of eighty-eight, after sixty-five years as editor of the *Vineyard Gazette*. He is, in my mind, a symbol of the country journalism that has been and still is the school where most of these prominent modern reporters got their training.

Mr. Hough was an old-fashioned man who believed that sticking to the news of the island was more important than worrying about the confusions of the mainland. He reported on the central questions of life—birth, marriage, and death, but really wasn't interested in reporting divorce.

After a few years in this business, I've never known anyone who had more grace or respect in dealing with the English language.

His main concern was the preservation of the unity, privacy, and beauty of this island. In sixty-five years, he seldom left it except once in a while to meet his responsibilities as head of the Thoreau Foundation in Boston, and go there to check in at Massachusetts General Hospital when he was in trouble.

One of his young colleagues on the *Gazette* asked him one day if he didn't long occasionally to see the world beyond the waters off the Vineyard.

"Not often," he said, "but when I feel the urge coming on, I collect a bunch of old *National Geographic* magazines, climb up to the attic of the *Gazette*, and stick my feet in a bucket of cold water until the feeling wears off."

Henry Hough worried about death and retirement.

"I suppose," he wrote in his famous book, *Country Editor*, "that death is the most characteristic of all the forces in a country town, because there are always so many old people living there, and the passing of an individual is so much more important than it is in the city. Besides, a town has a time to mourn. The obituary notice is a distinctive story-forum for the country weekly because it has to tell not only the stark fact of somebody's life, but it has to tell also a little of what that somebody was like, and what his career seemed to stand for. It has to tell even what a nobody was like, for the poorest citizen is in the eyes of the town a man."

It amused Henry Hough when one of our old newspaper buddies here on the Vineyard, Red Smith, of the old *Herald Tribune* and the *Times*, made a speech, saying: "Death is no big deal—almost any of us can manage it. Living is the trick we have to learn."

Henry Hough learned that trick very well. He thought the thing was to concentrate on simple things: on his family, his paper, his community, and nothing else. He made some enemies in the process, for he wanted to limit the growth of the island, while others wanted more people and more houses; and at the end he thought he was losing.

But in some ways he was wrong, and too pessimistic. Thirty-five years ago he worried about retirement and death. In 1950, he wrote the following in a lovely book called *Once More the Thunderer:*

How to resign the duties of a country editor—that is what we should like to know . . . apparently there is no way to taper off as there is some worldly occupations. It is all or nothing, until the end, whatever the end of country editorship may be. . . .

How to sweep the papers from the desk that have been there so long, and leave the heap of exchanges unopened and hear the telephone ringing but let it go unanswered as one steps through the door as an editor for the last time into a street of mellow twilight—twilight of course because quitting time must be fall, with the white houses of the town early in shadow and the stores already lighted as one walks home through the creeping, aromatic New England dusk.

Well, he wrote that thirty years ago, but he went on ever since until just a few days ago, when he wrote his last editorials. Then, he did what was very typical of him. He was always a punctual man. And he died at four o'clock on Thursday afternoon, just before deadline on his Friday paper. He always said that he would get his copy in on time, and that's precisely what he did.

---

73 BUSH'S VOODOO POLITICS

WASHINGTON, Dec. 15, 1985—Of all the horses at the starting gate for the 1988 Presidential race, Vice President Bush probably has the best track record. But he may be jumping the gun.

None of them can match his experience in the White House, in the Congress, in business, in diplomacy, as Ambassador to China and the United Nations, or in the subterranean world where he worked as head of the Central Intelligence Agency.

He has roots at Yale and in New Hampshire, which have few electoral votes, but now makes his home in Texas and that has more than a few. By birth, education, and tradition, he is part of that remarkable company of progressive Republicans from Teddy Roosevelt to Ike Eisenhower.

George Bush has been loyal to President Reagan, almost invisible as Vice President. But recently, he has come out of hiding and is beginning to run openly for the Republican nomination, and wondering where he's going and who's going with him.

He showed up here the other night as the principal speaker at a dinner in honor of the *Manchester Union Leader*'s former editor, the late William Loeb, an outrageous, bigoted man who had denounced him in the last Presidential election as a "hypocrite" for condemning Ronald Reagan's voodoo economics, as an "incompetent," and as a "spoon-fed little rich kid" who was "unfit to be President."

But Mr. Bush praised him anyway. That's the way it is in "the rough and tumble of politics," he said, and concluded that Mr. Loeb was "triumphantly right about the fact that Ronald Reagan is one of the greatest Presidents in our history." The tribute was worse than a disgrace. It was an embarrassment.

This tells us something about the corruption of ambition. George Bush is a good man in a big hurry. By stoking up the race so soon, he's probably not helping the President, who has three hard years to go, or himself.

He's not helping himself with the moderates who believe in him or persuading the conservative extremists, who, whatever he says, will never believe him or nominate him unless President Reagan doesn't live out his second term.

Obviously, he has a problem. To be nominated in a Republican convention dominated by the conservative wing of his party, he needs the support of the President, the conservative delegates, and the television preachers. But to win the election, if nominated, he needs the support of the moderates of both parties, all regions and factions.

This is the dilemma the Vice President hasn't yet resolved. George Bush is no bush leaguer. He has been in the big leagues for a long time, but clearly, he hasn't yet decided on his strategy. Maybe there are ways for him to make peace with the right wing of the Republican Party, but honoring William Loeb is almost like honoring Joe McCarthy.

The conservatives won't thank him for it, and the moderates will doubt him for being faithful to everything but himself.

He got in trouble with this in the last Presidential election when he put on the mucker pose and forgot his manners—"kicked a little ass," as he said about dealing with Geraldine Ferraro—for he was out of character, as he was in praising William Loeb.

He was dead honest in the 1980 campaign when he condemned Ronald Reagan's "voodoo economics"—the present record budget and trade deficits seem to prove his point—but now he seems to be following Mr. Reagan's voodoo politics: defending everything he opposed in the past; arguing for the Reagan policy of borrow and borrow, spend and spend; and hoping that he will inherit the Reagan mantle and be nominated in the process.

The guess here is that this won't work for George Bush. Ronald Reagan, like Eisenhower, didn't have an election with the American people but a love affair. Mr. Bush can carry on Mr. Reagan's failed economic and foreign policies, but later on—not now—has to come forward and be seen as his own man.

George Bush, in a way, has the same problem Hubert Humphrey had as Lyndon Johnson's Vice President. Comparisons are treacherous, but Mr. Humphrey probably lost the Presidency because he went along with President Johnson's disastrous policy in Vietnam when he didn't believe in it; and he was rejected by the voters in the end because they thought he had no vision of the future but was merely following the policies of the past.

George Bush is now in that same pickle: how to be faithful to the President without having any serious policy of his own.

PART VIII

CAMPUSES IN UPHEAVAL

BERKELEY, Calif., Oct. 22, 1966—Sproul Plaza is the center of political activity and controversy at the University of California: Bobby Kennedy will be here tomorrow; Stokely Carmichael has scheduled a big "black power" rally here on October 29; and Ronald Reagan is promising to stamp out wickedness at Berkeley if elected Governor next month.

The students here don't seem very worried at the prospect. It is true that Sproul Plaza is lined every weekday lunch hour with students advocating this and denouncing that, but most of the student body seems more intent on getting to the cafeteria than in stopping for the propaganda.

Not Uninteresting Subjects

This is not because the subject matter is uninteresting. At one table, a lovely young girl offers pamphlets on behalf of the Campus Sexual Rights Forum. It turns out that her organization favors legalized abortion. At another table, a conspicuously hairy young man represents Citizens Against Legalized Murder. He apparently wants to abolish the death penalty.

Then there are tables for the Independent Socialist Club, the Progressive Labor Party, and Black Power Workshops, plus one or two soapbox orators talking aimlessly about the Brown–Reagan election to the rapt attention of almost nobody.

A television camera could obviously make all this seem vaguely naughty. A good many of the students look like an unmade bed, but it is hard to imagine them as a race of moral monsters. In fact, there is an air of weary indolence about many of them, which makes one wonder whether they would get to the revolution on time or even whether they would really have the energy to take advantage of all the sexual freedom they advocate.

Nevertheless, the university is an issue in the California election, to the embarrassment of President Clark Kerr. Reagan has promised to investigate the uproar over the "filthy speech" incident here a couple of years ago. Governor Pat Brown has not been a very effective defender of the university's freedom, and both the extreme right and the extreme left in California politics have their own reasons for keeping Berkeley in the center of political controversy.

The extreme left, favoring what it calls "confrontation politics," would not mind seeing Reagan in Brown's place. It apparently prefers the contrast of a conservative Governor to the awkward ambiguities of opposing an old-fashioned liberal Democratic Governor. So it is raising funds for the Stokely Carmichael meeting, and one fear among university officials is that this event on the twenty-ninth may lead to violence, and force Governor Brown to bring the troops onto the campus.

The conservatives have their own ways of keeping the university in the campaign. For example, one of the leaders in the student action here in 1964 was a young man called Mario Savio, who left in good academic standing and has applied for readmission in the next term.

At a meeting of the University Board of Regents this week in Davis, California, two regents demanded to know whether Savio would be readmitted and made clear their opposition to any such decision. One of these was H. R. Haldeman, president of the University of California Alumni Association, who is also a member of the Southern California Finance Committee for Reagan.

The other was John Canaday, a retired Lockheed executive from Burbank.

The Moral Issue

Another issue raised by these two board members was whether the university would permit the San Francisco Mime Troupe to appear on the campus. This is an experimental theatrical group that apparently specializes in portraying sexual gymnastics, and when they appeared here at Berkeley a while ago, there was an outcry against them.

Anyway, raising these old controversies at the Board of Regents meeting keeps the issue of permissiveness at Berkeley alive and undoubtedly helps Reagan's "morality" campaign. For Reagan is not only benefiting from the so-called white backlash but also from what is called in California the "Berkeley backlash." There is undoubtedly considerable opposition to the race riots and to the notion of Berkeley as a den of moral delinquents and intellectual carpetbaggers, and the more this can be kept in the papers, the more it helps Reagan.

Actually, the moral and political situation here does not seem much different from that on any other large urban university campus in the United States. A great deal was made of narcotics arrests around here a while ago, but the Oakland police record shows that of 190 narcotics arrests in the last Oakland summary, 30 were high school students, 23 were students from other universities, and only 6 were Berkeley students.

There is probably more bohemianism at Berkeley than most places, more girls with black shoe polish on their eyes, and more beards, but California's climate encourages casualness. It is obviously more comfortable for a girl with a mini-brain to go around barefoot in a miniskirt in Berkeley than, say, in Boston.

On the other hand, over eight thousand University of California students are now working in their spare time on constructive projects in the schools and slums of the state, and very little is said about this. President Kerr put out a long report on these students to the Board of Regents this week, calling it the "untold story" of Berkeley.

"Filthy Speech" Issue

But when Regents Canaday and Haldeman raised the "filthy speech" and the risqué theatrical issues in the Regents meeting, this was again the controversy that caught the headlines.

Clark Kerr is handling the problem with more finesse this time, however, than he did in 1964. He is working quietly with his supporters on the board and trying to get rid of the nonstudents, who seem to have money enough to hang around the campus here and dabble in its politics without actually attending classes. In short, he is trying to repair the damage done by the last uproar, but this is hard during a political campaign when others are determined to keep the university embroiled in politics.

75 SUPPOSE THE YOUNG REVOLUTIONARIES REALLY WON

WASHINGTON, April 23, 1969—Let us suppose the student revolutionaries in America won all their specific demands, and the university presidents and faculties surrendered unconditionally. Where would we be?

The R.O.T.C. would be banished from the campuses along with the Dow Chemical Company, President Pusey of Harvard and probably Jim Perkins of Cornell. Black studies programs would be published in the autumn catalogs, and separate black dormitories would be introduced—both on the recommendation of black students.

In addition, the students would have a powerful voice in the administration, the philosophy, and the discipline of the universities, and would then not only have a "part of the action" but would have the opportunity of both spending and raising funds, selecting students, promoting, demoting, and firing faculty members, handling the alumni, the press, and other inconveniences, and dealing with the economic and biological problems of the young, including their own.

Who would be happy? What would the warriors of the S.D.S. do if they were administering instead of demonstrating? Without the R.O.T.C. in the universities, the Pentagon would have to raise an officer corps isolated from the civilizing influences of typical young men and women in a natural American university atmosphere. It is fairly obvious what Congress and the Pentagon would do: They would create more male military academies with more discipline, and probably end up with precisely the militaristic atmosphere the S.D.S. says it is opposing.

The Draft and the Blacks

The opposition of the campus revolutionaries to the military draft is even more interesting. Suppose the draft were abolished and we went to a "voluntary" well-paid army. The chances are that we would create in the process a well-paid military force of black mercenaries, and the social consequences of this would probably be quite different from the objective the S.D.S. has in mind.

Giving the young black and white revolutionaries everything they say they want is appealing until you think about whether they are really serious about taking on the responsibilities they demand. Do they really want to take on the struggle of creating a new society, or do they want the excitement of protesting against the old?

John Gardner, the former Secretary of Health, Education, and Welfare who is now giving his life to fighting for equality in the urban slums, went to Harvard before the recent tumult and defined the point.

He wondered, in the Godkin Lectures, whether the young revolutionaries really understood when they called for the destruction of the present social system in America that if they succeeded, the result would be chaos, which is "supremely antagonistic to any organized purposes, including the purposes of those who initiated the destruction."

Those who would destroy the present system, he said, fail to understand that periods of chaos are followed by periods of iron rule. They always dream that after their struggle, *they* will be calling the tune. The modern young revolutionary, Gardner suggested, will use any tactics to achieve his goal, without thinking about "what kind of dictator might emerge."

What we are facing now on the campuses, Gardner suggested, is the politics of derision and provocation:

Sad to say, it's fun to get mad and it's fun to hate. . . . That is today's fashion. Rage and hate in a good cause! Be vicious for virtue, self-indulgent for higher purposes, dishonest in the service of a higher honesty. . . .

There is no doubt that today's revolutionary is pursuing that goal with all the energy at his command. And in that pursuit, he is wholly cynical in his manipulation of others. The rights of the majority are irrelevant to him. . . . He has no interest in rational examination of the issues. . . . He will devise traps to demean those in authority, destroying their dignity where possible. He will exploit the mass media, feeding their hunger for excitement and conflict. . . .

But in the end, if he is given his specific demands, where will he be? Will the S.D.S. take responsibility if the universities submit? Will Harvard and Cornell, which have been more free than almost any other universities in the nation, really be much different without the R.O.T.C., Pusey, and Perkins?

What Do They Want?

There is a powerful argument for giving the students power. There is a tremendous argument for opposing the present level of military expenditures and for giving the blacks a sense of dignity, even in isolation, if that's what they want. But do the young radicals really want to go through the agony of exercising power or merely the excitement of fighting for it? An educated man is one who really thinks about the consequences of his actions, and this is the interesting question: Suppose university presidents and faculties gave them everything they wanted. Would the S.D.S. really deal with the hard questions, and would the rest of the country, after the politics of violence, tolerate them even if they tried?

76 THE NIXON ADMINISTRATION AND THE UNIVERSITIES

WASHINGTON, April 26, 1969—Almost everywhere we look these days, authority is under challenge: the authority of the family, the church, the university, the community, and the state. It almost seems to be the central issue of our time, but it is not really the main thing, and since the challenge is often to the hypocrisy and values of traditional authority, it may even be a good thing.

The main thing is the resort to physical force and threat of force and violence against the traditional authorities. It is the old question of ends and means. This is what has been going on at Harvard and Cornell in recent days, and this use of force by the young campus militants is what really interests the Nixon Administration.

Ends and Means

The Administration here is troubled by many things. It doesn't quite know how to reconcile its political, moral, and strategic interests in Vietnam. It is confused by the struggle over money for the cities and money for the Pentagon, but it is clear about one thing: None of these problems can really be resolved in an atmosphere of coercion and violence.

The picture of the blacks at Cornell coming out of the university building with guns on their shoulders the other day sent a shudder through this country, and the concessions by the faculties and administrators at Cornell and Harvard to the use of force by the campus militants have convinced officials here that justice is too serious a business to be left to university teachers and officials who submit to the use and threat of force.

The campus radicals, in their violent challenge to the law and the university and government officials, handed their political opponents a powerful issue. The Nixon Administration can scarcely believe it, and doesn't quite know what to do with it, but some things they do know.

The Political Pressure

They cannot make their way through their problems if coercion
and force are to settle things. This is a sincerely conservative
Administration, which believes in local political and police control. It came to power against the opposition of most university
communities, most intellectuals and blacks, and therefore has
been extremely cautious and almost timid about getting involved
in the campus conflicts.

In fact, President Nixon's first intervention in the university
controversy—in his letter supporting Father Hesburgh's tough
assertion of authority at Notre Dame—was quickly repudiated
by both Father Hesburgh and the President.

But now the Harvard and Cornell controversies have brought
the moral instincts and political interests of the Nixon Administration together. The last thing the Nixon officials felt they could
do or wanted to do was to get involved in the arguments in the
universities, where they knew they were not popular. And they
are still holding back.

The reaction in the country against what has happened in
Cambridge and Ithaca, however, is so critical of the universities
that officials here cannot ignore it and are now talking about how
the legal injunction process can be used against the militants.

The students and faculty on the left, paradoxically, are encouraging precisely the thing they fear the most. By their use of
force and concessions to force, they are encouraging the political
authorities they opposed to use the political and police power
they hate.

Even a few weeks ago, officials in Washington would not have
been suggesting that university officials rely on the courts to hand
down injunctions against student sit-ins, but now they are doing
so. And more than that. They are now asking why, if university
officials fail to ask for legal injunctions against the militants, why
should the moderate students not go to the courts and use the
legal authority to keep the universities open?

It so happens that the former dean of the Harvard Law
School, Erwin N. Griswold, is now the Solicitor General of the
United States, and it would be instructive for the militants to
read his lecture on this subject at Tulane the other day.

"Violent opposition to law—any law—or forcible disregard
of another's freedom to disagree," Dean Griswold said, "falls
beyond the pale of legitimate dissent or even civil disobedience
properly understood; it is nothing short of rebellion. . . .

I cannot distinguish in principle the legal quality of the determination to
halt a train to protest the Vietnam War or to block workmen from
entering a segregated job site to protest employment discrimination from
the determination to fire shots into a civil rights leader's home to protest
integration.

The Central Issue

The right to disagree—and to manifest disagreement—which the Constitution allows to the individuals in those situations—does not authorize
them to carry on their campaign of education and persuasion at the
expense of somebody else's liberty or in violation of some laws whose
independent validity is unquestionable.

This is the central issue—not of ends but of means—which
Harvard and Cornell confused, and which Washington and the
other political authorities are now taking up. It is a tragedy, for
political and police power on the campuses is offensive to almost
everybody concerned, but some authority must oppose anarchy,
and if the university teachers, administrators, and moderate students evade the issue, the politicians and police will undoubtedly
fill the vacuum.

---

77 FROM ANARCHY TO REPRESSION?

LOUISVILLE, Ky., May 3, 1969—The political reaction to the
campus disorders is now running very strong. The threat of anarchy is now producing the threat of repression, and politicians all
over the country are trying to put the university wreckers up
against the wall.

The wild wing of the Students for a Democratic Society has
done a remarkable thing. It has awakened all its proclaimed enemies. It has mobilized the squares, stirred up the Federal and
state legislators, weakened the anti-Vietnam War movement, divided the left, and pushed the country to the right.

Action and Reaction

This is quite an achievement. No other combination of political and moral forces in this country, from J. Edgar Hoover to Billy Graham, could possibly have aroused such a powerful coalition against the extreme left or made opposition to the demands of the white and black extremists so respectable.

In many ways, it is a sad story, for in the end, it could easily mean more political interference and control of the universities, more opposition even to legitimate dissent, reduced state and Federal funds for higher education, more separation and hostility between the races, and more trouble for the idealistic students who want fundamental but nonviolent changes in our society.

A Needed Challenge

The dangers of overreaction now are plain. The challenge of the young was not a bad but a good thing. They were questioning our materialism and hypocrisy, our policies and priorities in Vietnam and the cities, and the structure of many of our universities.

But the S.D.S. extremists who started by demanding "free speech" at Berkeley are now denying it to others. They want the right of dissent for the protesters, but no right of dissent for their opponents. They have gone well beyond Gandhi's or Thoreau's concept of civil disobedience; Gandhi and Thoreau were prepared to take their punishment for breaking the law, but not the young extremists of today.

They seize and destroy private property, shut down classes, interfere with scholarly research, and then demand amnesty and submission to their "nonnegotiable demands." They want "due process" for themselves, but not for their opponents.

It is not easy to shake the indifference of the quiet majority in this country, but the militants have achieved it. They forgot that students are not the only people who are troubled by the complexities, contradictions, and inequalities of American life. The middle-aged and the middle class—caught between their rebellious kids and their aging parents and between inflation and taxation—are really the ones in the middle. And the sight of guns on campuses and kids sneaking out of occupied buildings with covered faces, plus all these endless demands and headlines about the student rebellion, have finally produced great pressure on the politicians from the middle class to get this movement under control.

The politicians are delighted to respond. They have always enjoyed moralizing about the wickedness of the young and the permissiveness of the universities. President Nixon has had his say, and J. Edgar Hoover will be reciting on the radicals within the next few days.

Also, various Congressional committees are planning investigations under such pillars of philosophical meditation as Senators John McClellan of Arkansas and James Eastland of Mississippi— not to mention that other old friend of the S.D.S.—the former House Un-American Activities Committee.

Predictable Reaction

None of this is surprising, however. It is following the usual political scenario of violent action and extreme reaction. The odd thing is that the young militants who claim to know so much about human psychology and political tactics provoked such a predictable reaction. It is said they welcome the repression, for this will bring the moderates over to their cause. That at least is the theory, but that is not what is happening now; the militants are not getting stronger, but weaker, and the only thing that can really help them now is another angry lurch to the right.

78 THE CHANGING CAMPUS MOOD

CAMBRIDGE, Mass., June 11, 1970—There is something new in the air on the campuses of America at the end of this university year. All the same problems and arguments remain, but the moderates are beginning to challenge the extremists of the right and left and change the tone and maybe even the direction of the student debate.

Last year at this time, the battle in the universities was mainly

between the militants on the left and the university administrators. This is still largely true, but now the moderate university
students and faculty members are getting into the act and the
debate therefore is also between the extremist students and the
moderate students as well.

There seem to be three other changes: The campus debate is
spreading across the nation—it is now extending to Kent State
and Ohio State and other previously dormant or conservative
campuses—the moderate faculty members are beginning to speak
out against the more articulate teachers on the left, and the political movements in the universities are no longer isolated but are
looking for alliances in the larger movements of national politics.

This year's commencement activities at Harvard University
were not typical, but they indicate the trend. They were interrupted by a bull-horn demonstration by about thirty Cambridge
residents protesting against the expansion of the Harvard campus
into a poor residential neighborhood, but they were also marked
and even dominated by eloquent protests from the moderates
against the extremists of the left.

Pusey's Speech

President Pusey, who has been a modest and hesitant public
figure in the past, not only compared the tactics of the leftist
students to the fascist tactics of Senator Joseph McCarthy of
Wisconsin in the fifties but condemned the Harvard faculty members who sided with the leftists in last year's attack on the university administration. The Harvard faculty, which has hesitated in
the past to come out openly against the militants, voted against
interrupting classes next fall to put student political activities
ahead of academic studies, and the moderate students put up a
commencement-day spokesman from the graduating class who
attacked the student militants.

"Our biggest mistake," said Steven J. Kelman of Great Neck,
New York, to his Harvard graduating class,

has been to let the so-called New Left emerge as our spokesman. . . .
Can we wonder why the American people will continue to be hostile

towards students as long as we allow the rock-throwers, the burners, the totalitarians to represent us? Do we have a right to expect anything else?

There is only one way we can gain the respect and overcome the hostility of the American people. And that is by addressing ourselves to the unromantic and unexciting problems which just happen to be the problems which affect the ordinary American in his day-to-day life . . . for in the final analysis it can only be the American people, not a student elite pledged to one-party dictatorship [that can bring about change].

The Students' Choice
We, as Harvard students, can make the determination to overcome our isolation by speaking to the mundane problems of health care, jobs, and taxes—or we can continue to acquiesce to the wreckers among us. We can be part of the solution or part of the problem . . . the choice is ours.

This of course is not a new theme. The new thing is that President Pusey and the moderate students like Steven Kelman are now saying aggressively and out loud what they were saying defensively and privately a year ago.

Maybe the best symbol of the change at the Harvard commencement was the title of the Latin dissertation by Kirsten E. Mishkin, a Radcliffe student speaking for the young women graduates—*"De Maturitate"*—"On Coming of Age."

She was not only arguing against what she called the "iniquitous male supremacy" of American life but also for unity, and even civility toward other peoples and other generations, and she did it with a tenderness and generosity that has not been customary on university campuses in recent years.

"Together," she said, "let us establish a new society, the foundations of which will not be discrimination, but equality, not fear, but good will; not war between the sexes, but loyal brotherhood and sisterhood."

So something is happening. There is now a critical pause when the majority of students are not only turning back from violence and isolation but searching for a new theme and a new majority. Maybe it won't work, but there is at least a new and more hopeful tone to the campus debate at the end of this academic year, and it clearly should not be ignored.

PART IX

PERSPECTIVE

79 THE GIFTS OF PRIVACY AND BEAUTY

FIERY RUN, Va., July 4, 1967—President Johnson says we should forget about the "good old days" and "count our blessings," and while this is two clichés in one sentence, he has a point.

Country life in America today is a blessing worth counting. It may be worse for the very poor who have no money and the very rich who have less help than in former times, but it is obviously much better for the people in between.

The Advantages

The advantages are obvious. City people have more to run away from now than in the old days. They have to go through the suburbs to get to the country, which makes them grateful for living in town, and electricity has done more for the modern bucolic weekender than slavery did for the nineteenth-century plantation owner.

Could Mr. Jefferson tune in on *Gunsmoke* from Charlottesville? Could Mr. Lincoln listen to Beethoven from New York? Is it possible to imagine the Chicago Cubs in first place in the National League, let alone to watch them on television from some poison ivy cabin in the woods?

Professional and salaried families in America no longer have to choose between city and country life. They can have both on a modest scale. Much of what was available only to the landed gentry at the turn of the century is now available to the large servantless American middle class.

Of course, there are problems. "I can either get ready to go to the country or I can go to the country, but I can't do both," my wife said one Saturday morning. But if you can get past this awkward moment, the prospects are good.

Modern power, economics, transportation, and communications have now joined the conveniences of the city to the wider freedoms of the land, and the Gadarene rush to the cities is taking place in America just when life in the countryside is at its very best.

The Law of Compensation

The law of compensation in life works here as elsewhere. The more the people leave for the cities, the more shacks they leave behind for city folk who have the money to fix them up.

Even a hundred miles, and often less, from the main population centers, much land is empty, beautiful, and available. Elsewhere in the country the gifts of privacy and beauty—the two most precious and necessary things parents can give to their children in this distracted age—are more easily available, even for families of comparatively modest means.

Strange and paradoxical things are happening in the city and country life of America. Men built cities in the first place for safety. They wanted to get away from the danger of the countryside, from the fear of murder and robbery. Now the lonely countryside is safer than the cities.

Also, in the last generation, people went to the cities for conveniences and services. Now, at least here in the northern neck of Virginia, it is far easier to get a plumber in an emergency than it is in Washington. Call him on the party line, if it's free, and tell him you're in trouble, and he comes. He "visits" and tells you about his troubles, but he does the job.

Burroughs's Philosophy

There is a better reason than plumbers, however, for escaping from the city to the country. The city rapidly uses up men, John Burroughs, the naturalist, observed almost a hundred years ago.

"A nation," he said, "always begins to rot first in its great cities, is indeed perhaps always rotting there, and is saved only by the antiseptic virtues of fresh supplies of country blood."

Maybe so, but he makes a better point. "Paradoxical as it may seem," he says, "the city is older than the country. Truly, man made the city, and after he became sufficiently civilized, not afraid of solitude, and knew on what terms to live with nature, God promoted him to life in the country."

Capital and Cattle

America may have reached this point in its story, or if it is smart, will soon do so. Philosophically, it needs the country. Even commercially, the land—not much of it but ten acres, a cabin, and a spring that is both bold and true—is the best buy and blessing around.

Capital, cattle, cheap fertilizer, and barbed wire have transformed the American countryside. They have turned some of the coves and valleys of this part of the world into a park. Yes, Santa Claus, there is a Virginia. And as Lyndon Johnson says, it is one of the "blessings" worth counting.

---

80 THE NEW PESSIMISM: IS IT JUSTIFIED?

WASHINGTON, Feb. 16, 1969—In the vast disorder of human affairs today—private and public—something new is beginning to drift into the American spirit. Older societies have lived with it for many generations: It is the element of doubt that in this convulsive and contradictory age, we still have the capacity to master our problems.

The evidence of this pessimistic note is all around us. The men in charge of our Vietnam policy have no answer to the slow and relentless loss of life but to hold the bloody line and wait. The administrators of our universities are dismayed by the tactics of the campus militants and have to rely in the extremity on the police and the National Guard.

Gloom in New York

The Mayor of New York is overwhelmed by the rising torrent of welfare cases, which now total over a million in the five boroughs. And the Governor of New York is proclaiming a national fiscal crisis which in his view threatens the entire Federal system of government.

Even so optimistic and thoughtful a man as Caryl Haskins, the president of the Carnegie Institution of Washington, seems to be wondering these days. "Our most precious and perhaps our most threatened common possession," he says in his annual report, "is the quality of hope."

Out of Control?

If it is true that the most powerful and naturally optimistic people in the world are beginning to wonder whether events are out of control, the outlook for the future is gloomy indeed, but is this pessimism really justified?

It is true that a series of immense and tragic events over the past two generations have shattered the self-complacency of an earlier age. It is also true that the grandiose schemes for abolishing war and stamping out poverty and integrating the races have led to disillusion and reappraisal. But are these things bad?

There is great turmoil in the nation today mainly because it is really grappling with the most fundamental questions of human life. It is struggling, probably more seriously than ever before and probably more actively than any other nation on earth, with the contradictions of great wealth and poverty, with the selfishness of powerful factions and nations, and with the perplexities and hypocrisies of human relations in the church, the university, and the marketplace.

Also, we are finally coming to realize that wishes are not policies and that nations which have policies they are not prepared to pay for inevitably loiter down into deep trouble.

Thus, it can at least be argued that America is not rushing forward along a disastrous course, but is actually in the process of turning back toward safer ground. There is a whiff of anarchy on some university campuses, but in general there has actually been less violence in the universities this school year than last.

The Larger Perspective

The rich may be getting richer in America, but the poor are certainly not getting poorer. In fact, the paradox of this time is that the uprising of the poor has coincided with the period of their greatest progress, and the same can be said for the activities and the progress of the American blacks.

On the international scene, despite Vietnam and Czechoslovakia and the Middle East, the trend is not toward escalation and disarray but toward moderation and negotiation. The days of our moral indifference about foreign relations and race relations and university relations, while quieter, were not better but worse than the present, for they led to the conflicts we are now trying to compose.

Mood of Maturity

Maybe, then, the more solemn and cautious and even melancholy mood of the moment is not all bad. It could even be a sign of maturity. Lochinvar and the Sheriff are gone, and Washington has been taken over by less dramatic technicians, but expectations and realities, and ends and means, may be coming into better alignment.

Besides, the great majority of the American people were probably not bothering too much with these speculations about pessimism and optimism anyway. The main thing in America is not the political activities, but the nonpolitical majority that just goes on acting, and the quality of hope in them is too deep to be lost in a generation.

---

81 THE LEGAL AND MORAL ISSUES OF THE WAR

WASHINGTON, Jan. 6, 1968—The United States Government has now brought the fundamental philosophical issue of the Vietnam War into the courts. By indicting the chaplain of Yale University, William Sloane Coffin, Jr., Dr. Benjamin Spock, and others for their opposition to the war, the Johnson Administration has raised the question that goes back to Plato and before: When personal conviction and public law clash in a democracy, how far can the individual go in opposing the government?

This is not only a philosophical question and a legal question, but a practical political question, for charging the chaplain of Yale, among others, with wrongdoing in the name of justice is bound to excite political activity in the universities and the churches just at the beginning of the Presidential election campaign.

The Indictment

The conflict between personal conviction and public law is clearly defined, by the accident of legal language, in the indictment of the United States Court in the District of Massachusetts.

In this indictment, the grand jury charges that Coffin, Spock, Michael Ferber, Mitchell Goodman, and Marcus Raskin unlawfully, knowingly, and willfully urged Selective Service registrants to evade service in the armed forces of the United States. The evidence is fairly clear that they not only did this but that they asked publicly to be prosecuted for doing so.

But the indictment also charges that by doing so, they also willfully and knowingly combined and conspired together "to commit offenses against the United States." And this is the heart of the philosophical conflict. For they argue that the war itself is the major "offense against the United States," that they may be breaking the law of the land, but are upholding what they regard as the "higher" moral law, and are willing to pay the legal penalty for doing so.

The Nub of the Conflict

It is important to be clear about what is *not* at issue in this case. The Government is not challenging the right of Coffin, Spock, and the other defendants to speak out against the war. It is not challenging their right to say that the military draft is wrong or unfair. But it is saying there is a critical line between expressing an opinion and inciting and organizing young men to defy the law. This is the Government's case, and the Government may very well win it, but the conflict between the national law and moral conviction will remain.

Coffin, Spock, and the other defendants have been clear about this from the beginning. They came to Washington last October just before the Vietnam protest march on the Pentagon and said publicly at the Department of Justice that they were supporting the draft dodgers, and asked to be arrested for doing so. They questioned the draft law, but said that if the draft-card burners were to be arrested for breaking the law, then they were also guilty because they were inciting them to do so, and now the Government agrees.

The question, therefore, is, not whether Coffin and Spock are defying the law—they admit that they are—but whether the law is constitutional and even if it is, whether there is a higher moral law, which they choose to follow regardless of the consequences.

Coffin, Spock, and their associates are saying that there is a higher law. They are saying the war is morally wrong. They are insisting that the people who want to continue the war, including the Government, are committing "offenses against the United States," while the people who oppose the war, even if they are violating the law, are defending the moral principles of the United States.

That is why this case of *The United States of America* v. *Coffin, Ferber, Goodman, Raskin, and Spock* is so significant. It is a conflict of one view of what is right against another, of legalities and moralities, and the legalities are obviously on the Government side.

Coffin and Spock could have tested the question of right and conscience within the courts of a democratic system in a very simple way. They were not outside the legal or political realities of the country, like Gandhi in India, or the suffragettes in America, who had no vote. But they chose not to work within the system, not to oppose the war or the draft by advocacy and persuasion alone, but to paralyze the draft and the war by organizing defiance of the law.

Morally they may have been right, but legally they knew they were wrong and asked to be charged within the legal system, and the Government has now faced up to that challenge.

Maybe it is a good thing. The country has been arguing for months now about a great many other things: Is bombing effective or not? Should we negotiate with the Vietcong and the National Liberation Front or not? But this case of Coffin and Spock has raised even more fundamental questions: Is the policy of the United States in Vietnam morally right or wrong? Who is "committing offenses against the United States"—the people who oppose the war or the people who want to continue it or expand it?

A Good Case

Legally, the Johnson Administration obviously has a good case. It can undoubtedly prove that it went to war under the Constitution legally, if by stealth. Legally, it has the right to draft its citizens, no matter how unfair the draft system may be to the poor, and legally, citizens can oppose all this under the freedom-of-speech clause of the First Amendment. But Coffin and Spock have gone beyond this, and in the process, with the help of the Government's indictment, they have raised the basic question: Is the war not only legally but morally right? Is it an offense to oppose the war or to support it? Whoever wins the legal case, the moral case will obviously remain.

---

82   A NEW DIMENSION, A NEW VISION

WASHINGTON, July 21, 1969— *"And I saw a new heaven and a new earth, for the first heaven and the first earth were passed away."*—I Revelations xxi.

The great achievement of the men on the moon is not only that they made history but that they expanded man's vision of what history might be. One moon landing doesn't make a new heaven and a new earth, but it has dramatized the possibilities of doing so.

The leaders of men have in recent years been in a state of

profound depression over their inability to make more progress with the social, economic, and political problems of the world. Even in the United States, which has gloried in its capacity to do the impossible, men had begun to doubt their capacity to control events.

What the moon landing has done is to revive hope, but the old heaven and the old earth have not passed away. The stubborn facts of the human family remain the same. The population of the world increased by four hundred million in the decade of the sixties. It will grow, on the best estimates available, by about five hundred million, outside of China, in the seventies.

According to the United Nations, more than half of the people now living on earth are malnourished and therefore vulnerable to disease; five hundred million actually live in a state of constant hunger, and three million actually die of starvation every year.

Population Soars Daily

Meanwhile, the population of the earth increases by two hundred thousand every day, mainly in the underdeveloped countries, where 40 percent or more of the people are fifteen years of age and under.

Three wars were being fought on earth when the three astronauts landed on the moon—in Vietnam, the Middle East, and Nigeria. Rebellion and insurrection were common elsewhere. China, Germany, Vietnam, and Korea were divided between hostile political factions, and there were boundary disputes between the Soviet Union and China, East and West Germany, Italy and Austria, Israel and the Arab states, India and Pakistan, India and China, Thailand and Malaysia, Thailand and Cambodia, Cambodia and South Vietnam, and Mexico and Guatemala.

Of these danger spots, perhaps the most ominous is the conflict between the two Communist giants, the Soviet Union and China. Though the Middle East could get out of control, it is clearly in the interest of the United States and the Soviet Union to prevent it from doing so. The Sino-Soviet dispute, however, is deep and bitter, and could develop into a major conflict in which nuclear weapons would be used and threaten through atomic fallout the existence of human life far beyond the area of the fighting.

The nations of the earth were spending over $180 billion a year on military arms, a 50 percent increase since 1962, and an arms race of apocalyptic proportions was in progress between the United States and the Soviet Union, each of which had enough atomic weapons to threaten the very existence of human life.

A very large proportion of the human race was thus confronted by the intolerable paradox of great deprivation in the midst of plenty, existing between the two abysses of imposed political order in the totalitarian states and chaotic disorder in many of the fifty-six new countries that have come into existence since 1950.

Clash of Rich and Poor

It would perhaps not be too much to say that at this time, there was a kind of class war developing in the world between the rich and poor within many countries and also between the very rich industrial nations of the northern climes and the very poor agricultural countries of the southern climes.

In the week of the moon flight, U Thant, the Secretary General of the United Nations, issued a report, which was scarcely noticed in the excitement.

"I continue to be struck," he said, "by the magnitude of the stake and the relatively limited sacrifice, in financial terms, which would be needed to improve [the life] of the developing countries; only a slight reduction in expenditures on armaments would suffice to make available the external resources required for solving at least some of the gravest economic and social problems of today's world.

"On one or two occasions in the past, I have referred to the danger of the rich countries sinking into a kind of prosperous provincialism. But another danger should not be overlooked, that of sinking into a morass of poverty and despair. . . ."

Nevertheless, by the end of the sixties, which were supposed to be "the development decade" among the nations of the world, the large, rich nations were actually contributing a smaller proportion of their annual wealth to help the poor nations than they were at the beginning of the sixties. And as the seventies approached, there was increasing evidence of racial tension in the world and a kind of rising revolt among the educated young against the values of their elders.

In the relations between Moscow and Washington, there were some signs of progress. The Brezhnev regime has become increasingly repressive at home in the last year or so, and frightened of the rise of freedom in the Communist states of Eastern Europe, but it is preoccupied with the Chinese problem and therefore does not want too much trouble in the West.

Accordingly, it is at least willing to talk about bringing the arms race under control and working to avoid the spread of nuclear weapons. Moscow is still the arsenal of Communism and continues to arm the Arab states, but all indications are that it will cooperate with the United States at least to the extent of avoiding direct military involvement with the United States in the Arab-Israeli conflict.

The trend in Vietnam was clearly toward peace at the end of July. The United States had started withdrawing its troops from the battlefield, and while this policy of detachment promised to be long and painful for the American people, the outlook was for winding up a war that has divided the United States and limited its capacity to deal with its internal problems and help the underdeveloped countries.

Everywhere in the United States there was fierce debate and analysis of the nation's policies and priorities. Within the churches, the universities, and the Government itself, old assumptions were being challenged, and there was widespread anxiety that this was going to lead to division, disruption, and maybe even to a separation of the races into two hostile camps.

With the end of the Vietnam War, however, the chances for an easing of the tensions seemed fairly good. Between revolution and resignation, the trend of the moderate and rising middle class was toward reconstruction and peace. In fact, the major tendencies of policy within most of the advanced countries of the West were away from great adventures abroad and toward concentration on social and economic policies at home.

The moon landing undoubtedly dramatized the rapidity of change in the world and may therefore encourage new approaches, new attitudes, and new policies toward contemporary problems. In a way, this great achievement focused the mind of the entire race on a single event and said to the world what Mr. Lincoln said to the American people in 1862:

"As our case is new, we must think anew and act anew. We must disenthrall ourselves, and then we shall save our country."

83 THE PRIVILEGED SANCTUARY OF CONSCIENCE

WASHINGTON, June 20, 1970—The Congress, the Supreme Court, and the Director of Selective Service have now all spoken on what beliefs or convictions should relieve a man from serving in the armed forces of the United States, but the result is such a tangle of conflicting views that even a draft board of judges, saints, and philosophers would scarcely know what to make of it.

The three branches of the Government all agree, as they have from the beginning of the Republic, that there is, and should be, what one might call a private and privileged sanctuary of conscience. They acknowledge that for some men with certain deep personal convictions about the meaning of life and death, there is a "higher law" which forbids the killing of another human being and that this "higher law" must be respected.

The Basic Question

But which men and which beliefs? Here the Congress, the Supreme Court, and the Director of Selective Service fall apart. Must the test be "religious beliefs," or may the beliefs be ethical? Are you exempt from the draft if you were a card-carrying Methodist with a perfect attendance record at Sunday School and draftable if your philosophy of nonviolence came from Santayana or Huxley? How do you render unto Caesar the things that are

Caesar's and unto God the things that are God's if you don't honestly believe in either Caesar or God, but still believe with all your soul that killing is wrong and you can't rest in the night if you do it?

These are hard questions to answer in the middle of an undeclared war in Vietnam that has taken over forty thousand American lives and well over a million Vietnamese lives, South and North. But despite the emotion of the war, serious men and women in all branches of the Government here are struggling to deal with them objectively, and they are coming out with different answers.

The Basic Differences

The Congress passed a law exempting from military service any citizen "who by reason of religious training and belief is conscientiously opposed to war in any form." It added that "religious training and belief in this connection means an individual's belief in a relation to a Supreme Being involving duties superior to those arising from any human relation. . . ."

But the Congress drew a sharp distinction between religious and ethical beliefs. It said quite clearly that relief from military service did "not include essentially political, sociological, or philosophical views or a merely personal moral code."

What the Supreme Court has done in the last few days is to reject this distinction between religious and ethical objections to serving in war. The majority opinion of the Court was as follows:

> If an individual deeply and sincerely holds beliefs that are purely ethical or moral in source and content, but which nevertheless impose upon him a duty of conscience to refrain from participating in any war at any time, those beliefs certainly occupy in the life of that individual a place parallel to that filled by . . . God in traditionally religious persons. Because his beliefs function as the religion of his life, such an individual is as much entitled to a religious conscientious objector's exemption . . . as is someone who derives his conscientious opposition to war from traditional religious convictions. . . .

The Sharp Differences

This sharp difference between the Congress, which rejected nonreligious exemptions, and the Supreme Court majority, which approved them, sent the reporters running to the new head of Selective Service, Curtis W. Tarr, for his answer to the dilemma, and he was just young enough, honest enough, and foolish enough to try to resolve the conflict before he had time to think through all the legalities and moralities and get his guidelines down on paper.

Accordingly, he suggested some rules that must have startled most members of his draft boards in all the communities of this country, who have to pass judgment on draftees next Monday morning. Draftees who claim exemption, Mr. Tarr said, must be "sincere." There must be "no question" about it. Draftees must be opposed to all wars and not just the Indochina war. They must have more than a personal moral code, but must prove that they had consulted "wise men" and some "system of belief" and gone through "some kind of rigorous training."

On these laws from the Congress, decisions from the Supreme Court, and "guidelines" from the Director of Selective Service, young men of draft age in this country are obviously in trouble. They don't know where to turn, and the paradox of it is that the confusion favors the rich and hurts the poor.

There is something reassuring philosophically about the Supreme Court's support of ethical as distinguished from religious opposition to the war, something even exciting and ennobling about the American system that still struggles with life's great imponderables.

But the hard fact is that the Supreme Court's decision, obviously designed to be fair and strike a balance between religious and ethical objectors to the war, is unfair to the poor.

The sons of the rich and middle class in America can now appeal to the Supreme Court's decision for relief. As a matter of fact, they can flood the courts with appeals and even threaten the whole Selective Service system, but the sons of the poor are now in even more trouble than they were before. They don't have the money to hire lawyers. They don't have the education to prove that they went through a rigorous system of religious or ethical training or that they followed the counsel of what the Director of Selective Service calls "wise men."

One has to respect the officials of the Congress, the executive, and the Court for grappling with these fundamental human and philosophic questions, but while the aim all around is fairness and equality, the result is obviously unequal and unfair.

84   DEKALB COUNTY, ILLINOIS

DEKALB, Ill., June 10, 1976—DeKalb County, Illinois, is corn and Republican country. This is the home of the barbed-wire fence and hybrid corn—two inventions that revolutionized American agriculture. It is not worrying too much about Presidential politics these days. Its mind, as usual, is on the land.

In Chicago, the news is that Mayor Daley has assured the Democratic Presidential nomination for Governor Carter and that President Ford and Governor Reagan are still battling for the Republican nomination, but if you take North Avenue (Route 64) due west out of the city into DeKalb County, everything changes within a single hour.

The western Chicago suburbs on Route 64 are a disorderly jumble, dominated by new highways, with occasional glimpses of lovely old houses amputated by commercial "progress." It is never quite clear along this road when you enter or leave Melrose Park, Elmhurst, or Lombard. The dominant struggle is between the cars, the gas stations, McDonald's, and Kentucky Fried Chicken.

But at the village of St. Charles on the Fox River, less than an hour from The Loop in Chicago, Route 64 comes into gently rolling streets lines with big-roofed grandmother houses, with spacious porches and even porch swings, and on the westward uplands of the town, the world is suddenly all flat land and big sky.

Now we are in the abundant Middle Western plains, where all is lonely and orderly. The deep, fertile soil is black as coal, and the young green corn, now nine inches high, lines the fields into geometric patterns, right up to the manicured front lawns of the big farm houses and their huddled barns.

You don't see many people near these houses. They are out on their tractors, cultivating the long delicate rows of corn with their mechanical monsters—no more than little clouds of dust on the horizon.

These are the Americans who, even more than our industrial and computer giants, are leading the world in production, and they have obviously changed their old prairie and isolationist ways of other years: Their market now is the world. They want to sell their produce wherever they can—to the Soviets, the Chinese, or anybody else—and they are so busy in their fields that they have little time for gossip about Presidential politics.

The questions of a stranger coming down the empty roads seem strange to them, almost irrelevant. They know all about the news of the Ohio, New Jersey, and California primaries—they listen to the radio earlier in the morning than anybody else—and they hear that Mayor Daley has supported Jimmy Carter; but they have work to do, and will think about the election, they say, after the parties pick their candidates in New York and Kansas City.

The attitude of people out here, consequently, is not the same as in the cities or other parts of the country, but it may be significant. They don't know much about Carter or Reagan, but one gets the impression that when in doubt, they tend to favor President Ford.

He is a familiar and sympathetic character in these parts. He may stumble over his words or change his mind, but he is their sort of folks, and he is their President.

This is Ford's strength against both Reagan and Carter, and it shouldn't be minimized. The question out here is not about issues but about character and, primarily, in these Republican precincts, about who can win in November.

Ironically, Mr. Reagan does not seem to be gaining around here because he's against Washington, against détente, against Henry Kissinger, and for talking tough about Panama, Rhodesia, and the Soviet.

Quite the contrary, Ford's Washington experience seems to be helping him now, as against Carter and Reagan, who have no

Washington experience. Of course, all this may change as the diverse and confusing primary arguments give way to the nominating conventions and the two nominees.

Against all predictions, the Democrats, who seldom agree on anything, have been forced to unify behind Mr. Carter, while the Republicans still seem divided but will undoubtedly unify behind the President, when they really begin to think about it.

Even so, there will be four months before the November election—as long as the whole primary season. During this period, not only the people here in DeKalb County but the nonvoters in the rest of the country will begin to pay attention. And when they do, if the evidence here means anything, President Ford may seem much stronger in the autumn than he does now, at the beginning of the summer.

85   THE YEAR OF THE DANDELION

FIERY RUN, Va., May 9, 1978—The annual agricultural, or garden, report from this corner of the Blue Ridge is bad as usual, but not too bad. Everything in our garden suffered from inflation, except our production, and the deficit at the end of our fiscal year (May 1) stood at $106.56.

Even this does not wholly explain the extent of our losses. For taking into account the total number of what used to be called man-hours and calculating these at the existing minimum wage over the last twelve months, the actual deficit of our back-to-the-land experiment actually amounted to $603.27, non-tax-deductible.

Most of our disasters were self-inflicted, but not all. A winter storm, striking our electric wires in the night, destroyed eleven trees, including one magnificent sycamore almost as old as the Republic and leaving only its bony carcass. This is still a subject of controversy with the Virginia Electric and Power Company, which claims this tragedy was an act of God, a respected presence in these parts.

Over the entire spread of our domain (ten and three-fourths acres), however, there were some unexpected bounties this last year. The state of Virginia, which is always straightening out roads, if nothing else, decided that the old iron bridge over Fiery Run by the old miller's house was a menace and had to be replaced by one of those new wide cement bridges.

It was the judgment of the Commonwealth of Virginia that the old bridge had to be dismantled, plus all the honeysuckle vines and birds' nests that had accumulated over the years along its iron shoulders. This, of course, would cost the state time and money, so we negotiated one of the most significant waterway treaties since the Panama Canal.

Without expense or benefit of legal counsel, we proposed to relieve the Commonwealth of Virginia of the cost of dismantling the bridge, provided (1) it was deeded over to us by legal contract, (2) together with the little curve of state-owned land between the new bridge and the old, and (3) that the state abandon all claims of sovereignty, not only after the year 2000, but immediately and forever.

This was an executive agreement, not requiring a two-thirds vote of the Virginia Legislature, but the state did insist on a payment of ten dollars to cover telephone calls and paperwork. We thought about this, but in due course, the treaty was signed. Hearing of this, Henry Kissinger was astonished. Greatest diplomatic triumph by the weak over the strong, he said, or of individual over state since the Louisiana Purchase.

What, then, to do? We were now the owners, not merely of ten and three-fourth acres, but of ten and seven-eighth acres, with our own private bridge from the cabin to the miller's house. Our budget was more than balanced, so we plunged.

We put three steers in the pasture to eat it down instead of two (this costs less than cutting it with the old jeep and mower). We replaced a couple of old rotten logs in the cabin that were letting rain in on the books. We planted six fruit trees, and we bought a rotary plow so that this year we could make the stony hillside flourish.

You should see it now in the Virginia spring, with the dog-

wood and the red bud, and the silent mountains at dawn and
sunset—and if you try, we'll call the police. For of all things that
must be left to the children in this age, privacy and beauty are the
most important, and most difficult to preserve.

Every year, there is some new surprise in this remote triangle
in the Virginia hills. The dogwood is resting after a spectacular
display last year, but the wild flowers are recklessly beautiful,
and the violets and trillium are obviously running for office.

But above all, this is the year of the dandelion in these parts.
Never so many of them, never so big or brassy yellow or so
concentrated precisely in the middle of our lawn. So our glory
this spring is our dandelion garden, constructed by the simple
process of cutting the grass around it and leaving it there blazing
in the sun in the shape of a big D.

Lovers of rose gardens will no doubt regard this as somewhat
bizarre, if not vaguely suspect, but at the end of his life, G. K.
Chesterton thought the main lesson he had learned was not to
take simple natural things for granted, but to regard them with
gratitude, and he took the dandelion as the symbol.

"The pessimists of my boyhood," he wrote in his autobiogra-
phy, "when confronted with the dandelion, said with Swinburne:

> *I am weary of all hours*
> *blown buds and barren flowers*
> *desires and dreams and powers*
> *and everything but sleep.*

"And at this," added Chesterton, "I cursed them and kicked at
them . . . [and at] the strange and staggering heresy that every
human being has a *right* to dandelions . . . and need feel no
wonder at them at all. . . . The aim of life is appreciation," he
concluded.

He would not have liked this age. He took his philosophy out
of the old Penny Catechism that "the two sins against Hope are
Presumption and Despair"; but I like to think he would have
applauded our dandelion garden, and I know he would have
approved, on esthetic as well as economic grounds, our old ten-
dollar bridge.

86 BLUE RIDGE ELECTION

FIERY RUN, Va., Nov. 7, 1984—On Election Day, voting can seem to be either a routine duty or an intensely personal privilege; something that matters or—one vote among a hundred million— doesn't seem to matter at all.

Much depends on where you live and where you vote. Washington trembles with excitement over the result. Who takes over the White House and Congress determines the power, the atmosphere, the manners, and the talk of the Federal city for years.

Every race for the Senate and many for the House are watched and analyzed to see whether the old favorites or villains win or lose, who moves up to the chairmanship of the Congressional committees, and who will be in the Cabinet.

Elsewhere in the country, the Presidential elections, while interesting, do not dominate attention to such a degree. In Washington, with its clamor of voices predicting disaster if the other side wins, all seems chaotic and ominous, though most of the dire campaign prophecies and the glowing promises for the future never happen. Election Day in Washington and in the Virginia hills illustrates the contrast.

On Election Day, my wife and I walked down to the polling booth in the Episcopal Church at the corner of Bancroft Place and Connecticut Avenue in Washington and punched our votes.

It was different when we cast our first votes for President in that city forty years ago. Now, as then, women presided over the voting, but this time, about half of them were black, explaining the voting process to the old folks with patient kindness.

On the edge of the room, where we voted, a woman was explaining to maybe fifteen or twenty people, most of them Hispanic, what was going on, and they were listening with careful attention.

In the country, things are different. We came out here to our cabin in the foothills of the Virginia Blue Ridge and discovered in the silence that despite the election, everything seemed the same.

Fiery Run was still wandering toward the Rappahannock and the sea, carrying the autumn leaves.

This is Fauquier County, where Mr. Justice John Marshall lived and worshipped at the one-room Leeds Church up the road, going occasionally to the capital to help write the laws of the land. This little corner of Virginia is steeped in forgotten history, and has suffered and survived many trials.

For a hundred years, it was known as the Free State of Virginia, because General Washington, during the War of Independence, subverted the German Hessians who were fighting for the British by offering them land and freedom in these quiet valleys.

And there they lived isolated for generations with their own laws and churches, until they had the bad judgment to marry among themselves until the stock ran out.

For many years, this was Democratic, Harry Byrd country, always conservative like Harry. But now, like the rest of Virginia, it's for Mr. Reagan and the Republicans. Still, we don't talk politics with our neighbors at the cabin. Nobody is allowed to mention the subject for fifteen minutes, and thereafter nobody is allowed to spout off for more than three minutes. The rest of the time we talk about practical things closer to home.

For example, we lost Henry Baxley in the last year, one of the kindest neighbors I ever had. Don Allen, the manager of Bill Marriott's Fairfield Farm, a quiet man who understood the stupidity of city folk and always mended our fences and rounded up our stray cattle when they got out on the road, had retired. This was the main topic of our conversation.

There was also some discussion of a religious sect that proposed to establish the faithful in a cluster of houses outside the nearby village of Hume. More attention was paid to stopping that than to keeping John Warner in the Senate.

Also, somebody driving down the hill too fast on Route 635 hadn't made the turn over the Fiery Run bridge and had plowed through our fence into the pasture. The judgment of our neighbors was that it must have been some city idiot.

Having come back to this real world, we adjusted to the practical work at hand. I cut paths through the long grass in the pasture, and fixed a door that was off its hinges, and planted two hundred daffodil bulbs in the belief that they would flower in the spring no matter who won the election.

Thereafter, we returned to Washington in the gloaming and listened to the election returns, and somehow felt more confident that life would keep running along like Fiery Run, no matter what happened at the polls.

87   THE MISSING MEN

WASHINGTON, Dec. 26, 1984—And it came to pass in those days that three wise men attended the manger cradle in Bethlehem, but on the day after Christmas they disappeared. So there went out a decree from Caesar Augustus that the missing men should be found, but to no avail, for at that time, it seemed that wise men had vanished from the earth.

And there were at that place shepherds abiding in the field, keeping watch over their flock, and an angel saying unto them, "Fear not, for behold I bring you tidings of great joy. . . ." But Caesar Augustus was still dismayed. "Where are the Wise Men?" he demanded.

Let us go now to Jerusalem, he suggested, but when the search committee arrived upon the Holy Hill, there was much contention, for an election was in progress and no wise man was to be found.

From generation unto generation, the alarm was sounded among all the nations and peoples and faiths of the Old World, but there was no peace or good will on any front, and wars and rumors of wars prevailed, and so it was that in their despair, they turned to the New Jerusalem of the New World.

'Twas the night after Christmas (A.D. 1984) when the search committee arrived at the White House of the New World, but not a creature was stirring, not even a Meese. And when they arrived at the gate, they were turned away, having no driver's licenses or credit cards or other means of identification. The F.B.I. put out an urgent call to all departments of the Government to summon for consultation any man or woman on the Federal payroll. No response. The rolls of the press were called, on the odd chance. No luck.

When they traveled to Mother Russia, it was in mourning for the dead, and they sought entrance in the name of the common suffering and mortality of the human family, but heard only of wars on earth and in the stars, and no Wise Men.

So it was that the seekers after peace summoned all the prophets and philosophers of the nations to gather together, believing that peace was too important to be left to politicians and journalists. And here they found a glimmer of hope.

For this illustrious company looked forward to what Aldous Huxley called the Golden Age, in which there would be liberty, peace, justice, and brotherly love.

They quoted from the Bible and from their constitutions:

"Nation shall no more lift sword against nation."

"The free development of each will lead to the free development of all."

"The world shall be full of the knowledge of the Lord, as the waters cover the sea."

But lo, when they came to discuss the means to this ideal goal of human effort, they fell to quarreling among themselves.

Some believed that the way to the ideal world lay in the balance of military power, some in a redistribution of the world's wealth, or in the free exercise of the marketplace, or in military conquest, or armed revolution, or the dictatorship of a particular class.

And in the back of the room, the moralists insisted that the hope lay in the abolition of personal greed and the transformation of the human heart, and each argued with the violence of fanaticism that the road to the good and eternal life lay by a certain way and faith, but they could not agree on what way and what faith, and when a cry rose for the Original Question: "Where are the wise men?" only one voice was heard.

"I am the voice of Science," it said. "Your fate lies not on earth but in the stars. Seek not your salvation in principalities or the lies of politicians, or the theories of philosophers, or the dreams of poets, or the promises of divines.

"Look not to the heavenly hosts of the past, but to the scientific redeemers of the future. There between heaven and earth lies the only thing that offers any real hope to the world.

"We bring you tidings of great joy. For unto you is born this day, not the wise men of the earth, but a new race of scientific Wise Men, trusting not in the failed theology and philosophy of the past, but in the mathematics and computers of the future."

And so it was after this testimony that the quiet voice of a woman was heard to ask where these Wise Men of Science would come from, and to wonder whether after all there were any wise men.

Moral: Waste not thy time searching vainly for a wise man, for thou hast the right question but the wrong sex.

---

88   AMERICA IN A CHANGING WORLD

ALABAMA, Auburn University, Feb. 24, 1975—It is an honor to be asked to deliver one of the Franklin lectures, although I sometimes think that what this country needs these days, quite frankly, is not more lectures but thirty days of total silence. I refer you to the nineteenth chapter of the Book of Luke, the first to the third verses: "And Jesus entered and passed through Jericho, and behold there was a man named Zaccius . . . and he sought to see Jesus but could not for the press. . . ."

One of the problems of our time, maybe of any time, is to tell the difference between the important and the trivial. We reporters are so overwhelmed with information that we cannot sort it all out or get its meaning. We know the statistics of the economic slump at home, the food crisis in much of the world, and the energy crisis almost everywhere, but we do not feel them. It is not that we are indifferent or stupid, but simply that the clatter is too much for us, and also that reporters have not yet learned to reduce all this diversity to some understandable identity.

The theme I want to suggest for your consideration here is

that while the country is in a bit of a mess, it is getting about what it deserves, it is being brought back down to reality, and it will, as usual, probably make some progress as a result of its adversities. (You should remember as I go along that I'm a Scottish Calvinist, and nothing makes us happier than misery.)

We are now in the last year of the third quarter of the twentieth century (or the first year of the last quarter, depending on how you read the calendar), and there is a lot of moaning and even talk about another "Great Depression." This comparison with the thirties is a bad one, and it helps to create a very dangerous psychology.

During the real Great Depression of the 1930s, there were between fifteen to seventeen million people out of work. *Fortune* magazine reported in September 1932 that some thirty-four million men, women, and children were without any income whatsoever. The average weekly wage for those who had jobs was $16.41. Wheat was selling for less than twenty-five cents a bushel. Sugar was bringing three cents a pound, hogs and beef two and a half cents. Our present situation is bad enough, with over 8.2 percent of the people unemployed, high interest rates, and high prices, but comparisons with the last economic depression are ludicrous.

One of the paradoxes of this country is that we are a nation of optimists who seem somehow always to have loved pessimistic predictions. I suppose our most optimistic poet was Walt Whitman, but more than a century ago he wrote the following:

Never was there, perhaps, more hollowness at heart than at present, and here in the United States. Genuine belief seems to have left us. The underlying principles of the states are not believed in. . . . The spectacle is appalling. We live in an atmosphere of hypocrisy throughout. The men believe not in the women nor the women in the men. The great cities reek with robbery and scoundrelism. It is as if we were somehow being endowed with a vast and more and more thoroughly appointed body, and left with little or no soul.

So much for the good old days.

The present condition of America, according to President Ford, "is not good." The truth is that we've been on a binge and now the bills are coming in. We have assumed for the last generation that we could do almost anything we pleased all over the world, that we could fight and win a war on the Asian continent, ten thousand miles from home and in the shadow of China. We had the illusion then, long popular in America, that money and machines can settle almost anything, and we even thought that we could sell our products for whatever the traffic would bear but that other countries would not do the same.

Well, history seems to be trying to teach us something. It has at least tried to tell us in recent years that the days of limitless cheap gas and oil are over, that some peoples work harder than we do, notably the Germans and the Japanese, and that they have also mastered the arts of the modern computer and have almost as much advanced technology as we do. Meanwhile, we are no longer talking about the military superiority of the United States, but merely about arrangements of equality with the Soviet Union—particularly in nuclear weapons.

At home, our illusions about political leadership—such illusions as we still had—have been sadly shaken by Watergate, and when we look over the list of candidates for 1976, searching for some unsuspected savior, the draft picks seem a little thin. This has shaken the spirit of many people, some of whom go fishing and some of whom go crazy, but in the perspective of history, these developments are not surprising, and it may be that they are not all bad.

It was never really reasonable for us to suppose that we could play forever as dominant a role as we did in the immediate postwar generation, or that we would retain a monopoly on the advanced science and technology of the world, or that Richard Nixon and his gang were going to lead us into an era of prosperity and peace, or that we could run deficits into the hundreds of billions and not suffer the consequences. So we are having to adjust and change, and cut down and do hard things with our minds. As General Andrew Jackson ordered—I think at the Battle of New Orleans—"Elevate them guns a little lower!"

But this is far from being a tragic or, in comparative terms, even a depressing situation. In the first quarter of this century, our civilization had to endure a terrible world war. In the second quarter, a worldwide depression and a second world war that destroyed the old empires and the old order of the world. And in the third quarter, the Korean conflict, the Vietnam War, the collapse of the Communist alliance, and the emergence of China and of over a hundred new nations.

No doubt the fourth quarter will be tough. The Middle East is now the flash point of the world. Democracy is in trouble all over the world, threatened by inflation, political instability, and a crisis of leadership. Even the British are wondering whether their ancient liberties can withstand the pressures of inflation, and all across the Mediterranean, from Portugal and Italy to Greece and Turkey, the North Atlantic alliance is obviously in deep trouble.

But unlike the first two quarters, we are not now threatened, as our fathers and grandfathers were, with world wars. Rebellions, uprisings of all sorts, intricate economic and financial problems, yes—but atomic weapons have at least terrified the nations into some kind of restraint. Never in history have two great powers, with such different philosophies and interests, faced each other with such armaments as the United States and the Soviet Union have done since the last world war. Yet always, when one of them went too far, as Moscow did in Cuba and we did in Vietnam, the other great power has held back. I merely remind you that during the Vietnam War, our aircraft carriers in the South China Sea were always within range of missiles that Russia could have provided the North Vietnamese. But the weapons were not provided, for that would have changed a limited war into a world crisis.

It is very largely the fault of the press that we always seem to concentrate on things that go wrong and tend to distort history in the process. You will remember that there were only twenty years between the two world wars—from 1919 to 1939—yet we have avoided general war for over thirty years since 1945 and are, albeit very slowly, making some progress in getting control of the nuclear arms race.

The surface of the waters of the world is very troubled now, but underneath strong tides are running There *are* some hopeful trends and tendencies. We are beginning to realize that we cannot by ourselves solve all the problems of finance, of trade, of the price of oil and food, of pollution, of piracy in the international airways. A new world economy has come into existence and cooperation across borders is increasingly essential in the national lives of all peoples.

Not so long ago we were saying we couldn't "recognize" China. (How can you fail to recognize fully one-fifth of the people living on the earth today?) Germany is no longer pretending that Europe is not divided or trying to defy the power of the Soviet Union. Even Prime Minister Harold Wilson is no longer pretending that Britain is closer to the United States than to Europe, and so he is joining the Common Market. Israel is no longer pretending that it can hold on to the Sinai, and even the Arabs (the more moderate ones, at least) are finally accepting the fact that Israel exists and has a right to live behind secure and internationally guaranteed borders.

Finally, the Soviet Union is no longer pretending that all Communists will be comrades and allies, but is talking more to Washington than it is to Peking, and instead of boasting that it can outproduce us, is counting on the agricultural production of the United States and the advanced technology of other non-Communist states.

I am not trying to put a rosy glow on all this. Pollyanna is dead, and good riddance. There is no way to foretell what will happen after the end of the present leadership in China and the Soviet Union. Mao Tse-tung is in his eighties and did not even appear at the last Communist Party Congress. Chou En-lai was reported to be under house arrest or very ill during the last few months, but he suddenly emerged as the principal spokesman at the latest party meeting. Also, Leonid Brezhnev has lately been seen at party functions, after a long period of invisibility.

The one thing we know is that the Communist system has never mastered the problem of passing power smoothly and calmly from one clique or one generation to another, and as we had a Stalin follow a Lenin, it is always possible, though it is not likely, that the hard-liners will regain power again in Moscow and Peking and perhaps even restore the old Sino-Soviet alliance.

In watching these developments in China, Moscow, and else-where, it might be well to remember the advice Sir Ernest Satow used to give young British Foreign Service officers before they went to the Orient. "Do not waste too much time," he said, "trying to imagine what is in the Oriental mind. For all you know, there may be nothing in it. Just be sure you know what is in your own mind."

We are a little unsure about this in Washington these days. For a long time, the Congress had abdicated much of its power to the President. This trend began in the early thirties under Roosevelt, when the Federal Government, in reaction to the de-pression, assumed much greater responsibility for running a planned economy. The President had to be given far more power in the forties with the invention of the atomic bomb and the intercontinental ballistic missile. For after that, it was possible for the Republic to be destroyed from overseas before you could even get the Congress through the traffic in downtown Washington. That trend toward centralized and hidden power in the White House reached frightening heights, or depths, under President Nixon, and now the reaction has set in.

Maybe it is swinging too far the other way. Although the Congress has the right and the duty to help policy abroad, it does not have the capacity, being so large a body, to execute policy. Lately, it has been trying to do so by insisting on conditions for trade with the Soviet Union—specifically, insisting on the release of Soviet Jews to Israel—and this has of course been regarded by Moscow as an interference in its internal affairs. Likewise, the Congress has insisted on cutting off military aid to Turkey be-cause of that nation's actions in Cyprus, and the result has been merely to make things worse in Cyprus while weakening Wash-ington's relations with both Greece and Turkey at a time of crisis in the NATO alliance.

None of these problems, however, is insoluble or a threat to the Republic. They can be endured if not solved, for I must say that despite all the present fussing between President Ford and the Congress, the atmosphere is much better now than it has been for some years. You may not agree with Mr. Ford's energy program or with his budget or his planned deficits, but when he says something, you don't have to wonder what he means or what he's trying to hide. He even dramatizes his weaknesses. He knows the difference between yes and no and between right and wrong, and after the last few years, this is a tremendous advance.

Of course, the Presidential campaign of 1976 has already started, and it is not possible to toss a cuspidor out of the Senate press gallery without hitting a potential Democratic candidate. Sooner or later, they all hear "Hail to the Chief" in the night. This does not contribute much to balanced, reasonable debate on public issues, and the campaign is likely to lose altitude as it picks up speed. We may even loiter down into a dreadful campaign concentrating on tragedies of Watergate versus Chappaquiddick. I hope not, but it could happen.

It might also happen that Ronald Reagan and Governor Wallace will become disenchanted with the two major parties, as so many other people have, and put together the most serious challenge to the Democrats and Republicans since the days of Old Bob LaFollette. Again, I think this is unlikely, and besides, it is all speculative and not very helpful.

If we keep in mind that it is less than a year until we celebrate the two hundredth anniversary of the Declaration of Independence and concentrate on the strength and ideals of this great country, we will have a reliable guide, I think, for our conduct as individuals and a nation. We have watched our institutions work well under extreme duress in the last couple of years. They *are* reliable. They will see us through, if we avoid choosing up sides on hard, ideological issues and concentrate on the facts. A time of extraordinary change is a time of flexibility, of charity for ideas we oppose, since nobody can be sure in such a shifting world precisely who or what represents the best course for the nation.

Historically, this nation has made its greatest advances after times of extreme tension. It was only when the British confronted us with intolerable demands—and intolerable, at that, to only a minority of our people—that we finally demanded and gained our national independence.

We knew that the institution of slavery was a contradiction to the religious and political ideas of the nation, but it took a tragic civil war to get rid of it.

We know now that it was impossible for this vast continental country to isolate itself from struggles elsewhere in the world, struggles that threatened the very existence of Western civilization and the hope of all free societies, but it took two apocalyptic wars, which we entered late, before we finally put our power behind our ideals and the creation of some order in the world.

The same was true of the modernization of our economy; we had to endure the Great Depression before we adapted our growing industrial society to the new social and political remedies of the twentieth century.

Finally, it took Vietnam and then Watergate before we began to restore the balance of power among the executive, the legislature, and the courts, and while this was one of the ugliest chapters in the history of the Republic, it achieved something more. It forced a revision of our campaign financing and gave rise to some new safeguards against bugging, wiretapping, and political espionage and sabotage. Much remains to be done in all these fields, but the old story has been repeated: We have made progress through adversity.

The immediate question before us, then, is whether we can also learn from our present economic difficulties and find remedies that will restore the balance, prosperity, and confidence of the nation. For the moment, we are obviously divided and are even shouting at one another, but there is more quiet negotiation going on between the White House and the Congress than appears on the surface, and the chances of a compromise on gas and oil prices in the short run are not too bad.

The next few years, however, are probably going to be tough—tougher on some regions and some classes of our people than on others. The slump is uneven. It is more serious in industrial New England and in most of the South than elsewhere. It is particularly hard on the urban areas that live on the production and assembly of automobiles, and while it is going to be hard on this year's graduates looking for jobs, it is going to be harder still on the old folks living on pensions and on the poor blacks and whites.

Even a government that is not usually guilty of undue pessimism estimates that we are going to have abnormally high unemployment for at least three years, and even now, again by official count, 41.1 percent of all black teenagers are out of work. I find that a scary statistic, for if anybody thinks we can sustain that level of black-teenage unemployment without trouble in the streets, I have yet to meet him.

In closing, let me say a word about the limited powers and responsibilities of political leaders. They like to pretend, of course, that they have the answers to our problems, and we journalists contribute to this illusion by concentrating on their activities, their families, their hobbies, and other things that have limited importance. They do many things in the public interest, and they get credit for many other things they have very little to do with. But they are also often blamed for a lot of things that are beyond their control.

For example, many of the struggles of nations today that seem to be foreign problems are actually domestic problems. Henry Kissinger cannot do anything about the inflation and industrial troubles of Britain, though these affect the strength of the NATO alliance. He cannot influence the wide gap between the very rich and the very poor in Latin American and other underdeveloped areas of the world, though these are likely to lead to serious struggles, spilling across borders in the future. Nor can he do anything much to arrest the alarming population explosion in the world. Yet these may very well be our problems, too.

Beyond this, the fundamental fact is that it is not the political leaders who are changing the world. It is being transformed primarily by the fertility of the human mind and the human body. All over the world, medical science is dramatically reducing infant mortality and prolonging the lives of the aged. And in between, as expectations rise in the poor nations, the population increases alarmingly. In short, we are changing the world faster than we can change ourselves or adapt our institutions to the changes. The experts tell us that here at home we are approaching zero population growth, but in my own years as a reporter, the population of this country has increased by about eighty million—by almost as many people as the total populations of Great Britain and France combined.

The stress of providing jobs, houses, schools, hospitals, universities, welfare, social security, transportation, and all the other necessities of life in such a short space of time for such a multitude has been very great, even for so rich a country as ours. No matter where I travel in the world, I find leaders of all cities, states, and nations, no matter what system they operate under, baffled by the magnitude of these human and political problems. This is why I suggest a little patience and even compassion for the men and women who have to struggle with these questions. Lord knows they have plenty to answer for, but they didn't produce all these people: They are merely trying to get their votes.

The main difference in America is that here, in contrast to the Soviet Union and China, whose political masters conceal and suppress the facts, we are now grappling with all these conflicts in the open, as a free people should. In this country today, there is not a single human relationship that is not being carefully analyzed—whether that of husbands to wives, parents to children, employers to employees, teachers to students, preachers to parishioners. It is a tremendous challenge to a free society at a very difficult time, but my faith, indeed my conviction, is that we will meet the challenge, if we can hold together at home.

Index